Contents

Notes on the Authors   vi

Preface and Acknowledgements   vii

1 East European Welfare: Past, Present and Future
   in Comparative Context   *Bob Deacon*   1

2 Social Policy in the Soviet Union and its Successors
   Nick Manning   31

3 Social Policy in Bulgaria   *Bob Deacon and
   Anna Vidinova*   67

4 Social Policy in Czechoslovakia
   Mita Castle-Kanerova   91

5 Social Policy in Poland   *Frances Millard*   118

6 Social Policy in Hungary   *Julia Szalai and
   Eva Orosz*   144

7 The Future of Social Policy in Eastern Europe
   Bob Deacon   167

Index   192

Notes on the Authors

Mita Castle-Kanerova, who was exiled from Czechoslovakia in 1968, is Senior Lecturer at the Polytechnic of North London. She currently teaches and researches into the history and politics of social policy in Eastern Europe and on women in Eastern Europe. She taught in the spring of 1991 at the Charles University, Prague.

Bob Deacon is Reader in Social Policy at Leeds Polytechnic. He is author or editor of four volumes on aspects of East European social policy and a member of the editorial board of *European Social Policy*.

Nick Manning is Reader in Social Policy at the University of Kent. He is author or editor of eight volumes including, with Vic George, *Socialism, Social Welfare and the Soviet Union* (1980), the classic study of Soviet social policy. He is at present co-directing an ESRC research project on environmental and housing movements in Estonia, Russia and Hungary.

Frances Millard is Principal Lecturer in Soviet and East European Politics in the School of Social and Historical Studies at Portsmouth Polytechnic. She is co-author of *Pressure Politics in Industrial Societies* (1986), editor of *Social Welfare and the Market* (1989) and has written a number of articles in the area of Polish health care and social policy.

Eva Orosz is a Senior Lecturer at the Social Policy Department, Eötvös Loránd University, Budapest.

Julia Szalai is Head of the Social Policy section of the Institute of Sociology of the Hungarian Academy of Sciences. She is also a founder member of the Centre for European Studies in Budapest.

Anna Vidinova was until recently a member of the Institute of Sociology of the Bulgarian Academy of Sciences. She now lives and works in London and was recently engaged on an Anglo-Bulgarian study of workplace organization.

The New Eastern Europe

The New Eastern Europe

Social Policy Past, Present and Future

Bob Deacon

Mita Castle-Kanerova
Nick Manning
Frances Millard
Eva Orosz
Julia Szalai
Anna Vidinova

SAGE Publications
London · Newbury Park · New Delhi

First published 1992
Reprinted 1993

SAGE Publications Ltd
6 Bonhill Street
London EC2A 4PU

SAGE Publications Inc
2455 Teller Road
Newbury Park, California 91320

SAGE Publications India Pvt Ltd
32, M-Block Market
Greater Kailash – I
New Delhi 110 048

British Library Cataloguing in Publication Data

Deacon, Bob
 The New Eastern Europe: Social Policy Past,
 Present and Future
 I. Title
 361.610947

 ISBN 0–8039–8438–3
 ISBN 0–8039–8439–1 pbk

Library of Congress catalog card number 92-53698

Typeset by Photoprint, Torquay, Devon
Printed and bound in Great Britain by
Biddles Ltd, Guildford and King's Lynn

Preface and Acknowledgements

This book is the product of the labour of several people. It is the fruit of several seeds sown some years ago. It is, however, merely a moment in the development of an intellectual and political analysis of the evolution of social policy in Eastern Europe.

The strands that have led to this volume are numerous. The remote origins lie in my visit to Hungary in 1982, where I met Julia Szalai, who helped me confirm that Hungarian social policy had little in common with an idealized socialist social policy (Deacon, 1983). Julia Szalai and I, together with other colleagues in the United Kingdom and Hungary (Sidney Jacobs, Fiona Williams, Janos David and Peter Gyori), went on to undertake an Anglo-Hungarian study of attitudes to the welfare state between 1985 and 1988, with the help of an Economic and Social Research Council grant. During that study it was already evident to us that the bureaucratic state collectivist system of welfare in Eastern Europe had outlived any useful role it had ever played. We also became convinced that the dialogue that needed to take place between the East and the West was not one of economists who were blind to the negative consequences of unbridled marketization, nor of socialists who were deaf to the negative lessons to be learned from the Eastern European and Soviet experience for the socialist project, but one of critical social policy analysts concerned to focus on the common problem of the alternative and diverse ways human needs might be articulated and met.

This fruitful Anglo-Hungarian dialogue extended to encompass an Anglo-Polish dialogue funded by the Suntory–Toyota International Centre at the LSE which was reported in a volume edited by Frances Millard (1989). During the 1980s I also began to establish a working relationship with colleagues at the University of Kent, where Nick Manning and Vic George had already published their volume on Soviet social policy (1980). Immediately prior to the upheavals of 1989 in Eastern Europe, again with the help of ESRC funds, Leeds Polytechnic played host in 1988 to an international conference on Social Policy and Socialism. (The continuing East–West dialogue of social policy analysts that took place then was reported in Deacon and Szalai, 1990.) By this time the dialogue had widened to include Bulgarians, including Anna Vidinova, whom I had met several years earlier in Sofia, and a number of Czechoslovaks. Jirina Siklova was prevented from leaving Prague at that time to attend the conference but her place was, so to speak, taken by Mita Castle-Kanerova, who had been unable to return to Czechoslovakia after she found herself in London in 1968. Mita finally was able to return to Prague in 1990 and spent several months there in the Charles University in 1991, preparing her contribution to this volume and helping to extend the East–West dialogue of social policy into Czechoslovakia. The dialogue also continued to take place in other international conferences, notably the World Congress of Soviet and East European Studies held in Harrogate in 1990, which generated a further volume of papers embracing several of the countries of Eastern Europe (Deacon, 1992).

This volume therefore represents the collective work of colleagues who have personally, politically and academically been deeply involved in the collapse of the previous communist regimes in Eastern Europe and whose knowledge and direct experience of the past have enabled them to provide an insightful analysis of the present and to make reasoned projections into the future. It represents, to our knowledge, the first systematic attempt to sum up the experience of the now historical bureaucratic state collectivist system of welfare, to analyse the problems of social policy in the period of transition to capitalism and to chart and project the future development of social policy in Eastern Europe in the 1990s. This task is undertaken by situating the discussion in the context of a review of the state of the art of comparative social policy, so that we hope the volume is not only a contribution to the study of social policy in one region but also a contribution to the development of the discipline of social policy.

The separate chapters carry individual authors' names and this reflects the division of labour. Each of the chapters has, however, benefited from the comments of other contributors. This is especially the case for the opening and concluding chapter. While not everyone would endorse all the details of the analyses in all of the chapters, we are in general agreement with the broad drift of the analyses and conclusions of the volume. Some of the country-specific chapters conform to a standard format. Others, notably the Hungarian and Bulgarian ones, depart from this. This is a reflection of the fact that these chapters were written by Hungarians and Bulgarians who were immersed in the immediacy of the analysis and political development of policy in these two countries. What the book loses in comprehensiveness it gains from analytical insights that more detached and less well-informed UK-based writers would have missed.

No special funds were available to underpin the preparation of this volume but each of us has managed to find time and personal or sometimes institutional resources to see the project through. Mita would like to record her thanks to the Social Policy Association for funding her visit to Czechoslovakia. We would all like to record our thanks to Karen Phillips of Sage for her enthusiastic support and to Alastair McCauley of the University of Essex for his helpful comments on draft chapters.

Bob Deacon, Leeds
on behalf of all the authors

References

Deacon, B. (1983) *Social Policy and Socialism*. London: Pluto.

Deacon, B. (ed.) (1992) *Social Policy, Social Justice and Citizenship in Eastern Europe*. Aldershot: Gower.

Deacon, B. and Szalai, J. (eds) (1990) *Social Policy in the New Eastern Europe*. Aldershot: Gower.

George, V. and Manning, N. (1980) *Socialism, Social Welfare and the Soviet Union*. London: Routledge and Kegan Paul.

Millard, F. (ed.) (1989) *Social Welfare and the Market*. London: London School of Economics (STICERD Occasional Paper, 15).

1

East European Welfare: Past, Present and Future in Comparative Context

Bob Deacon

The collapse of the communist regimes across Eastern Europe in 1989 and the replacement of the Soviet Union in December 1991 by a loosely co-ordinated body of newly independent states has brought to an end not only a particular type of political and economic system but a particular type of welfare state. The bureaucratic state collectivist system of welfare that became established within the Soviet Union under Stalinism and exported to the countries of Eastern Europe after the Second World War is no longer. It is the purpose of this book to sum up the characteristics of that particular type of welfare regime, to describe the legacy of social welfare problems it is bequeathing to successor regimes and to begin to map and chart the diverse ways in which the new governments of Eastern Europe and the former Soviet Union are approaching the development of a new social policy.

In this first chapter we begin by setting out the main characteristics of the pre-1989 system of welfare that, individual country variations notwithstanding, existed in a fairly standard form across Eastern Europe and the Soviet Union. We then describe in general terms the immediate social policy problems that the successor regimes are confronted with. These are problems that are a compound of the legacy of unfulfilled promise and actual neglect, on the one hand, and problems of the transition to market economies and political pluralist systems on the other. Here the chapter will focus on the twin emergent issues of facilitating both an active civil society and a new and acceptable conception of social justice in the period of transition.

The later part of the chapter will situate the study of the newly emerging and diverse post-communist welfare regimes in the broader comparative and cross-national social policy literature. There are two elements to this. The first consists of a review of the developing literature on welfare state regime types and suggests ways in which the new developments in Eastern Europe might be studied and analysed within the framework that now exists for studying capitalist welfare states. An element of this discussion will be the increased and evident importance of transnational agencies in shaping national welfare states. The second consists of the establishment of a set of criteria by which new social policy developments might be evaluated. The final chapter will return to these issues and draw interim conclusions based on the more detailed descriptions of emerging social policy in each of the country-specific chapters.

Bureaucratic state collectivism: a balance sheet

Had we been present in 1989 and able to stop the clock of Soviet perestroika or the revolutions of Eastern Europe, what, as critical analysts of capitalist welfare states, would we have wished to preserve? For some internal critics of the old regime the answer was simple, very little. Julia Szalai stated in 1989, before the end of communism in Hungary, that what 'social policy today gives its subjects are the many irritating, humiliating and painful experiences of unfairness, defencelessness and chronic shortage. Social policy has come to be associated with widely unsatisfied needs, of unacceptable bureaucratic regulations, of haphazard provision of services at more and more unacceptable levels' (Deacon and Szalai, 1990: 92).

On the other hand, some social analysts based in the West (Feher and Arato, 1989) have drawn attention to the ways in which heavily subsidized foods and rents, full employment, relatively high (as a percentage of average) wages of workers and provision of free or cheap health, education and culture services represented a type of welfare contract between the party-state apparatus and the people which was marred only by its inefficiency and the hidden privileges of the nomenklatura. Below we try to draw up a balance sheet of positive and negative features of the pre-1989 system.

The right to work was generally enshrined in the constitution. A place of work was indeed available for the vast majority of the population, both men and women. Often, however, this was a way of hiding unemployment. Little productive work actually took place in many workplaces. The regimes pretended to pay such workers and the workers pretended to work. In many countries, most notably Hungary (but the practice existed elsewhere), wages from official workplaces were so low that an adequate standard of living could only be secured by taking a second or even third job in the unofficial economy which was often dependent on the utilization of resources formally belonging to the official place of work. For those who lost their jobs for political and other reasons no system of unemployment benefit existed. For those regarded variously as work-shy or rejecting the socialist work ethic little was provided. Gypsy minorities lived in the margins of these societies as a reserve army of labour with no rights and entitlements by virtue of citizenship.

The relatively high (as percentage of average) wages of sections of the working class – miners, transport workers, construction workers – could be seen as one of the justifications for these societies to be regarded, in a very limited sense, as workers' states. Certainly the relatively privileged position of miners compared to that of middle-ranking professionals (doctors and teachers) was a source of much resentment among the latter. This feature, however, co-existed with the hidden privileges of many within the party-state apparatus who had access to hidden incomes and welfare services. It was the 'unjustly' deserved privileges that became a source of much anger, especially in the GDR, during the revolutions of 1989.

Many services, including medical care, were provided free at the point of use. There was often an extensive system of work-based medical provision. The number of doctors and hospital beds was higher than in comparable West European countries. The service provided was, however, totally inefficient, undercapitalized and often lacking in basic equipment. Only in specialist enclaves did excellence exist. While often professing a prophylactic approach to health, the governments of Eastern Europe and the Soviet Union systematically injured the health of their populations by requiring work in health-damaging environments, by polluting the earth and atmosphere and by presiding over a social system that indirectly encouraged alcoholism, unhealthy diet and suicide. The mortality rates for Eastern Europe compare very unfavourably with those of comparable capitalist societies, and throughout the sixties and seventies and most of the eighties these were worsening. Recent data from the Soviet Union (Mezentseva and Rimachevskaya, 1990) suggest improvements following in the wake of the anti-alcohol campaign. Only in the Central Asian republics of the Soviet Union did health indicators compare favourably with neighbouring and equivalent Iran and Turkey. McAuley (1990) reported life expectancy for males and females in Central Asia in 1979/80 as 63.2 per cent and 69.8 per cent respectively, compared with figures of 55.8 per cent and 55.0 per cent for Iran and 60.0 per cent and 63.3 per cent for Turkey. Soviet socialist imperialism does seem to have had beneficial impact on aspects of the quality of life of its southern colonial republics, but this, of course, was at the expense of the right of the republics to self-determination.

Benefits and services provided to ease the situation of working women were quite extensive in many of the East European countries. The three-year child care grant in Hungary and comparable benefits in the GDR had attracted the approval of comparative analysts. An extensive system of creche and kindergarten services complemented the cash benefits. Except in Romania, abortion legislation was liberal. The other side of the coin was the obligation upon women to work and be carers, the unreconstructed division of labour in the home between men and women, the poor quality of the communal services and the lack of user involvement in them. Abortion was often the most available form of contraception.

Housing was cheap. Rents represented a very small proportion of income. The right to a place to live was a policy actively being implemented by many East European governments. The inefficiency of the construction industry and the lack of priority given to it in earlier years has led, however, to extensive shortage. Twenty-year waiting lists were not uncommon. Enforced three-generation and post-divorce communalism was common. Even enforced communal kitchens and bathrooms, a distorted legacy of the idealized communalism of the early Bolsheviks, was common. Recently councils built Gypsy houses with no running water, no sewage disposal systems and no lighting, and with no pavement outside. The better flats were often allocated to the party-state apparatus. The redistributors benefited from the redistribution. Evidence from the Soviet Union (Zaslavskaya, 1990) suggested house building was becoming a major priority in the early perestroika days.

Certainly the system of social security against the financial consequences of sickness and old age was well developed and often provided for benefits that, initially, represented a high proportion of wages. The absence of inflation-proofing, however, turned these benefits over time into gifts of the state that might or might not be uprated periodically. There was a heavily work-related element in the benefits system. Retirement could, however, take place at a relatively young age. The other side of the coin of the social security systems was the paternalistic, parsimonious, cash-limited social aid system administered by local authorities. For those falling outside insured categories of risk, provision was totally inadequate. Allocation according to work record rather than necessity led to unmet and extensive need among widows, the young, disabled, single parents, alcoholics and other outcasts of society.

The state, often through the agency of the workplace or trade union, did indeed exercise a paternalistic concern for those in established workplaces with good work records. Holiday homes, sanatoria, housing and other benefits came with the job. The

Table 1.1 *A system of welfare across Eastern Europe and the Soviet Union*

Advantages	Disadvantages
Job security for many	Inadequate or absent unemployment pay
Workers' wages represent high percentage of average wages	Hidden privileges of party state bureaucrats
Free health services (but oiled with bribes and gifts)	Underdevelopment of preventative approach to health. High mortality/morbidity rates
Three-year child care grants for working women and the right to return to work (especially in the GDR and Hungary)	Obligation upon women to work and care. Sexist division of labour
Highly subsidized flats	Maldistributed flats so better-off live in most heavily subsidized
State-organized social security pension and sick pay system	No index-linking of benefits, and heavily work-record regulated. Totally inadequate back up social aid
Party-state/workplace paternalism	Total absence of rights to articulate social needs autonomously from below

obverse of this system was the virtual absence of any right or facility to articulate welfare needs from below, either in the workplace or outside it. Prior to 1989 pressure groups and charitable organizations working for the poor were outlawed throughout Eastern Europe.

The summary description of the system of welfare existing up to 1989, and continuing in part subsequently, is elaborated in more detail for particular countries in the following chapters.

Table 1.1 summarizes the 'advantages' and 'disadvantages' of the bureaucratic state collectivist system of welfare. Table 1.2 provides some summary social data for the 1980s: a snapshot of the later days of bureaucratic state collectivism compared with similar data for countries within the OECD.

We arrive at the paradox that if they existed in the context of the democratic pluralist politics of the capitalist economies of Western Europe, certain aspects of some social policies of the old Eastern Europe (child care grants and the guarantee of work for mothers and fathers, liberal abortion legislation, subsidized housing, benefit levels set at a high percentage of average earnings) would be heralded by many as the progressive achievements of the social

Table 1.2   *Some social indicators at the end of bureaucratic*
state collectivism

	Soviet Union	Bulgaria	Czecho-slovakia	German Democratic Republic	Hungary	Poland	Romania	OECD
Population (millions)	286.4	9.0	15.6	16.6	10.6	38.0	23.0	824.8
GDP per capita (US dollars)	5,552	5,633	7,603	9,361	6,491	5,453	4,117	14,637
Cars per 1,000 inhabitants	50	127	182	206	153	74	11	385
Life expectancy (average m/f)	70	72	71	73	70	72	70	76
Infant mortality per 1,000 live births (0–1 year)	25	14	13	8	16	16	24	8
Workers with secondary education (%)	27.3	–	29.4	–	33.8	28.8	–	61.0

All data are for 1988, except cars per population which is 1987.
Sources: World Bank, 1990; European Commission, 1991

democratic regulation of market capitalism, whereas within Eastern
Europe they are perceived as part and parcel of the totalitarian state
project of forcing work out of reluctant citizens for purposes which
seem to benefit only the privileged party-state apparatus.

We are also faced with two central conclusions. One is that the
positive (from the Western critics' standpoint) features of East
European social policy – its formal egalitarianism for example – sit
side by side with an underdeveloped and inefficient economy. The
East European experience does underline the point that a balance
of advantages has to be struck between economic efficiency and
distributive justice. We are reminded of Kornai's (1986: 124)
conclusion that

> It is impossible to create a closed and consistent socio-economic
> normative theory which would assert, without contradiction, a political-
> ethical value system and would at the same time provide for the
> efficiency of the economy. . . . What compromises are brought about
> between the different normative principles by the social forces of
> different social systems . . . is a scientific question.

The balance that has been struck historically in Eastern Europe
and the Soviet Union has favoured an egalitarianism of underdevelopment. This understanding prompted Gorbachev (1987: 100)
in the very early days of perestroika to pronounce against crude
egalitarianism and social levelling:

> Equalizing attitudes crop up from time to time even today. Some citizens understood the call for social justice as 'equalizing everyone'. . . . On this point we want to be perfectly clear: socialism has nothing to do with equalizing. Socialism cannot ensure conditions of life and consumption in accordance with the principle 'From each according to his ability, to each according to his work'. This will be under communism.

The inefficiency of the economy which reduced the resources available to fund social measures also, of course, operated *within* the social services so that those free services, such as health, were themselves inadequate by Western standards.

The second general conclusion is that the system of welfare had taken the strategy and logic of Fabian paternalism as far as it could go and it was found wanting. What Sidney and Beatrice Webb admired so much in Stalin's Russia in the thirties was this system of providing *for* people. As important as the issue of inefficiency in the welfare systems of bureaucratic state collectivism was the issue of the absence of the rights to articulate and to lobby for needs autonomously from below. Welfare recipients were objects of provision and never active subjects in defining needs and running services that met needs. The opportunity to exercise influence either through the marketplace or the ballot box or by direct consumer involvement was absent except for a privileged nomenklatura layer. Kornai's concerns about the trade-off between efficiency and equality can be reformulated into a parallel statement about the trade-off between guarantees and autonomy. Here we are reminded of Jordan's conclusion that

> In future societies . . . the debate might be about . . . state services as less the expression of society's compassion and concern, or fear, of the deprived and unfortunate and more the expression of democratic participation itself – the active and politically aware involvement of equal autonomous citizens in the process of designing their societies. (1985: 348)

We return to these trade-off's between equality and efficiency, autonomy and guarantees in the last part of this chapter when we consider the criteria that might be used to evaluate old and new social policy developments.

We shall now turn to the problems bequeathed to new social policy-makers by this legacy and outline the main policy issues to be faced in the period of transition for communism.

Social policy in transition: the issues

Numerous accounts exist elsewhere (Ash, 1990; Dahrendorf, 1990; Glenny, 1990; Sword, 1990) of how the political era of bureaucratic state collectivism in Eastern Europe came to an end. Similarly there has been much discussion already of the economic problems faced by the new governments of the former Soviet Union. Here we are not concerned directly with the political and economic issues. Our focus is on the problems faced by social policy-makers and those who seek to influence social policy in the period of transition. The nature of the emerging political systems and the problems associated with the marketization of the economies will, however, shape both social policy and our discussion of it. At the outset let us assert quite clearly that we believe that the transition we are witnessing now in Eastern Europe and the former Soviet Union is the transition from a type of social and political system we have called bureaucratic state collectivism to capitalism. How quickly this process will take place is not yet clear. Little state property has yet been privatized. The emerging capitalist class of entrepreneurs has yet to establish itself. Whether the transformation will be accompanied by the flowering of pluralist political democracy familiar in Western Europe is also not yet firmly established. Other non-democratic capitalist options exist. These are points we address below and also in the next section of the chapter, which focuses on different capitalist welfare state regime types.

The problems faced by social policy-makers in the period of transition are four-fold. Each of these separate problems compound each other leading to an initially very bleak prospect for the establishment of a set of policies that would engender consensual support and begin to tackle and effect urgent issues.

The first problem is that the past promises of decent housing, good health services, security in conditions of sickness and old age, and other provisions might now be expected to be realized and met. The old inefficient command economies could not deliver, the new market ones will be expected to. Popular expectation combined with a heavy degree of reliance by some beneficiaries of state collectivist welfare on these services and subsidies constitute the first constraint on policy. The second, and related problem, is the legacy of inadequacies and inefficiencies of the past. The populations of Eastern Europe and the former Soviet Union are inadequately housed, suffer more morbidity and die earlier than they need, are ill educated and live in poverty. To bring standards up to West European levels requires that social policy be given a high priority. Third, and compounding cruelly the legacy of problems from the past, are the new welfare problems flowing directly from the first steps being taken across Eastern Europe towards market and eventually capitalist societies. Unemployment is presently about 10 per cent of the workforce. The 'collapse' of the Soviet economy upon which Eastern Europe depended for trade will push these figures higher during 1992 and 1993. A new unemployment benefit system is having to be constructed and funded to meet this situation. As prices rise, either by the impact of market forces or by decree to reflect the real value of products, wages and benefits are failing to keep pace. Real wages and benefits are required to fall to match equivalent real wages for the actual market worth of the products produced in any unit of labour time. During 1990 and 1991 a fall in living standards by around 30 per cent was common across Eastern Europe. A similar, if not larger, fall in living standards will occur in the countries of the former Soviet Union in 1992 and 1993. Compensatory measures are needed, but not often provided, to protect the most vulnerable groups from this impoverishment. Finally, of course, there are fewer funds available to the new governments to meet these requirements constituted of popular expectation, of past neglect, and of new problems of marketization. Government budgets are reduced as the productive tax base shrinks and as requirements of international lending agencies dictate.

Within and alongside this matrix of problems for policy-makers two issues deserve further attention. These are the ones of justice and citizenship. Earlier we discussed the tension and trade-off that exists between egalitarianism and efficiency, and guarantees and autonomy. These issues face East European government and society in the period of transition in particularly acute ways. We address these in turn.

Marketization, inequality and social justice
The revolutions of 1989 were clearly at least partly motivated by the wish of significant sections of the population to join in the fruits of Western capitalist consumerism. A more or less rapid introduction of market mechanisms with a pluralization of forms of property is an inevitable outcome of these social changes. The consequences for social policy are likely to be as follows:

1   A shift in the pattern of social inequality from those based on bureaucratic privilege to those based on market relations. There will be a consequent widening of social inequalities that will be acceptable only insofar as capitalist conceptions of social justice replace egalitarian ones in popular consciousness. The hated injustices of the old regime will give way to the more ready acceptance of some aspects of the inequality of the new regimes. There may, however, be significant sections of the working class who will continue to be attracted by egalitarian sentiments and therefore by a politics of levelling aimed at restoration of the old order or something similar.

2   An incursion of market relations directly into the welfare sphere. Degrees of privatization in the health sector, reduction in subsidy for state housing and an increase in the role of private housing, the replacement of state social security schemes by fully funded enterprise or sectoral schemes, are all likely to emerge. An issue will be whether any of the previously anonymous state property will be converted into communally owned and controlled citizens' property rather than simply privatized. This marketization process will feed the new social inequalities.

An urgent issue, therefore, for policy-making in this field is the determination of what would be regarded as acceptable in terms of new inequalities. What price will the poorest be expected to pay for the general expected improvement in the standard of living of all? How far should benefit levels in periods of incapacity from work reflect new wage inequalities? What minimal degree of compensation for the removal of subsidy will be politically necessary? These and other comparable bread and butter considerations of social policy-makers in the West will be played out in the new situation of Eastern Europe in the 1990s.

Later chapters will review early developments country by country and the concluding chapter will evaluate and comment on emerging trends. It would be reasonable to expect the attraction of egalitarian sentiments to be stronger in some countries than others. Relative power balances will shape the development of these issues in each particular situation. Wnuk-Lipinski (1992) has suggested for Poland that there are those whose interests were blocked under the previous regimes who will use the new situation to satisfy their needs, while those whose interests were relatively well satisfied in the past will be less positive about the new emerging capitalist conception of justice. Sections of the working class and the nomenklatura who were well adapted to the old regime may favour little change. Professional groups and flexible members of the nomenklatura will find advantages in the new order. Debates between Ministers of Finance favouring rapid marketizations and Ministers of Labour and Social Affairs arguing for compensatory social measures, such as is reported in Chapter 4, reflect the crystallization of these new social group and class interests.

Citizenship, civil society and welfare
The revolutions in Eastern Europe of 1989 and the popular resistance to the August 1991 coup in the Soviet Union were symbolic of the frustration of a citizenry which demanded a voice in the future of their country. The articulation of social need from below and the democratic expression of such need in the political

and social sphere were hallmarks of the events of the period. There were exceptions of course. Mass movements played a much greater part in the political changes in the GDR and Czechoslovakia than they did in Hungary. In Poland the Solidarity movement had lost much of its mass character when it finally found itself in power. Perestroika, initially a movement of revolution from above unwelcome to some, provoked the 'conservative' coup of August 1991, which, in turn, generated mass protest and diverse social movements throughout the Soviet Union.

In all these countries, therefore, we would expect fo find a social policy of the future which engages citizens much more actively in running and controlling policy and provision. We would expect to see a flourishing of new social initiatives of a self-help and philanthropic kind. A pluralization of welfare agencies is likely to emerge. We would expect to see political contestation about what and whose social needs to meet.

However, it would be foolish to anticipate an unproblematic ripening of an active and self-managed civil society everywhere. This is more likely in some countries than others. There will be a differentiation of social policy between countries reflecting the extent to which the revolutions from below in each country had a mass character. There will be a differential capacity to make use of the new possibilities of citizenship between various social groups. This will feed the emergence of new inequalities mentioned above. One of the sadder legacies of totalitarian state socialist paternalism will be precisely the dependence of significant sections of the population on the benefits of the old regime. The state will still be looked to to provide even as it gives up this role. On the other hand, the providers of welfare – doctors, teachers and lawyers – will be able to state their terms of provision.

Countries will be distinguished one from the other as to whether all, some or none of the population are ready to become active political, economic and social citizens ready to shape their own and their groups' interests. This diversity will reflect historic and cultural factors. For the Polish situation Kolarska-Bobińska (1992) has noted the low level of self-activity, communal initiative and entrepreneural activity in the early months of 1990. Passivity, apathy, mutual dislike and hostility characterize the new situation. Wnuk-Lipinski (1992) has commented that

> More freedom means greater individual responsibility for one's own life and a more individualized choice of one's life career. For some this may be an unbearable burden. This is a potential social foundation of the 'escape from freedom' syndrome which may result in some kind of populist movement under authoritarian leadership. To help the helpless

seems to be, in this context, the most serious challenge to social policy in a post-communist society.

Hungary represents a different picture. Here bourgeois activity by citizens in the interstices of Kádárism has led to a dualized society in which one half is ready and able to become active subjects of a new welfare capitalism and the other half finds no solution to its problems in the new situation. Julia Szalai (1992) is inclined to suggest the choice is between some form of European welfare future and some form of 'Third World' future.

How the two related issues of social justice and citizenship are resolved over the coming years will be crucial in determining the broad nature of the new social policy regimes. The goal of socially just capitalist economies with flourishing civil societies within which the state reinforces the citizenship rights of the less powerful is by no means a guaranteed outcome. Under the umbrella of these two overarching issues are located a number of more specific social policy issues that will emerge and be addressed in the period of transition. We deal with these briefly now. Each will be addressed in various degrees in the specific country chapters.

Women and liberation from work   Most upsetting from the stand-pont of Western feminists is likely to be the ready embrace by significant sections of the female population of Eastern Europe of the opportunity to escape the double burden of work and mother-hood by giving up work. Unemployment will encourage this process and the pressures will mount for the abandonment of the child care and child grant arrangement which followed from the labour force requirements of the previously full employment economies.

Coupled with this will be the restoration of the influence of the church and the threat this will pose to liberal abortion policies, already a source of conflict in Poland and former East Germany. A countervailing pressure will, of course, be the possibility of the emergence of new autonomous women's movements across Eastern Europe, but the speculation must be that these will be slow in ripening.

Unemployment, poverty and racism   Unemployment will be created everywhere in the countries that replace the former Soviet Union and in Eastern Europe. Hurried, *ad hoc*, uncovenanted benefits not funded by insurance contributions, schemes to establish new enterprises with enterprise allowances to ex-workers and appeals to the voluntary sector to relieve the poor have been the first response of the new governments to the problems created.

There is likely, then, to be a considerable differentiation in policy strategy. In some countries training schemes and fully funded benefit schemes will emerge. In those more wedded to the shock therapy and rigours of market discipline, impoverishment of the few is likely to be tolerated in the interests of the majority.

Existing racist sentiments, as between, say, Hungarians and Gypsies, new (but previously hidden nationally based) racist sentiments, as between, say, Hungarian and Romanian, and even newer racist sentiments derived from the migration of workers across Eastern Europe are certain to flourish in the context of unemployment and impoverishment. The break-up of the Soviet Union will bring with it a myriad of ethnic clashes. A real test of the social policy of the new regimes will be whether they challenge this racism and seek to ameliorate the social consequences or whether they capitulate to it.

Health, ecology and production　The need to rescue populations from premature death and from undue levels of morbidity could be regarded as the paramount social policy question faced by Eastern Europe. The developments both in terms of medical care provision and of preventive health policy are likely to be slow in coming. Privatization of aspects of medical care for some will bring early access to treatment but the level of public spending required to reach the bulk of the population will not be easy to find. Certain particularly health-damaging industrial plants are likely to close quickly but people will continue to live off the polluted soil around them. The introduction of more ecologically sound production techniques in those factories that stay open will take longer-term investment. This slow development, coupled with the new health-threatening consequences of unemployment, new groups entering poverty, growing racism and stressful intensified work, suggests a further decade of early mortality and excessive morbidity for parts of Eastern Europe and the former Soviet Union. In a recent comparative study of Bulgaria, Poland, Hungary and the Soviet Union, Wnuk-Lipinski and Illsley (1990: 889) concluded similarly that

> East European countries are abandoning their non-market economies and taking a radical look at their health systems. Transition to more effective and efficient services will be difficult. They have no appropriate models, they do not possess the organizational and management skills required to establish and maintain new effective institutions; and of course they have very few resources. In the future it will be possible to measure monitor and publish, but the bad health statistics . . . cannot quickly be turned round.

We turn now from considering some of the immediate social policy issues to be faced in the period of transition to a consideration of the welfare regime types that are likely to become established over time in Eastern Europe.

East European social policy in comparative context

Once the immediate post-crisis period of transition from centrally planned to market economies has been overcome, what type of welfare regimes are likely to be established in Eastern Europe and the several countries of the former Soviet Union? How will the characteristics of the newly emerging and probably diverse systems of welfare compare with existing models of welfare capitalism? Will the East eventually merely copy the West, at best, or will new variants of social and economic political strategy emerge?

To set the context for this discussion we need to review the attempts that have been made to classify social policy or welfare state regime types among the developed capitalist nations. The most recent has been Esping-Andersen's (1990) three-fold typology into 'liberal' welfare states, 'conservative corporatist' welfare states and 'social democratic' regime types. He described the essence of these in the following terms.

Liberal. In one cluster we find the 'liberal' welfare state, in which means-tested assistance, modest universal transfers or modest social insurance plans predominate. Benefits cater mainly to a clientele of low-income, usually working-class, state dependants. In this model, the progress of social reform has been severely circumscribed by traditional, liberal work-ethic norms: it is one where the limits of welfare equal the marginal propensity to opt for welfare instead of work. Entitlement rules are therefore strict and often associated with stigma; benefits are typically modest. In turn, the state encourages the market, either passively – by guaranteeing only a minimum – or actively – by subsidizing private welfare schemes.

Conservative corporatist. In these conservative and strongly 'corporatist' welfare states, the liberal obsession with market efficiency and commodification was never pre-eminent and, as such, the granting of social rights was hardly ever a seriously contested issue. What predominated was the preservation of status differentials; rights, therefore, are attached to class and status. This corporatism is subsumed under a state edifice perfectly ready to displace the market as a provider of welfare; hence, private insurance and occupational fringe benefits play a truly marginal role. On the other hand, the state's emphasis on upholding status differences means that its *redistributive impact is negligible*.

But the corporatist regimes are also typically shaped by the church, and hence strongly committed to the preservation of traditional familyhood. Social insurance typically excludes non- · working wives, and family benefits encourage motherhood. Day care, and similar family services, are conspicuously under-developed; the principle of 'subsidiarity' serves to emphasize that the state will only interfere when the family's capacity to service its members is exhausted.

Social democratic. The third, and clearly smallest, regime-cluster is composed of those countries in which the principles of universalism and de-commodification of social rights are extended also to the new middle classes. We may call it the 'social democratic' regime type since, in these nations, social democracy is clearly the dominant force behind social reform. Rather than tolerate a dualism between state and market, between working class and middle class, the social democrats pursued a welfare state that promotes an equality of the highest standards, not an equality of minimal needs as is pursued elsewhere. This implies, first, that services and benefits be upgraded to levels commensurate with even the most discriminating tastes of the new middle classes; and, second, that equality be furnished by guaranteeing workers full participation in the quality of rights enjoyed by the better-off.

Mitchell (1991), following Castles and Mitchell (1990) has suggested that the income transfer data for several welfare states do not easily fit this three-fold typology and suggests a fourth 'Labourite' welfare regime into which she would fit the United Kingdom and Australia. Ginsburg (1992) also presents a four-fold typology of capitalist welfare states. His typology encompasses welfare in a corporate market economy (e.g. the USA), liberal collectivist welfare systems (e.g. the UK), social market economy welfare systems (e.g. Germany), and social democratic welfare systems (e.g. Sweden).

Mishra, in his study of welfare states in crisis (1984) and of the responses of different developed capitalist countries to welfare crisis (1990), distinguished initially differentiated welfare states (DWS) from integrated welfare states (IWS) in which there was a close and planned relationship between economic, labour and social policy. In his later study countries were divided into those that had reacted to economic crisis in terms of a strategy of welfare state retrenchment (e.g. the USA) and those that adopted a more or less successful strategy of welfare state retention (e.g. Sweden). Catherine Jones (1985) attempted a four-fold typology in which regime types were distinguished along two dimensions: one, the level of spending, and two, the extent of welfare commitment identified by universal as distinct from residual provision. At one extreme high-spending universalist regimes were described as high-spending *welfare* capitalist. At the other extreme low-spending residualist regimes were described as low-spending welfare *capitalist*. Table 1.3 compares these typologies.

In arriving at these typologies Esping-Andersen, Mishra, Castles and Jones have, in general, focused their attention on only *some* of the full range of questions we might wish to ask of the social policy of a country. These questions are the level of spending on welfare, the agency (e.g. state or market) of provision (in Esping-Andersen's terms the degree of de-commodification of welfare provision), the distributional impact of welfare activity and the degree of integration of economic, labour and social policy. Mishra (1990) does attempt to address the question of whether women's interests are better served by a social democratic, corporatist or liberal residual welfare policy, but does so only in terms of level of benefit and wages available to women and children and the extent of employment of women rather than the degree to which women are also involved in the formulation and management of policy (Showstack Sassoon, 1987), or in terms of the social relations of welfare policy. When put to tests posed by these questions such regime types might be found wanting (Gould, 1988). Ginsburg (1992) addresses a far more comprehensive set of questions that include the implicit and explicit impact of social policy on the gender division of labour and the extent of racist or ethnic exclusion from welfare rights implicit or explicit in the interrelationship between social policy and immigration and labour market policy. Dominelli (1991), in her feminist comparative text, also addresses many of these issues. We will return to this wider agenda of comprehensive question-setting in cross-national social policy analysis later in the chapter.

Our discussion of the comparative social policy literature has focused entirely on models of welfare capitalism in Western Europe and North America. Although it is likely that variants of these models will emerge in Eastern Europe, it has been argued (Ruzica, 1991) that the price of capitalist development within Eastern Europe might be the loss of democratic pluralism. Regimes that are authoritarian liberal (like Chile) or authoritarian populist (like Peru) may emerge as the only ones that meet the needs of the situation – the need to ruthlessly marketize while not meeting popular welfare expectations or allowing free political activity. It could also be argued that the heavy emphasis on paternalistic occupational and workplace welfare within Eastern Europe might

Table 1.3 *Welfare state regime-types*

Country	Castles and Mitchell (1990)	Ginsburg (1992)	Esping-Andersen (1990)	Jones (1985)	Mishra (1990)
USA	Liberal welfare states	Corporate market economy	Liberal welfare states	Low-spending welfare *capitalist*	Policy of welfare state *retrenchment*
UK	Labourite welfare states	Liberal collectivist	–	Low-spending *welfare* capitalist	Policy of welfare state *retrenchment*
Germany	Conservative corporatist welfare states	Social market economy	Conservative corporatist welfare states	High-spending welfare *capitalist*	–
Sweden	Social democratic regimes	Social democratic	Social democratic regimes	High-spending *welfare* capitalist	Policy of welfare *maintenance*

provide a suitable environment within which the Japanese model of employer welfare could find a natural home should Japanese investment make major inroads into these economies. Other authoritarian and strongly government-led models of capitalist development familiar in South East Asia may also fit the needs of the new Eastern Europe and some of the countries of the former Soviet Union. As Kazakhstan embarks on the privatization of its housing stock, it is seeking the advice of the South Korean business and political community. (A discussion of some of these non European models of welfare capitalism can be found in Jones, 1992.)

We turn now to developments in Eastern Europe and discuss these in the context of the typology set out by Esping-Andersen, but bearing in mind the limitations of his typology and the reservations of the previous paragraphs.

For Esping-Andersen the questions asked and the criteria used to distinguish welfare state regime-types fell into three clusters. These were as follows:

1   The degree of *de-commodification* of provision. He asked to what extent were services and benefits available without price, or independent of insurance contribution or work record, or available on the basis of citizenship entitlement.
2   The *distributional* impact of services and benefits. He asked to what extent the net effect of tax and benefit systems contributed to the generation of inequalities, the maintenance of existing social stratification, or the redistribution in an egalitarian direction of goods and services.
3   The *state/market* mix in pension provision. He asked to what extent were pension entitlements dependent on state systems, occupational systems or market systems.

At this stage in the unfolding of the new Eastern Europe it is clearly not possible to collect the array of data that would be necessary to replicate Esping-Andersen's study in relation to these countries. Nevertheless, on the basis of the accounts of the development of policy described in Chapters 2 to 6, we shall, in the final chapter, begin to suggest whether the countries of Eastern Europe and the former Soviet Union are likely to settle down into one of the three Esping-Andersen's regime-types, or whether a historically new post-bureaucratic state collectivist regime type is emerging, or whether social policy regime types are emerging that have more in common with those of South East Asia or of South America, or elsewhere.

In order to make the tentative predictions of our final chapter we will be guided not only by the descriptions of actual emerging policy in these societies but also by those factors that have been shown by cross-national research to be capable of explaining the variation that exists between existing developed capitalist welfare states. If systematic cross-national research has already demonstrated the explanatory power of certain economic, demographic, political and cultural factors, then it would be reasonable to use these to predict the impact of these variables acting within the newly unfrozen post-communist societies of Eastern Europe and the former Soviet Union. These new developments will provide a testing ground for the adequacy of the theories of welfare state development in the West to accommodate and explain new developments in the East.

The first generation of empirical studies that used factor analysis to try to explain the development of welfare states was epitomized by Wilensky's (1975) cross-national study. This pioneering analysis used data for sixty nations, including less developed and state socialist countries. It was found that economic capacity ('level of economic development'), need ('proportion of the population that was elderly') and administrative momentum ('age of the programme') explained about 80 per cent of the variance in welfare effort ('social security expenditure') which was converging as countries experienced economic growth. Political factors were found to be of little relevance.

In direct response a second type of study, typified by Castles and McKinlay (1979), has attempted to highlight political effects by restricting the sample to Western industrial countries. This method was adopted on the grounds that wider samples have such a large range of economic levels and social structures that it is difficult to detect the effects of political factors. This cross-sectional study of 'advanced democratic states' for 1974 found that, by restricting the sample, political factors such as left-wing mobilization, and the absence of right-wing government, do indeed become predominant, although only about half of the variance in public welfare ('transfer payments, educational expenditure and infant mortality') can be explained. Other studies of the period up to the 1970's came to the same conclusion (Stephens, 1979; Castles, 1982; Esping-Andersen and Korpi, 1984; Rice, 1986).

A third family of studies has taken the obvious step of considering the relationship between economic/social structural factors and political mechanisms in an attempt to synthesize the previous findings. A notable early example was the study by Hicks and Swank (1984) of the impact of both political and economic 'capitalist and working-class-linked actors' on changes in direct cash

Table 1.4 *Explanations of the development of the welfare state*

	Functionalist theory	Conflict theory	
Pluralist	Requirements of (capitalist) industrial system	'Bottom up' reaction to democratization and to worker organization	'Top-down' reaction to failing legitimacy of political elites
	'Integrated Pluralist Model' (combines all above elements)		
Marxist	Need to safeguard capital accumulation, compensate for its negative effects	Response to collective working-class demands	Attempts to win over and integrate workers into accepting existing political system
	'Integrated Marxist Model' (combines all above elements)		

Source: Adapted from Alber, 1982

transfer payments for income maintenance between 1960 and 1971 in 'rich capitalist democracies'. Notwithstanding changes in need (the aged, unemployed and dependant), economic growth and political actions by both right of centre parties and trade unions were the main determinants of transfer spending, explaining 95 per cent of the variance. Similar conclusions about the combination of political and economic determinants were reported in more recent studies in this group (O'Connor, 1988; Castles, 1989; Hicks et al., 1989; Pampel and Williams, 1989; Schmidt, 1989). Both Marxist- and non-Marxist-inspired cross-national studies have tended to converge in terms of the factors invoked. Mishra (1990) suggested a conceptualization of welfare policy flowing from democratic class struggle to embrace the accounts now being offered. Similarly Jones (1985) reported Alber's (1982) review which attempted to show the similarity of Marxist and pluralist explanations for welfare development. Table 1.4 summarizes this consideration.

The factors in these studies that have been invoked as having explanatory capacity on welfare effort have included the following.

- Degree of working-class strength.
- Degree of homogeneity of populations.
- Degree of centralization of state authority.
- Degree and nature of religiosity.

- Degree of social mobility.
- Demographic factors.
- Historico-cultural differences.
- Differential impact of external factors.
- Political choices.
- Political ideology of leading party.

The next step in systematic cross-national research was to invoke factors such as these not just to explain some measure of welfare effort but to use them to explain the diversity of welfare state regime types described earlier in this chapter. Using bivariant and multivariant regression analysis, Esping-Andersen (1990) has demonstrated the power of several variables to explain the divergence between liberal, conservative corporatist and social democratic regime-types. The variables tested that might have been considered to afford a degree of explanatory power are listed below. The means of operationalization of these variables is indicated in parenthesis.

- Demographic need (percentage of population over 65).
- Economic development (GDP).
- Economic growth (percentage real growth between 1960 and 1980).
- Working-class mobilization variable (left political party measured by cabinet share of seats).
- Influence of Catholic teaching on social policy (proportion of parliamentary seats).
- Historical impact of absolutism and authoritarianism (three-fold classification and year of universal suffrage).

Neither population structure nor GDP nor rate of growth of GDP were particularly significant in explaining the variation between developed welfare state regime types. Their explanatory power had been exhausted in the first generation of cross-national studies that had compared underdeveloped, middle-income and developed countries (Wilensky, 1975). There was some evidence however to suggest GDP is linked positively to liberal welfare state regime types.

Conservative corporatist regime types were more likely to exist where there was a combined influence of Catholicism and a legacy of authoritarian statehood. Liberal welfare regimes types were more likely to exist where left political party representation was low and when, combined with this, economic growth was high. Social democratic regime types were only likely to exist where left-wing political power was high and Catholicism low (Esping-Andersen, 1990: 133–8).

Any initial attempt to 'test' the capacity of these variables, and others, to predict and explain the emerging divergence between welfare state regime types in Eastern Europe and the former Soviet Union is bound to be tentative. Even a retrospective analysis in a few years' time will be provisional. One of the immediate problems to be faced will be how the variables might be interpreted and hence measured in these very different circumstances. GDP, rate of growth and population structure present fewer problems but we might expect GDP to play a greater part in explaining variation because of the relative underdevelopment of some of the countries of Eastern Europe and the former Soviet Union. A more complicated question is what is meant by working-class mobilization, Catholic party influence and the strength of the absolutist and authoritarian tradition and practice in the context of the new Eastern Europe, and how should these be measured? In terms of left political party representation do the transformed communist parties count along with the old and newly created social democratic parties as the only left parties? What about other forms of working-class strength via direct links with the nomenklatura unmediated by political party? Do the radical free democrats of Hungary which have few links to the old trade union movement but progressive social policy ideas count here? Where do Civic Forum and Solidarity – initially eschewing party political ideology and form but now breaking up into parties – fit into this picture? The degree of working-class mobilization associated with the two movements was quite different. Similar problems arise in terms of counting the number of Catholic seats where Catholicism is expressed indirectly through Solidarity in the eyes and practices of some members of the *Sejm*. Where does the Orthodox Church within some of the Balkan republics fit here? It is less concerned with social issues and more with scripture and hence will not have the social impact of Catholicism. Absolutism and authoritarian tradition represent a fascinating question. Do we count the overthrow of the Tsar as the end of absolutism or has absolutist rule continued until today? Similarly in Poland there is a thread of continuity running through the pre-war dictatorships and the post-war Stalinists. Czechoslovakia had a longer lesson in democracy.

In addition to the problems in interpreting and measuring these variables in these new circumstances one could suggest the importance of other factors absent from Esping-Andersen's model which are likely to play a part in shaping the social policy futures of Eastern Europe. The nature and character of the 1989 revolutions is one of these. Another is the direct and indirect political impact of transnational agencies (IMF, European Community, World Bank).

A third is the experience gained through societal learning from other countries. The countervailing pressures of the IMF, on the one hand, requiring the reduction of public expenditure as the price for loans, and the European Community, on the other, requiring for membership the existence of a set of policies and provisions compatible with the requirements of the Social Charter will clearly influence the tactics and strategy of East European governments. The new political actors of Eastern Europe will be influenced by and choose from already existing social policy strategies. We consider all of these issues and set out our initial prediction of emerging welfare state regime types in Eastern Europe in the last chapter.

Evaluating new policy developments after 'communism'

Another approach to the study of the new social policy of Eastern Europe would be to evaluate developments as they take place against a set of criteria that have common currency among analysts of comparative social policy.

In the extensive social policy literature there have been in fact very few attempts to set out systematically a typology of criteria that might attract wide agreement. Sometimes normative concerns with equality preoccupy an author. At other times there is focus on levels of public expenditure. Comparative studies have often adopted somewhat uncritically (Wilensky, 1975) those criteria which are readily measurable, such as the age participation rates of the population in higher education. Specialist studies of particular services have developed useful outcome indicators. Obviousy the comparative tables published by the WHO, UNESCO and the World Bank on, for example, mortality rates are of value. An earlier study (Deacon, 1983), in an attempt to move away from a limited focus on expenditure levels and develop criteria that addressed the way in which welfare services were experienced, suggested six criteria:

- Priority afforded to welfare.
- Form of control over provision.
- Balance of agencies (state/market/family, etc.) providing welfare.
- Relationship of user to provider.
- Distribution and rationing principles.
- Assumptions of policy concerning family policy/sexual division of labour.

This approach to systematic question-setting in cross-national analysis was endorsed by Higgins (1986), who developed the approach further in a definitive review of comparative social policy.

More recently Williams (1989), in a concern to inject into the mainstream of the social policy discipline issues flowing from feminist and anti-racist critiques, has added the following criteria:

- Relations implied between, family and women.
- Basis of women's eligibility to welfare.
- Relationship between state policy and migrant labour.
- Extent to which social policy is racist.
- National or international basis to welfare entitlement.

It is interesting to note Inkeles's suggestion (1989), in a study comparing welfare policy in the Soviet Union and USA, that comparative criteria should move away from a reliance only on measures of expenditure to incorporate measures of experience, but that even here there is a blindness to feminist and anti-racist concerns. In this case four criteria are argued for:

- Level of expenditure on welfare.
- Degree of social justice embodied in provision.
- Subjective evaluation by welfare users.
- Outcomes (e.g. mortality rates).

In all of these and other more partial contributions there tends to be an elision between the search for additional criteria and the value judgement of the author of the criteria. Social relations between provider and user are added because it is believed they should be of reciprocal co-operation. The basis of a woman's entitlement to welfare is added because it is believed it should be on the basis of independent citizenship and not as a dependant or as a mother. In Table 1.5, where we offer a list of ten criteria against which we might judge social policy developments, we separate clearly the criterion from the value judgement which we personally choose to bring to bear on that criterion. Simply to suggest, as we do, that the distribution principles of a social policy should be considered does not imply that these principles should embody a degree of egalitarianism. We could applaud a social policy that let the tall poppies grow. Equally to include as one of the criteria the form of control over welfare provision does not necessarily imply that they should be democratic. We could applaud an autocratic form of control.

Table 1.5 lists, then, on the one hand, all the criteria that we could imagine being used to evaluate a social policy, and on the other, the value judgements and beliefs we would choose to bring to bear on each of these criteria in turn. These value judgements derive from our belief that they represent the interests of the many rather than the few, that they represent the interests of welfare

Table 1.5 *Criteria for evaluating social policy*

Criterion	Our value judgement
1 Degree of self-activity by *civil society* in shaping policy and provision	High
2 Relationship between social policy and *economic policy*	Integrated with social concerns dominant
3 *Priority* afforded to welfare provision (includes outcome measures)	High but with degree of individual choice above universal standard
4 What social group *interests* served by social policy	All
5 *Agencies* of provision (i.e. state, market, citizens, family, employer, etc.)	Mixture and diversity in civil society
6 Form of *control* over policy and provision	Democratic (both direct and indirect representation involving workers, users and citizens)
7 *Relationship* of welfare provider and welfare user	Reciprocal co-operation
8 *Distribution* and rationing principles	Degree of equality consistent with economic efficiency and individual choice
9 Implications for *family* form and sexual division of labour	Variety of family forms with no assumed gendered form of care
10 *National* and *ethnic* basis of policy and provision	No national or racial basis to entitlement, but with diverse ethnic forms of provision

users rather than providers, that they represent the interests of women and black people rather than white men only.

It would be a simple matter if we could leave it there and add all our preferred attributes of an ideal social policy together (the ten criteria coupled with our values) and look for the strategy that contributed all of these. In fact, in reality choices have to be faced as to which of the attributes are more valued than others because strategies that score high on some seem always to score low on others. Concretely and centrally, as we suggested earlier, there are to some extent choices between (1) efficiency and equality, and (2) autonomy and guarantees.

Historically we might conclude that the varied welfare states of the West provide for more autonomy of citizens to articulate and provide for their needs (although not enough) at the expense of the guarantee of provision to all, whereas the opposite tendency is true in the East. Similarly the welfare states of the West provide more efficiently for housing and health care and other social provision but with less equality both inside and outside the welfare sphere, whereas the opposite tendency is true in the East. The extent of nomenklatura privilege does, of course, qualify this over-simple assertion.

The above can be set out in diagrammatic form as in Figure 1.1. Here we describe the extent to which this is true, first, as a self-image (or official ideology) of the system, and, second, in reality, insofar as we can draw on empirical evidence to demonstrate the image/reality gap in the case of bureaucratic collectivism. We include here only liberal welfare state types (the USA), social democratic welfare state types (Sweden), bureaucratic state collectivist types (the Soviet Union). The model would need to be more complicated to accommodate the idea of conservative corporatism.

Our task could be, therefore, to imagine a social policy system that is, if possible, both just and efficient and provides for both autonomy and social guarantees. In fact, of course, we have to argue, following Kornai (1986), that in any imaginable society of the immediate future there will be *choices* to be made between competing values, albeit these choices will, in practice, be a reflection of different interests and social forces operating in that society. At present social democratic regime types seem to best combine these conflicting desirable features.

As far as these sets of values and criteria for judging social policy developments are concerned, we would applaud a strategy that tends towards both more equality and more efficiency and more autonomy and more guarantees but where the foresaking to some extent of one for the other in either case is the outcome of a democratic political process where the interests and the will of the majority in society are expressed. In other words that political strategy is to be preferred that allows the maximum degree of informed choice about these questions to be exercised by citizens both for themselves and for the society. Here we follow Doyal and Gough (1992) in their discussion on basic human needs and the constitutional and personal prerequisites for these to be met.

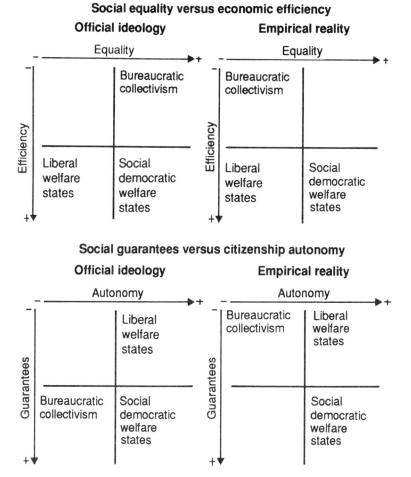

Figure 1.1 *Systematic choices between social equality and economic efficiency, social guarantees and citizens autonomy*

Conclusion

In this chapter we have summarized the characteristics of the system of social welfare that existed in the bureaucratic state collectivist regimes of Eastern Europe prior to their collapse in 1989. We have set out the immediate issues to be faced by social policy-makers in the period of transition with which these regimes are now confronted. We have situated our study of the newly emerging welfare states of Eastern Europe in the context of the comparative social policy literature within which various welfare capitalist regime types have been described. Finally we have set out criteria against which new developments in East European social policy might be evaluated.

The subsequent country-specific chapters will indicate where the pre-1989 policy and practice of these countries departed from the general model of bureaucratic state collectivism described above. They will describe the new developments in social policy addressing implicitly or explicitly the issues highlighted in this chapter. Some of the chapters begin a country-specific assessment of the new policies both in terms of welfare capitalist regime types and the criteria set out for evaluating developments.

In the final chapter we will review and summarize these accounts of social policy in transition, note the diversity of development, make an initial prediction of the type of welfare regimes that are likely to emerge over the next few years and offer an initial evaluation of some of the post-communist developments. We will also return to the theme of an ideal socialist social policy and discuss what might now be meant by such a concept in the light of the 'anti-communist' revolution of 1989.

References

Abrahamson, P. (1991) *Welfare and Poverty in the Europe of the 1990s*. Roskilde University, Denmark.

Alber, J. (1982) 'Le Origini del Welfare State: Teorie, Ipotesi ed Analisi Empirici', *Rivista Italiana di Scienza Politica*, XII (3): 361–421.

Ash, T.G. (1990) *We the People*. Harmondsworth: Penguin.

Castles, F. (1982) *The Impact of Parties*. London: Sage.

Castles, F. (1989) *A Comparative History of Public Policy*. Cambridge: Polity.

Castles, F. and McKinlay, N. (1979) 'Public welfare provision, Scandinavia, and the sheer futility of the sociological approach to politics', *British Journal of Political Science*, 9: 157–71.

Castles, F. and Mitchell, D. (1990) *Three Worlds of Welfare Capitalism or Four*, Public Policy Discussion Paper No. 21 Canberra Australian National University.

Dahrendorf, R. (1990) *Reflections on the Revolution in Europe*. London: Chatto and Windus.

Deacon, B. (1983) *Social Policy and Socialism*. London: Pluto.

Deacon, B. and Szalai, J. (eds) (1990) *Social Policy in the New Eastern Europe*. Aldershot: Gower.

Dominelli, L. (1991) *Women Across Continents*. Hemel Hempstead: Harvester-Wheatsheaf.

Doyal, L. and Gough, I. (1992) *A Theory of Human Needs*, London, Macmillan.

Esping-Andersen, G. (1990) *The Three Worlds of Welfare Capitalism*. Cambridge: Polity.

Esping-Andersen, G. and Korpi, W. (1984) 'Social policy as class politics in post-war capitalism', in J.H. Goldthorpe (ed.), *Order and Conflict in Contemporary Capitalism*. Oxford: Oxford University Press.

European Commission (1991) *The European Community and its Eastern Neighbours*. Brussels: Office of Official Publications, European Commission.

Feher, F. and Arato, A. (eds) (1989) *Gorbachev: the Debate*. Cambridge: Polity.

Ginsburg, N. (1992) *Divisions of Welfare*. London: Sage.

Glenny, M. (1990) *The Re-birth of History*. Harmondsworth: Penguin.

Gorbachev, M. (1987) *Perestroika*. London: Fontana.

Gould, A. (1988) *Conflict and Control in Welfare Policy: the Swedish Experience*. London: Longman.

Hage, J. (1989) *State Responsiveness and State Activism*. London: Unwin Hyman.

Hicks, A. and Swank, D. (1984) 'Welfare expansion: A comparative analysis of 18 advanced capitalist democracies, 1960–71', *Comparative Policy Studies*, 17 (1): pp. 81–119.

Hicks, A., Swank, D. and Ambuhl, M. (1989) 'Welfare expansion revisited: 1957–1982', *European Journal of Policy Research*, 17 (6): 401–30.

Higgins, J. (1986) 'Comparative social policy', *Quarterly Journal of Social Affairs*, 2 (3): 221–42.

Inkeles, A. (1988) 'Re-thinking social welfare: USA and USSR in comparative perspective', in G. Lapidus and G. Swanson (eds), *State and Welfare USA USSR*. Berkeley, CA: University of California Press.

Jones, C. (1985) *Patterns of Social Policy*. London: Tavistock.

Jones, C. (ed.) (1992) *Comparative Social Policy: Trends and Prospects*, Routledge.

Jordan, B. (1985) *The State: Authority and Autonomy*. Oxford: Basil Blackwell.

Kolarska-Bobińska, L. (1992) 'Civil society and society anomy in Poland', in B. Deacon (ed.), *Social Policy, Social Justice and Citizenship in Eastern Europe*. Aldershot: Gower. pp. 55–69.

Kornai, J. (1986) *Contradictions and Dilemmas*. Cambridge, MA: MIT Press.

McAuley, A. (1990) 'The Central Asian economy in comparative perspective'. Paper presented at the World Congress of Soviet and East European Studies, Harrogate, England, 21–6 July 1990.

Mezentseva, E. and Rimachevskaya, N. (1990) ' "The Soviet Country". Profile: Health of the USSR population in the 70's and 80's', *Social Science and Medicine*, 31 (8): 867–77.

Mishra, R. (1984) *The Welfare State in Crisis*. Brighton: Wheatsheaf.

Mishra, R. (1990) *The Welfare State in Capitalist Society*. Hemel Hempstead: Harvester-Wheatsheaf.

Mitchell, D. (1991) *Income Transfers in Ten Welfare States*. Gower.

O'Connor, J.S. (1988) 'Change in welfare effort in OECD Countries: 1960–80', *European Journal of Policy Research*, 17: 401–30.

Pampel, F.C. and Williams, J.B. (1989) *Age, Class, Politics, and the Welfare State*. Cambridge: Cambridge University Press.

Rice, T.W. (1986) 'The determinants of Western European Government 1950–1980', *Comparative Political Studies*, 19 (2): 233–57.

Ruzica, M. (1991) 'Post-Communist states, transition, social policy'. Paper presented at a conference on the Welfare State: Transition from Central Planning to Market Approaches. Budapest, June.

Schmidt, M.G. (1989) 'Social policy in rich and poor countries: socio-economic trends and political-institutional determinants', *European Journal of Policy Research*, 17 (6): 641–59.

Showstack Sassoon, A. (ed.) (1987) *Women and the State*. London: Hutchinson.

Stephens, J.D. (1979) *The Transition from Capitalism to Socialism*. London: Macmillan.

Sword, K. (ed.) (1990) *The Times Guide to Eastern Europe*. London: Times Books.

Szalai, J. (1992) 'Social participation in Hungary in the context of restructuring and liberalisation' in B. Deacon (ed.), *Social Policy, Social Justice and Citizenship in Eastern Europe*. Aldershot: Gower. pp. 37–55.

Wilensky, H. (1975) *The Welfare State and Equality*. Berkeley, CA: University of California Press.

Williams, F. (1989) *Social Policy: a Critical Introduction*. Cambridge: Polity.

Wnuk-Lipinski, E. (1992) 'Freedom and equality: an old dilemma in a new context', in B. Deacon (ed.), *Social Policy, Social Justice and Citizenship in Eastern Europe*. Aldershot: Gower. pp. 178–89.

Wnuk-Lipinksi, E. and Illsley, R. (1990) 'International comparative analysis: main findings and conclusion', *Social Science and Medicine*, 31 (8): 879–89.

World Bank (1990) *World Development Report 1990*. Washington, DC: World Bank.

Zaslavskaya, T. (1990) *The Second Socialist Revolution*. London: I.B. Tauris.

2

Social Policy in the Soviet Union and its Successors

Nick Manning

To understand Soviet social policy, it is necessary to understand the nature of the Soviet Union, as it was until December 1991. Conversely, social policy is also an important and much neglected source which can help to inform more general theoretical debate about Soviet society and the society of the republics which succeed it. This theoretical debate has developed in two fairly separate streams.

On the one hand, the totalitarian model was initially used by political scientists, followed by its collapse. In its wake, attention has shifted to a variety of middle-range theoretical foci such as interest groups, corporatism, development/industrialism and a functionalist use of systems theory (White and Nelson, 1986). These have been tested with increasing care through the slow accumulation of case study and quantitative data. While the development of the economy is acknowledged to be of great importance, much of this work takes this as given and analyses the political system as a relatively autonomous phenomenon.

On the other hand, a variety of approaches drawing on Marxist theory have been elaborated. Marxist work explicitly includes economic development as an integral element in the analysis of political change. In addition to the official Soviet view of itself as 'developed socialism under conditions of scientific-technological change', Marxists have traditionally split over whether the Soviet mode of production was capitalist, socialist or in some state of transition in between. In the absence of satisfactory proof either way, more recent work has posed the possibility of a new mode of production (bureaucratic collectivism), and hence a new route between pre-industrial society and socialism-communism (Manning, 1984).

The latter views contain an important loosening of the Marxist assumption about the place of economic factors in the explanation of political change. In other words, they are primarily concerned with the apparent autonomy of the political system and to that extent have begun to use ideas more familiar to the political science tradition. Hence terms such as bureaucratic collectivism (Melotti, 1977; Machover and Fantham, 1979), dictatorship over needs (Feher et al., 1983), centralized state redistribution (Szelenyi and Manchin, 1987) and organic labour state (Harding, 1984) are being used to analyse the way in which political direction seems to resist expected economic constraints. Nevertheless, these models remain distinct in that they assume that Soviet society consisted of an integrated totality, in that there appears to have been a stable and therefore reproducible pattern of social relations for which in principle a primary dynamic can be identified.

The crucial question here is about stability and change, both because this theoretical debate can only be advanced through the study of change, and more immediately because of the question of the significance of perestroika, the attempted coup in August 1991, and the collapse of the Soviet Union in December 1991. Two opposing views frequently appear in the literature. On the one hand, Soviet society is seen as the site of remarkable continuities, so that even where change occurred, it was interpreted as a variation on a long-standing cultural or political tradition. On the other hand, imminent radical change is predicted, often in the form of the collapse of the system. In fact neither of these views is really concentrated in any particular theoretical tradition, although political science has moved from an emphasis on Soviet stability to the acknowledgement of change, while Marxist work has developed its new models for precisely opposite reasons – the absence of change seemed to require new thinking about stability.

Not only are these debates crucial to an adequate analysis of Soviet social policy, but such debates can be usefully advanced through the study of these policy issues in the Soviet and post-Soviet setting. A glance through the journals and literature on Eastern Europe reveals immediately a relative neglect of such domestic fare. Such an analysis, using the changing development of Soviet social policy, has been used to discuss the relative strengths of competing models elsewhere (Manning, 1984; George and Manning, 1980), and will be developed further in the course of this chapter.

Needless to say, it is important to remember the differences between the former Soviet Union and the other nations of East/ Central Europe. The dimensions of time and space indicate immediately the unique situation Gorbachev's Soviet Union was in. The pre-Stalin era had effectively disappeared into history as a shared popular experience and hence source of inspiration, and the size of the Union made 'capital city-dominated' politics, typical of Central Europe, immeasurably more complicated. Consequently, civil society activism, whether political, entrepreneurial or self-help, was, compared with East/Central Europe, relatively muted, while the traditional struggle for power, particularly over regime succession, such as the failed coup against and final resignation of Gorbachev, continued, albeit now open to public view.

Soviet society, social issues and social policy: the old regime

Picking up the point about the relative longevity of the Soviet era, and as a necessary prelude to a discussion of the process of social policy change under perestroika and beyond, we can usefully begin with a brief review of social conditions and social policy in earlier times. Using criteria of policy aims and resources, implementation and policy effects, it has been suggested (Manning, 1984) that Soviet social policy could be divided into four periods: utopian (1917–21), urban (1921–9), industrial (1929–57), welfare/productivity (1957–84). Distinct patterns of social policy are associated with those periods.

The first brief period can be suitably described as one in which problems were seen to be the result of social disorganization brought about by the twin problems of war and capitalism. Although this was a time of wide debate about the future of social policy, there was no particular difficulty in identifying the objective conditions which were problematic and there was general agreement on the values which were felt to be threatened. For example, about 50 per cent of the population was illiterate, and Lenin argued that 'an illiterate person stands outside; he must first be taught the ABC. Without this there can be no politics; without this there are only rumours, gossip, tales, prejudices, but no politics' (quoted in Pinkevitch, 1929: 375). Similarly, epidemics were rife: cases of typhus rose from 22 per 10,000 in 1918, to 265 in 1919, and 394 in 1920. As Lenin put it, once again succinctly: 'either the lice will defeat socialism or socialism will defeat the lice' (Lenin, 1965: 185). Mass campaigns were mobilized to deal with these threats.

The next period runs from 1921 to 1929. Here we begin to see the development of greater debate about the nature and existence of social issues, and therefore the kind of solutions which should be adopted. Bettleheim (1978) has graphically captured the struggles of this period in his portrayal of the party as falling into the hands of the middle class. Along with this process we begin to see the way in which sectional interests come to affect perceptions. Having survived the immediate problems of war communism, the overriding concern was about the future direction and pace of economic development. Since the source of capital had to be the agricultural worker, the main social issue of the day became the recalcitrant farmer, who was blamed for resisting collectivization, eating too much food and developing a taste for capitalistic agriculture.

The analysis of problems shows a clear shift from an assumption of value consensus to a struggle over value conflict. Not surprisingly, the imagery changes from a struggle with objective conditions to a struggle to label problem groups. It was this change which paved the way for Stalin's 'Urals-Siberian method' for procuring grain. Problem groups justified the use of violence, since a more familiar method, namely education, was unlikely to produce the desired changes quickly enough. The conflicts about this policy in the party at the time are well enough known, and illustrate graphically both the decay of consensus and the process adopted of re-establishing it, that is, the isolation of opponents.

During the next period, which covers the years of Stalin's power, the main focus of concern was with industrialization. This is the framework within which social concerns were analysed and dealt with. Debate about the problematic nature of social conditions withered. For example, the inadequate production of housing for the rapidly growing and urbanizing population resulted in a steady fall in average urban per capita housing space, to dip below four square metres by 1940. Yet this never came to be seen as a problem.

In contrast the supply and discipline of labour was a perennial concern. Anything that appeared to get in the way of this objective was liable to be seen as deviant. Thus the rules which defined rights at work, social security entitlements, security of tenure and sickness absence were all progressively tightened during the thirties, so that their infraction came to be seen as an individual failing. The obsessive drive for rapid industrialization as a key defence of the Revolution against the fear of 'capitalist encirclement' made possible, as it turned out, the defeat of the invasion by Germany. The subsequent destruction of people and property would have been far worse without this policy, as Gorbachev and others have suggested since. But in this period up to the 1950s there was little room for the perceived luxury of social problems.

In the previous analysis of social policy (Manning, 1984) no divisions were made within the post-Stalin era. This is no longer justifiable. Whatever the limitations of Khrushchev's concrete achievements, he opened up debate in a remarkable manner which encouraged consideration of a whole range of issues. The tone was set by his 'secret speech' which raised Stalin's policies in their entirety as problematic. This change was not merely the whim of a new leader. The late fifties and early sixties were significant economically, and, in parallel to the twenties (and, one should add, to the eighties), this gave rise to intense debate about the future direction policies should take; it also gave rise to new debate in the West about the real nature of Soviet society.

Between 1957 and 1964 Khrushchev sought to re-establish early ideals as his guide to policy, particularly through the 20th Party Programme, 'The Road to Communism'. This entailed the rebuilding of a vigorous party after the decimation of the 1930s in order to overcome the interests of groups like industrial managers committed to existing patterns of investment and social policy. He used the media in an innovative way, both to raise issues for debate and to muster support for his ideas. However, his success was limited. For example, housing was successfully promoted as a social problem in one respect, namely the development of mass production through pre-existing economic mechanisms. However, control over the distribution of housing and the commensurate provision of environmental services necessitated a significant shift in power from industrial managers to local soviets. This was never achieved, despite legal directives.

It was suggested earlier that in the twenties the opening up of debate indicated a lack of consensus over which social conditions were a problem, and therefore how they should be dealt with. One consequence was that perceptions changed from social problems as objective conditions to the identification of problem groups, in the competition to establish a particular viewpoint. Earlier this group had been the farmers. Now it was to be the new middle classes, made up of industrial managers, senior intellectuals and party careerists. This can be seen, for example, in Khrushchev's education reforms, which prioritized workers at the expense of more privileged groups precisely in this, the most important site for class reproduction in Soviet society.

This was a time of the politicization of social issues. Khrushchev deliberately sought to provoke debate, even crisis, as a means of melting political structures in the hope that the resulting changes would crystallize into a pattern which more closely resembled his ideal. As it turned out, he took on more than he could control, and in 1964 he himself became defined as the problem and was removed by the very groups he criticized.

The following twenty years, while exhibiting relative continuity in social policies, could not have been more of a contrast. Stability rather than change was paramount. There was a return to consensus about the problems facing Soviet society. 'Developed socialism' was to be built slowly and methodically. No great leaps forward, or in any other direction! Social problems therefore became departures from a common norm of steady progress. Rather than a struggle to identify and label problem groups, perceptions shifted as in the thirties and forties to the rooting out of deviant individuals. While this never attained the paranoid depths of the thirties, the pursuit of dissidents and the misuse of psychiatry in the firm belief that dissent must be *de facto* a form of madness indicates the absence of legitimate debate in the 'years of stagnation'. In a sense there were no social problems in the 1970s. While, of course, social conditions changed (divorce rose, the population aged, the economy slowed and life expectancy faltered), increasingly unreal assurances were given of business as usual.

The development of social debate since 1985 is not difficult to predict from this pattern. There seems indeed to have been a periodic swing in Soviet domestic political activity which is quite clearly reflected in the way in which social policy has been perceived and dealt with. This can be specifically associated with two different models (Manning, 1985): on the one hand, problems are seen to be located in objective social conditions, or deviant individuals, at odds with the dominant consensus; on the other hand, problems are the site of political struggle over the right path to pursue for social development. The latter seems to be the case for the twenties, the fifties and the eighties. Whereas in the former case individual victims are blamed and changed, in the latter case there is an intense political debate. The objective on the part of the contending groups is, ironically, to vanquish opposing perceptions and hence usher in a new era of consensus by relegating the problem to the realm of a technical solution.

Problems of social policy, pre-perestroika

Under Brezhnev social policy exhibited the relative stability that was characteristic of most aspects of government from the late 1960s to the early 1980s. This was the achievement of 'developed socialism' (Evans, 1986) – a description adopted to signify the technological modernization of Soviet economic life. The term, however, also acknowledged the absence of any of the fundamental changes in social relationships towards full communism that Khrushchev, in the 1959 party programme, had claimed would be achieved by 1980 (Gilison, 1975). Deacon (1983, and Chapter 1 above) has described the limited achievements of Soviet social policy in this era. In general it may be characterized as the pursuit of the gross expansion of 'intermediate' welfare indicators, such as the numbers of doctors or nurses, or the numbers of flats, or the numbers of teachers, or the early retirement age. The figures for these were proudly displayed as signs of the inexorable upward growth of 'developed socialism', although even these were subject to the restraint of the 'residual principle':

> In the last fifteen years, as an aspect of the negative processes mentioned above, the fall in the rate of growth and in economic efficiency has been especially painfully reflected in our inability to solve our social problems. Resources were allocated to the social sector according to the so-called 'residual principle', whereby capital investment was firstly directed towards industrial goals, while housing, the raising of living standards and other improvements in people's lives only received what remained. (Aganbegyan, 1988: 15–16)

Thus 'final' welfare indicators, such as the meeting of social needs, or the quality of the goods and services provided, or the kind of social relationships that were produced or reproduced, were not so impressive. For example, the position of women as both workers in and consumers of welfare received relatively little analysis, and elicited relatively little concern within the Soviet Union. This was the result of a very weak women's movement, official equality for women and the general lack of opportunity and resources for issue-based politics. Again, the conflicts of interest between different ethnic and national groups, so dominant in recent Soviet internal events, were assumed to be dissolving within a superordinate socialist society. Yet the mechanism for this, migration and russification, was deeply resented.

Kornai (1980) has suggested that this overshadowing of quality by quantity is a logical result of the Soviet model in which individual enterprises and organizations operate in a 'shortage' environment, thus enabling output to be distributed regardless of quality, and with 'soft' budgets as to the resources used. Indeed anyone who systematically questioned whether these gross production figures were sufficient indicators of the achievements of 'developed socialism' was likely to experience harassments of varying severity by agents of the state. There developed therefore a growing gap between everyday experience and the official version of the nature of social policies (Goldfarb, 1989). It is this general gap which underlies the specific problems that we can now identify in different social policy areas. We will briefly review one or two of the most significant problems in each area which built up in the years following the 1960s.

Social security

Social security is in all modern societies the most expensive social service, costing almost as much as all other services together. It is closely related to the labour market, either in the sense of the earning of entitlements, or in the sense of concerns about the general incentive to work. It is also relatively simple, in that it involves relatively little of the labour intensity or production activities of the other social services. It is consequently a relatively pure site for the expression of official preferences and *de facto* status differences within the population.

One of the great achievements claimed in the Soviet Union was that there was no unemployment, since work was a guaranteed right under Article 40 of the Constitution. Unemployment benefit disappeared in 1930 at a time of greatly tightened labour codes under Stalin's drive for industrialization. This achievement was a mixed blessing for workers, however, since the employment that was guaranteed may well be in unpopular parts of the country or in unpopular industries. Pensions were also closely shaped to labour requirements in that they were insufficient for many years, driving most pensioners out to work. However, the Brezhnev years inherited from Khrushchev a dramatic improvement in the basic level of pensions (George and Manning, 1980), sufficient for the majority of pensioners to withdraw from the labour market for the first time, and at an earlier age than in most industrial countries. Nevertheless, this severance of the link between labour conditions and pensions was not complete, for inequalities of working income were reproduced in pension rates. Moreover, for most pensioners, with a 1986 per capita average of 89 roubles a month (and not index-linked), the basic level was insufficient to bring them much above 70 roubles – in effect the semi-official poverty line, established by the survey results made possible under Khrushchev (Matthews, 1986).

This link between work history and social security in the Soviet Union illustrates the heavily 'insurance-based' design of the system, which was essentially geared to entitlements carefully accumulated as a result of a good employment record. By contrast, the 'social assistance' function, designed to provide income in response to a test of need, was unsystematically developed. This helps to explain why the social security system was neglectful of a number of 'pure need' groups, such as poor children, the disabled, the unemployed:

> Thirty years of almost uninterrupted growth in the standard of living of workers and collective farm workers, although at a very slow rate, have been accompanied by a scandalous backwardness in social allocations. The result is the appearance of a widespread layer of 'new poor' in the country. Tens of millions of people, including invalids, the disabled, widows, single mothers (they are still called 'deserted wives' in the Soviet Union), alcoholic down-and-outs, and youth on the fringes of society, are living well below the breadline. (Mandel, 1989: 12)

Health care

Health care seems at first blush to have been a great achievement of the Soviet Union. It had more doctors, nurses and hospital beds per capita than any other major industrial country (Mezentseva and Rimachevskaya, 1990). It had a rational structure of health facilities, which started with the allocation of doctors to local housing areas (where they could undertake some quasi-social work activities). Patients were registered at the local polyclinic where 'their' doctor was based, and possibly also registered at the health station at their place of work – some of which, such as the railways, had highly regarded facilities. Specialist hospitals were regionally based (George and Manning, 1980).

However, criticisms about Soviet health care steadily accumulated. Resources devoted to health care by comparison with international trends, even compared with the UK which is at a relatively low level, were extremely meagre in the Soviet Union: about 4 per cent of net material product (NMP) (equivalent to about 2.5 per cent of 'GNP' calculated on a market basis), compared with 6 per cent of GNP in the UK, and 10 per cent of GNP in the USA (Davis, 1990). The consequence of this is that well-known medical procedures were not available in the areas of technology, antibiotics, the control of cross-infections in health facilities, and the public health control of infectious diseases and other public health problems such as alcoholism. These criticisms are supported by the stagnation, and then degeneration, of both overall and infant mortality rates from the early 1970s onwards (Mezentseva and Rimachevskaya, 1990).

In a wider sense there were also deficiencies in health care arising through the effects of other policy priorities. The most infamous was the misuse of psychiatric hospitals and treatment to both detain and punish dissidents. This resulted in the expulsion of the Soviet Union from the World Psychiatric Association in 1983 (Dossett-Davies, 1988b). A second example is the development of workplace health stations. These are typically presented as a generous extra dimension to Soviet health care in comparison with the West, such that Soviet workers' needs could be met more effectively. However, an alternative interpretation is that the prior policy concern was about labour discipline and labour turnover/absenteeism (Navarro, 1977). Thus work absence on health grounds was to be sanctioned by medical personnel at the place of work; or at least good quality health care, in the context of an under-resourced general health service and a tight labour market, could be a powerful form of occupational welfare with which to attract and retain labour.

Finally, social relations in such a labour intensive service as health care have been questioned in terms of the experiences of women as patients, and the career structures which left women as predominant among nurses and junior doctors, while most senior positions were held by men (Navarro, 1977). The low status of women health workers is starkly illustrated by the fact that their wages had by 1989 drifted down to about 70 per cent of the average by 1984 (Davis, 1989: 435).

Notwithstanding these deficiencies, it must be acknowledged that the benefit of central control improved the provision of health care, and hence the morbidity and mortality rates, of Soviet Central Asia to a level well above what would have otherwise been the case. By 1970 inequality in the distribution of resources had fallen steadily to the British level, and well below the American figure (the coefficient of variation in the distribution of doctors in the 1970s for the USSR, UK, USA, respectively was 0.19, 0.15, 0.31: George and Manning, 1980: 117).

Housing

Housing provision has been a continuous source of dissatisfaction since the October Revolution, as has already been mentioned. For much of this time urban living space per capita has been below the sanitary norm of nine square metres. This has been a result of three factors. First, the housing stock inherited after the October Revolution was meagre. Second, rapid industrialization and the consequent urbanization resulted, despite substantial housing production, in a steady decline in per capita living space from an already low level. Third, the Second World War destroyed a further 15 per cent of housing stock, and it was only then that there was a sustained effort to remedy the situation, with an effective doubling of housing investment in the 1950s and 1960s. By 1961 the sanitary norm, set forty years before, was finally exceeded in urban areas (Andrusz, 1984).

This shortage of space has had a number of consequences on domestic life. Young couples can rarely find their own flat in which to begin married life, and normally have to share with one set of parents. In addition a significant proportion of tenants are still in communal flats, sharing cooking and bathing facilities. This stressful situation stimulates divorce, and inhibits reproduction (Shlapen-tokh, 1989; Chinn, 1977).

However, the crude production of space was always going to be rapidly succeeded by further dissatisfactions. These include poor finished quality, resulting in damp, cold, and large repair costs. Associated infrastructure development, such as roads, sewerage, schools and shops were also poorly co-ordinated. Beyond these, and now coming into its own as the major current housing problem, is the question of who owns and controls the stock. There were four tenure types of housing stock in the Soviet Union: local soviet, 'departmental' (owned by enterprises and organizations), co-operative and private. The first two account for a large and growing proportion of the total stock: in 1991 about 25 per cent was local soviet stock, and a full 50 per cent in the hands of enterprises. They supply housing on two entirely different bases: the first according to need (family size, waiting time), and the second according to merit (the interests of the enterprise in rewarding its labour force). Over the years there have been periodic attempts to transfer stock from enterprises to local soviets on grounds of principle, but these failed simply because control over housing has been too valuable a resource for enterprises in a situation of chronic labour shortage. Clearly, with half the housing stock in a quasi-'tied cottage' tenure, labour market flexibility, let alone an individual sense of security and autonomy, is going to suffer.

Education
Education is of particular importance in all societies, both as an investment in human capital and as a site for the reproduction of social relations. It was regarded with pride in the Soviet Union. At the time of the October Revolution, half the people were illiterate. As noted above, this was seen by Lenin as a major barrier to mass political involvement, and great efforts were made to develop education. This necessarily involved adult education – a tradition that became highly developed by Western European standards, and which in principle was extended to all social groups.

As in the case of health care, the size and scale of the education sector, including nurseries, was impressive. Again, while quality and sensitivity to individual needs frequently gave way (to political education and russification), central control made possible the development of education in Soviet Central Asia to a level that would not otherwise have happened.

The main problem in education stemmed from the simple point that in the Soviet Union the main access to more desirable jobs and social status was the higher education system, yet the main work available was in blue-collar production. There was thus an inevitable conflict between the aspirations of the majority of pupils and the reality of working life for most of them, that is, between the two functions noted earlier of human capital investment and social reproduction. Competition for the scarce resource of higher education was intense, and for a variety of family-based reasons a steep class gradient appeared in the opportunities available (Yanowitch, 1977).

One response, particularly embodied in the 1958 Khrushchev reforms, was to expand the opportunities available in schools for university preparation, in order to maximize the chances for workers' children, while trying to retain a production-oriented curriculum. The effects of this policy, not unlike similar expansionary policies adopted in the 1960s in the UK and USA, was to secure the chances of all middle-class pupils, while making very few inroads into the inequality of access. The education system was thus seen to suffer a double failure: it allowed, at 60 per cent, too many pupils to enter the general academic school oriented towards university entrance, and hence wasted education investment for the majority of those pupils who would never proceed to higher education; moreover, it failed to reduce class inequalities.

Occupational welfare
In conclusion to this section on the accumulated problems of social policy before the advent of perestroika, it appears that Soviet welfare was, in Titmuss's terms, largely reminiscent of occupational welfare. Strictly speaking this is entirely compatible with the socialist principle of 'each according to their work', with social need being the guiding principle for distribution only under communism. Nevertheless, despite the Brezhnev re-timetabling of the 1959 'road to communism' via the period of developed socialism, it would be reasonable to expect the beginnings of prefigurative communist distribution in the field of social policy if anywhere. But to make it more need-oriented would be to break the links with the labour market, and ironically labour incentives were seen under perestroika as one of the major priorities, with social policy regarded as a key avenue for the improvement of the 'human factor' (Zaslavskaya, 1990: 96).

Collapse of the old regime

The origins of the desire in the Soviet Union for far-reaching changes lay in three problems. First, and paramount, was the slowdown in economic growth during the 1970s. Second was the erosion of the popular legitimacy of the state. Third was the fear of a decay in family and community life. The specific expression of these problems, however, varied.

The slowdown in economic growth was partly the result of the inability of the Soviet economy to raise worker productivity, itself caused by the peculiar incentives for waste and poor quality of the 'shortage model' (Kornai, 1980), and the 'partial ignorance' (Ellman, 1989) that comes with highly centralized planning with poor data processing in a complex economy. While this was partly a technological weakness, there was also an absence of any politically acceptable means of intensifying work activities. Gorbachev's chosen solution was the adoption of full cost accounting and limited marketization in an attempt to decentralize economic decision-making and thus close the 'information gap'.

In the political area the erosion of the popular legitimacy of the state was evident in the disaffection revealed in the activities of dissidents of various persuasions – what Goldfarb (1989) has characterized as the collapse of the 'totalitarian mind'. Towards the end of the Brezhnev era this was compounded by the growth of corruption throughout government. In order to win back the interest and trust of citizens, a new policy of openness about public affairs and new democratic mechanisms were constructed.

The third problem was the evidence of decay in family and community life. Both infant and adult mortality were rising, and such classic social problems as divorce, crime, drug misuse, and particularly alcoholism, were growing to the point where they could no longer be ignored. This set of issues generated a reaction in terms of the re-moralization of social life, particularly expressed in the vigorous campaign against alcohol consumption instigated soon after Gorbachev was elected secretary, and discussed in detail below.

It is clear that while the immediate concern was with economic performance, a number of other and seemingly interrelated problems had accumulated. Whether this was coincidence, or the result of some more general systemic crisis, will be discussed further in the final section of this chapter. First, it is necessary to detail the story of the changes that have developed since the early 1980s.

While, of course, these general problems emerged from the 1970s onwards, and first began to shape policy noticeably with the leadership successions of Andropov and Chernenko, it was the election of Gorbachev in 1985 that marked the beginning of a very different era. However, if any date is needed for the appearance of the seedling which grew into perestroika, it can be taken as the presentation by Academician Tatyana Zaslavskaya (later President of the Soviet Sociological Association, elected deputy, and scholar of social policy issues) of the notorious report known as the 'Novosibirsk Manifesto' two years earlier, in April 1983, to a closed seminar of the economics departments of the CPSU Central Committee, the Academy of Sciences and Gosplan (Zaslavskaya, 1984).

Existing officially in just seventy numbered copies, the report argued that the main obstacle to improved economic performance was the economic system itself. In this she was doing no more than many other liberals in asking for decentralization and quasi-markets. But the real innovation in her report was in its social rather than economic analysis. In a nutshell, she argued that economic and educational levels had reached the point at which the social characteristics of workers no longer corresponded to those required by strategic and technical mechanisms unchanged since the 1930s command economy. There were widespread frustrated aspirations which undermined motivation at work (Shlapentokh, 1989). Moreover, and this has been her main and repeated analytical tool, she contended that sharply felt contradictory social interests had developed between different groups in Soviet society, which may even have amounted to the development of social classes. Without an adequate understanding of these interests, and their support for or opposition to change, she argued little could be done to solve any of the pressing social and economic problems.

Zaslavskaya and the head of her Novosibirsk Institute (Aganbegyan) came to Moscow as key advisers to Gorbachev in the mid-1980s – the 'mother and father' of perestroika. He advised on economics, and she set up the Soviet Centre for Public Opinion Research to try to identify those very social interests which would support or oppose perestroika. In the ensuing seven years change has been frenetic. Keane (1990) identifies four phases up to April 1989, to which we could add three more to bring us up to date at the time of writing (January 1992). These phases are of roughly annual duration. First was a period of *preparation* (March 1985–July 1986), during which Gorbachev launched the now well-known concepts of perestroika, glasnost and uskorenie (acceleration). He also swiftly set about securing coalitions and allegiances at various levels of the bureaucracy, and launched one specific domestic change – the battle against alcohol. Second was a period of *struggle for political ascendancy* (July 1986–July 1987), in which democratic procedures, such as multiple electoral candidates, were promoted as the mechanism for loosening and overcoming entrenched resistance to economic change. Glasnost also began to show real results in the exposure of corruption, disinformation (e.g. over Chernobyl) and the existence of a wide variety of cultural interests at odds with the old Brezhnev line.

By this time, more than two years on, the inevitable upswelling of new or long dormant social and political forces began to appear, such that the next phase of *consolidation* (July 1987–June 1988) was increasingly threatened. Independent political clubs, demonstrations, new social movements and popular fronts were either formed or planned around issues of socialism, environmentalism, nationalism, democracy and freedom of speech. Significantly, Boris Yeltsin was sacked as Moscow party chief. From the 19th Party Congress onwards (July 1988) Keane detects the *disintegration of the party*. This Congress initiated the proposal for an elected Congress of

People's Deputies, and an executive-style presidency. In October 1988 the Baltic Popular Fronts were founded, in March 1989 People's Deputies were elected, and in May 1989 the first Congress of People's Deputies took place. This is important both because of the organization of the Inter-Regional Group of Deputies (destined to become a social democratic opposition to the CPSU), and because social policy issues were widely debated (Rogovin and Ivanov, 1989).

The summer of 1989 witnessed widespread miners' strikes and the highly symbolic staging of the Baltic human chain. From this point on we can add a fifth period, borrowed from Kagarlitsky (1990), who presciently identified the beginning of the *end of perestroika*. By 1990 the party is in an insoluble dilemma: 'no legally guaranteed civil society, no democracy; no democracy, no meat or decent vegetables in the shops, no freedom from fear, no independence for nations, no freedom for Soviet citizens to travel' (Keane, 1990: 348).

The party could proceed no further without opening itself up to real competition, whether from a social democratic or conservative direction, yet to do so could mean losing the power to continue to direct the pace and direction of perestroika. This is why perestroika became bogged down, and lost its momentum. Thus 1990 heralded both the final preparation of the social democratic alternative, in the shape of the Democratic Platform manifesto which appeared in April, and the growing power of the conservative opposition, which successfully scuppered the Shatalin '500-day' plan for radical economic restructuring in September, and engineered the military suppression of Baltic autonomy at the turn of the year.

The year 1991 witnessed a continuing struggle between conservative groups, centred partly in the military and partly in the party, and the pressure for liberalization coming from a mixture of republican nationalism, professional and managerial interests, and the West. Early in the year it seemed indeed as if perestroika was on the wane, yet the early summer witnessed real price reform, a reduction in travel restrictions, the election of Yeltsin to the Russian presidency, and every likelihood of substantial aid from the West. With this oscillation between progressive and conservative forces it is not difficult to see why the coup in August 1991 took place, nor that Gorbachev and Yeltsin saw it coming. There was thus a sixth phase, *the dissolution of the Union*, which began with the collapse of the coup, Gorbachev's resignation from the Communist Party, and the banning of its activities. The initial aim was for a united economic zone amongst the republics designed to replace the old command structures, but Gorbachev's desire for a new political union always looked unrealistic. During the autumn power began to ebb from Gorbachev as Yeltsin annexed more and more Union functions for

Russia, culminating in the establishment of a new Commonwealth of Independent States, completely separated from the old Union. Clearly there was no further function for Gorbachev who in the end was denied the dignity of a formal, legal transfer of power, and he finally resigned late in December.

This marks the arrival of a new phase in Russia, *authoritarian populism* marked by the search for a positive alternative to communist ideology, and political and economic structures. Yeltsin wasted no time in decreeing a relatively widespread price liberalization in January 1992, although it is as yet unclear how much popular dissatisfaction this will generate, and indeed whether it will in turn threaten Yeltsin's own position. Politically, there appears to be a retreat from democracy, at least for the time being, for although Yeltsin was popularly elected, others in senior posts are appointed; and local government (in Moscow and St Petersburg for example) has moved from elected soviets to appointed prefects.

Aid from Japan, the USA (mainly medicines, which are now in very short supply) and the EC as part of a G7 package has finally appeared to help with the immediate problems of the 1991/2 winter, exacerbated by a poor 1991 harvest. In the longer term, associate membership of the IMF will impose market discipline as the price of integration into the world economy, and the imposition of a 'triangulation' condition, whereby 50 per cent of aid credits have to be spent in East/Central Europe, will help to re-establish trade patterns disrupted by the collapse of the CMEA (the old 'common market' in Eastern Europe). As a net subsidizer of the other former republics, however, it makes no economic sense for Russia to stay in the new Commonwealth of Independent States, which Steele predicts will collapse within months (*Guardian*, 21 February 1992, p. 19). Either way, the social costs of these changes in terms of unemployment, poverty and medical supplies will be punishing. We can turn to the details in the next section.

New crises of social policy

As we noted in the discussion of the origins of perestroika, social policy in the form of the 'human factor' was seen by Tatyana Zaslavskaya as having a vital part to play in revitalizing Soviet society. In common with other writers, such as Ferge (1979), she distinguishes social policy, as a mechanism for compensating for misfortunes resulting from the market or other social institutions, from societal policy. The latter refers to the use of social interventions to engineer change in the general social structure

(Zaslavskaya, 1990: 99). On the whole it was argued that perestroika needed to reintegrate social/societal policy as a central element in social development, rather than confining it to the distribution of 'residual' resources left after more important priorities had been · satisfied. Hence, theoretically, Zaslavskaya remains still within a societal policy approach.

For example, problems for societal policy include the gender and ethnic inequalities mentioned earlier, which were either unaffected or exacerbated by the mass production of health or education workers. In these professions, as in Western countries, women predominate particularly in the junior and middle levels, while men control the top positions (Navarro, 1977). It seems no coincidence that the typical level of pay, even for middle-ranking posts, has been around 30 per cent below average rates. Moreover, as consumers of these services, women's specific needs are a low priority. For example, the widespread use of multiple abortion as a form of contraception damages women's health unnecessarily (Buckley, 1990: 196–8).

As far as ethnic inequalities are concerned, it is true to say that, for example, welfare provision in the Central Asian republics is higher than it would otherwise have been without Soviet influence. Nevertheless, in terms of quality, there are notable problems. In health care there are high rates of infant mortality, infectious diseases and poor hospital provision (Buckley, 1990: 195–6). In education the most vexed question is over the relative status of minority- and Russian-language teaching, since a disproportionate amount of published material, official documents and even alphabet development has been in Russian rather than native languages (Gitelman, 1990: 152–3).

In practice, since the advent of perestroika, social policy has been characterized by a combination of pre-existing policy problems, new solutions and new problems thrown up by the information and politicization that glasnost has generated. Activity has been more pronounced in some spheres than others, and perhaps a detailed examination of one area (health) after a briefer reference to the other issues (social security, housing and education) is most useful here.

As a general background to this, it should be remembered that Soviet social policy commentators, such as Natalia Rimachevskaya of the Institute of Demography, are saying that as of 1991 there is a widespread sense of disorganization and chaos such that policy prescriptions and their implementation are extremely uncertain in terms of their effects. Moreover, as we concluded at the end of the section on social policy before perestroika, there is a close connection between the labour market and social policy priorities. Social policy is thus inevitably bound up with attempts at economic change. For example, if, as many argue, economic restructuring will have to come from small and medium enterprises (SMEs), then a flexible labour market will have to be made possible throughout the economy. However, there are likely to be obstacles to this. It is worth reviewing these before looking at specific policy areas, as an indication of the likely interaction between social and economic policy.

The first obstacle to a flexible labour market is the absence of true unemployment, the result of a right to employment enjoyed since the abolition of unemployment benefits by Stalin in 1930. This situation is changing rapidly, as has been the recent experience in Poland, as economic reform occurs. However, there are attempts, detailed below, to cushion this effect, and if possible nullify it, by offering sufficient retraining schemes to enable every displaced worker to move jobs without extended spells of unemployment.

Second is the attitude to work activity itself. It was the experience of anyone who stayed in the Soviet Union for any length of time that there was   low commitment to the quality of daily work. As the popular saying went, 'we pretend to work, and they pretend to pay us!' This is not just a matter of low pay, however, but also the time-consuming nature of goods and service distribution. Many workers have to spend work time each day either shopping or making arrangements through friends and contacts for the acquisition of everyday requirements (Shlapentokh, 1989). There is also the urgent problem of alcohol abuse in work time that leads to great loss of efficiency.

Third is the attitude to income distribution. Although Gorbachev in 1987 stressed his dislike of 'levelling tendencies', using the principle from Marx that under socialism the criterion is 'from each according to his abilities, to each according to his work', there was widespread support amongst workers for the principle of wage equality, that is, that differential effort should not be rewarded with differentials in pay. Recent survey evidence suggests that this attitude is deeply entrenched, and as yet unchanging (Mason and Sydorenko, forthcoming).

Fourth is the attitude to general economic restructuring, particularly price reform. Cumulative all-union representative sample surveys carried out in 1989 and 1990 by the Soviet Centre for Public Opinion Research showed little public support for the kind of radical restructuring of prices and ownership proposed in the Shatalin '500-day' plan. This included a rapid reduction in the large existing subsidies for food, travel and housing, and the general movement of prices to a level which more accurately signalled the real costs of production. It also planned for the widespread privatization of enterprises, housing and land. Initial reaction to Yeltsin's actual price reforms introduced in January 1992 confirms this view although little overt resistance has as yet materialized.

In Gorbachev's time there was growing hostility to such changes, with a large minority of citizens claiming that they would 'actively' resist them. The abandonment in 1990 of 'shock therapy' in favour of a more gradual programme of price reform and privatization by Gorbachev may well have been a more democratic decision than was apparent to Western observers. More specific surveys of particular factories in and around Moscow confirm that there was a clear variation in attitude according to social class: managers supported change, but the shop floor did not (Toshchenko, 1987; Chichkanov, 1987). A 1992 survey by the Soviet Public Opinion Research Centre (unpublished) shows that public attitudes towards housing privatization remain stubbornly hostile. There has also been sharp public criticism of the new co-operative ventures, which are now legal, since they are felt to be exacerbating supply shortages through their superior purchasing power, and hence have become associated in the public mind with unjust privileges. These are in effect the nascent SMEs of the future, and such antipathy towards them cannot be encouraging.

Fifth is the absence of new sources of labour. The history of other societies in the midst of rapid industrial expansion, or restructuring, suggests that a good supply of new labour is essential. Traditionally there have been four sources: rural workers, migrants, women and structural unemployment. None of these have so far been available. Women are already economically active, and mass immigration is unlikely. While widespread unemployment is feared, it seems likely that there will be significant efforts to protect workers, possibly using the resources released by the reduction in military expenditure. Nevertheless, if, as expected, unemployment rises past 10 per cent, this will constitute a major change in labour supply. Another source might be from the rural workers of the Central Asian republics; but the end of the Union and uncertain future of the Commonwealth of Independent States makes this source very uncertain.

Sixth are difficulties around the reproduction of labour in terms both of the urban birth rate and of education and training. Here there is a well-known conflict between the high rate of economic activity of women, designed to increase the short-term labour supply, and the consequently diminished size of urban families, as a result of which longer-term supply may be threatened (Chinn, 1977). Furthermore, shortages of young workers are exacerbated by the difficulties of matching educational output to economic requirements, a problem whose 'solution' (the 1984 education reform) has not yet worked.

This is of great significance as a measure of the problem-solving capacity of the system, and will be discussed in more detail below.

It can be concluded, before turning to conventional social policies, that there is an as yet unresolved tension between current levels of social justice and attitudes towards work, and a flexible labour market which may hamper the introduction of SMEs on any large scale.

Social security

The time of perestroika saw improvements in pensions, and a commitment in the first Congress of People's Deputies to monitor the standard of living of poorer groups, although it was still not easy for the government to discuss poverty openly. As far as pensioners are concerned, evidence about their economic difficulties resulted in the raising of minimum pensions to the level of the minimum wage (70 roubles per month – but see the poverty lines mentioned below) in October 1989, to take effect from January 1990. This was described as the 'small pension law' (Tsivilev and Rogogin, 1990: 186) since it was supposed to be merely a stop-gap before a more comprehensive reform (necessary not least because of the appearance of significant inflation). As far as poverty is concerned, the relative improvement in published statistics in the late 1980s enabled Ellman (1990) to calculate that in 1988, using a poverty line of 78 roubles per month (compared with a line of 75 roubles accepted by the Soviet Parliament), about 14 per cent of the population was in poverty. Spiralling inflation since then has led some to speculate, that as of February 1992, over 90 per cent of families are technically in 'food poverty'.

There is no doubt, however, that the cornerstone of social security under the Soviet system was the right to work (Article 40 of the Constitution), upon which other policies for income maintenance were based. Therefore the main current problem is the possibility of mass unemployment as the economy sheds the estimated 30 per cent of labour that is economically unnecessary (Urban, 1987: 3). An early example was the experimental 12,000 redundancies on the Belorussian railway in 1985/6, all of whom it was reported were found other employment (Trehub, 1987: 11). However, it is difficult to decide very clearly what unemployment actually is. For example, Adirim (1989) showed 'joblessness' in the region of 6 per cent, but that relative 'worklessness' in existing employment which results in incomplete wages might account for another 10 to 15 per cent, while a desire for a better job was expressed by the majority of the population.

This process generated a new Employment Law, formally adopted on 15 January 1991. This officially signalled the end of the right/duty to work by imposing a 1 per cent payroll levy to generate funds to finance unemployment benefit, retraining, public community work and career guidance (Standing, 1991). Twenty-five per cent of the funds were earmarked for a central all-union fund available for low-income high-unemployment republics, the rest staying at republic level, although the dissolution of the Union will probably cause this inter-republic flow to largely disappear. As elsewhere, the usual problems of practical implementation exist here, most notably the scarcity of employment offices. In addition, of course, there may be insufficient funds generated to pay for benefits set at or near the minimum wage for six months, or to support those who have exhausted their entitlements. The latter group are expected to exceed 50 per cent of the future unemployed, and in the absence of a national scheme of income support, poverty will spread rapidly. Standing (1991: 392–3) argues that only a basic income/social dividend scheme will accomplish both the alleviation of poverty and the flexibility of labour supply which will dominate social security policy in the 1990s.

Housing
The period of perestroika saw few new problems, although homelessness and begging was, as in London, on the increase (Stetina, 1990). But the old ones of access, quality and infrastructure remained. The main effort to tackle them was the commitment in the 1986 Party Programme (27th Congress of the CPSU) to provide all families with their own flat by the end of the century. Since an estimated 20 per cent live in communal flats, this implied a massive increase in housing investment (Trehub, 1987: 29). As noted earlier, in 1991 half of the stock was enterprise-owned, and some enterprises echoed the party promise, and also pledged to provide all of their workers with separate flats. Rents, which even together with energy costs rarely absorb more than 3 per cent of household income, have not yet been raised in any of the republics (as full cost accounting requires) as a prelude to a more flexible housing market.

The changes Gorbachev planned for the housing market can be deduced from three important decrees issued in 1988 that gave carte blanche (and bank credit!) for the expansion of private, and co-operative, housing construction (Andrusz, 1990). The final decree, in December 1988, granted the right for organizations and soviets to sell their housing stock, as a result of which the Moscow Soviet in July 1990 decreed that all of its tenants (about 25 per cent of all households) had the right to buy their flats through a complicated formula which entitled families to a basic space allowance, over and above which the price rose steeply. Informal opinion in the Centre for Public Opinion Research about this potentially dramatic change, however, is that at the moment this kind of decree is not and could not be effectively implemented in Moscow. However, an example can be seen in pre-independence Estonia, where flats were put on sale in late 1990, and prices were set in the region of 150,000 roubles per flat. The Estonian Academy of Sciences has estimated that, with annual salaries at around 5,000 roubles, less than one hundred local residents could raise such funds (Niit, 1991). In 1991, fearing an influx of North American money from returning expatriate Estonians for whom such a price was only $5,000, this market has been suspended. The recent announcement of the end, in January 1992, of the 'propiska' system of controlling the right to live in a city such as Moscow will heighten this tension between public and private property, since a new influx of hopeful city dwellers will emerge from the satellites and suburbs that have been held at arm's length beyond the city limits.

Education

The main effort here was directed towards raising the salaries of teachers (by about 30 per cent), continuing the slow process of implementing the 1984 school reform. While this was laid down a year before Gorbachev's elevation, he publicly committed himself to it. Once again we can identify the issue as a conflict of interests, and hence (following the discussion at the beginning of this chapter) we would expect it to be perceived in terms of groups labelled as problems, rather than in terms of deviant individuals. The basic difficulty here is that too many pupils want to get into higher education. They therefore resist learning a useful production-related skill which they and the economy actually need, since most of them will not be able to realize their ambitions.

The 1984 reforms made a bold attempt to solve the first failure by planning for a reduction of the proportion of each cohort entering the general academic school from 60 per cent to 29 per cent. In addition, all children were to get experience of real work as part of their curriculum. As a political safety valve, the 60 per cent who were now to go through vocational school would be given the right to apply for higher education and take the relevant entrance exams (Zajda, 1984). This change looked very much like a move away from a comprehensive principle towards selective schools, in which the cream would be identified early and the rest are consigned to the factory. It was unlikely to have anything other than a negative effect on the class distribution of access to higher education, although it would bring education more closely into line with the requirements of the labour market.

Public debate reported about this issue concentrated on three things. First, the availability of 'production-training' facilities is too limited. Second, the quality of vocational schools was too low for pupils to have any real chance of getting into higher education. Third, the vocational schools were seen as merely the place where weaker pupils were expected to go; they have little positive image. Indeed a report in December 1986 made an explicit comparison with the 1958 reforms, observing that then only 5 to 10 per cent of school graduates were placed in jobs that they were trained for.

The conflict of values between educational opportunity and manpower planning is very clear in this education debate. However, the level of politicization of the problem could be higher. Indeed Gorbachev said at the 27th Congress of the CPSU that: 'The reform of general education and vocational schools has started. It must be said that the tempo and depth of implementation of the measures envisaged by the reform cannot yet satisfy us' (Connor, 1986: 36).

These reforms occurred with little real effect on the opportunities of more privileged children, and thus faced little opposition. After all, there is still in reality an educational division of labour between the upwardly mobile and the majority of workers, through which the conflicting aims (of educational opportunity and manpower planning) can be kept apart. The problem group in this case, those pupils who have inappropriately aspired to higher education, are being cooled out at an earlier point in the system through technical adjustments, while the whole question of the reproduction of inequalities is being avoided.

Health

Here, the main policy problem Gorbachev faced was the underfunding of the health service that has already been discussed. Substantial wage increases were granted in 1986 to bring medical staff pay up to average levels, and promises were made in the twelfth five-year plan to inject substantial increases into funds for new technology, drugs and so on. As elsewhere, these remained largely unfulfilled. However, as with the example of the railway labour shake-out, experiments in service restructuring were set up. For example, in April 1988 the Leningrad health service was turned over to a strict internal market – well before the equivalent mechanism was even contemplated in the UK. Hospital budgets were set to zero, and polyclinics given the task of purchasing the services that they needed from hospitals, and paying a 'market price' through which hospitals were to earn their revenues. It did not work without major hiccups

(Roberts, 1990), but there were some who could see the potential benefits in terms of greater efforts on all sides to think through the consequences of referrals.

However, the main activity in the health field lay not inside the health services, but rather in an attempt to remedy the serious stagnation and decline in life expectancy and infant mortality that developed in the late 1970s (Mezentseva and Rimachevskaya, 1990). This, without doubt, was the most serious health problem of the period, notwithstanding other notable issues such as the Chernobyl nuclear disaster, AIDS, the disabled, children in care and environmental pollution (*Economist*, 1990: 25–8; Dossett-Davies, 1988a; Steele, 1991; Pierson, 1988; Harwin, 1988; Perera, 1990). Indeed it was so troubling that the publication of the relevant statistics was suspended from 1972 to 1986 (Trehub, 1987: 13). The main reason for this pattern – unique to the industrialized world – was felt to be alcohol abuse, although it is likely that environmental pollution has been an as yet unquantified and under-recognized contributor. In any event alcohol abuse is the easier problem to handle, and it was Gorbachev's immediate priority on being elected General Secretary. While, of course, alcohol consumption had been recognized as a problem before (there was an active temperance movement in the 1920s), Gorbachev identified himself strongly with this new and vigorous campaign. Less than two months after being elected, he launched the anti-alcohol campaign on 7 May 1985 with a decree and a flurry of media activity in the following two months. These measures were adopted (*Current Digest of the Soviet Press*, 30 (20): 3–5):

1 Sales to young people under 21 banned.
2 Alternative sports, leisure and entertainment planned.
3 All-union temperance society planned.
4 Production of alcoholic goods to be reduced.
5 Production of non-alcoholic goods to be increased.
6 Alcohol sales banned from work, education and travel.
7 Alcohol sales restricted until 2 pm.
8 More tearooms and snack bars planned.
9 More treatment and rehabilitation centres planned.
10 Penalties for drink-related misdemeanours increased.

There is little doubt that this amounted to a major effort. The concerns expressed, and therefore targets for change, apart from the general production and consumption of alcohol, were child and adult deaths, accidents, alcoholism and absenteeism.

The evidence on the effectiveness of this campaign is mixed. First is the success of the campaign over time. Improvement could take place at four separate stages in the problem: production, sales, consumption of alcohol, and the effects of these on individuals in terms of health and behaviour.

Production. This is the 1986 out-turn as a percentage of 1985 levels:

Liqueurs, vodka, wine	65 per cent
Fruit juice	147 per cent
Non-alcoholic beverages	130 per cent
Mineral water	114 per cent

These changes appearing in the 1986 plan results reported on 18 January 1987 are a notable contrast to almost all of the myriad other figures, which rarely moved more than 5 to 10 per cent.

Sales. Reported as reduced by 40 per cent in Moscow in April 1986, and in November 1987 as having fallen by an unspecified amount for 1986 and 1987.

Consumption. Figures are as follows: commercial beverages, reported to be down by 50 per cent in June 1987; average total alcohol consumption, down by over 50 per cent (Mezentseva and Rimachevskaya, 1990: 872); perfumes and industrial alcohol, reported to be growing in August 1985; home-brew, reported to be up in terms of sugar sales (up by one and a half million tons) and yeast thefts (doubled).

Health. Deaths from accidents, poisoning and injury were reported in October 1986 as down by 24 per cent, and from cardiovascular diseases as down substantially. In January 1987 a small rise in the birth rate and reduction in the death rate of 1.1 per thousand to 9.7 for 1986 was reported. In May 1987 average life expectancy was reported to have risen for the first time in a decade to 69 (Mezentseva and Rimachevskaya, 1990). In November 1987 reports appeared of a 37 per cent reduction in alcohol-related car accidents, and a 50 per cent reduction in deaths attributable to alcoholism to 23,300 (this figure fits well with earlier estimates by Treml, 1982).

Behaviour. In June 1987 absenteeism was reported as down by an unspecified amount, 'sobering-up's down by one-third, and crimes involving alcohol down by 26 per cent. However, in December 1987 a report of more than double the cases of drunkenness at work to a quarter of a million appeared.

These figures appear to indicate a substantial improvement in the kinds of conditions which were provoking concern before 1985. However, this is most closely linked to the simple reduction in the availability of alcohol. Anecdotal evidence such as letters to the press suggests the absence of a substantial change of public attitude. This is corroborated by indications that the public was actively seeking to undermine retail control. There was also a major failure of will at the Ministry of Trade reported in September 1986 relating to the proper regulation of alcohol allocations. That is they were too high. Similarly, the production of cognac by the Soviet State Agro-Industrial Committee actually rose in the first half of 1987, and the planned reductions in vodka were too small. As a result senior officials were disciplined in both cases.

More worrying was the evidence reported in November 1987 that unforeseen problems were appearing as some of the public attempted to avoid the tighter regulations. Home-brewing was booming: sugar sales had mushroomed, and were now controlled through rationing coupons. Thefts of yeast, as mentioned above, have doubled. This was matched by the spread of alcohol 'dens' in apartments, and the rise in poisonings occasioned by the increased use of alcohol-based perfumes and industrial alcohol. A report in December 1987 also claimed that while cases of drunkenness at work fell in 1986, they had more than doubled in 1987. Clearly a considerable portion of this evidence is attributable to increased efforts by the police and the courts, but not all of it. In addition there were repeated calls for greater efforts by the relevant agencies to support the campaign, alongside the acknowledgement that there were too few real activists. There was even some sympathy expressed for pensioners who made alcohol to supplement their income, or to tip the providers of small services that they needed!

In sum, it seems that while Gorbachev was not winning the argument with the public, he may have been winning a battle. Politicization had enabled a change in the production and consumption of alcohol to be tolerated, but it had not succeeded to the extent that the problem could be relegated to the back-burner. Indeed the 1991 price law excluded price rises for vodka. Although space precludes a detailed comparison with the experience of other countries, this pattern may well mirror American experience with prohibition and West European experience with tobacco control (Calnan, 1982).

To conclude this section, we can try to estimate the direction in which social policy has been travelling by comparison with the critieria identified in Chapter 1 (Table 1.5) as supportive of socialist ideals in welfare, for which analysts such as Zaslavskaya have argued, and briefly in terms of the Esping-Anderson (1990) typology described in the same chapter.

First is the 'degree of self-activity by civil society in shaping policy'. It is clear that in the examples of education reform and alcohol control popular views count for little. In the areas of employment and price reform, and probably housing, however, public opinion has been heard, although self-activity may well be restricted to those already relatively advantaged.

Second, the 'relationship between social and economic policy' has been frequently observed in the Soviet past to result in the use of the former to support the latter. The 'human factor' in general has now been acknowledged to matter in its own right in terms of people's needs and expectations, and there was a genuine attempt to improve expenditure on social services, as a result, for example, of the efforts of the first Congress of People's Deputies.

Third, the 'priority given to welfare' was correspondingly higher, in that economic hardship, lack of housing access, and mortality appeared to stimulate new policy efforts.

Fourth, 'group interests' served by policy changes were beginning to emerge, both literally and analytically, as the concept of 'social interest' became accepted. The clearest evidence to date is through the various attitude surveys available. These suggest strongly that amongst ordinary workers there was deep suspicion about the changes that perestroika promised. Managers were by contrast eager supporters.

Fifth, 'agencies of provision' were beginning to multiply, as Tsivilev and Rogogin (1990) identified for the elderly. No doubt social movements developing, for example, in the areas of environmental concerns and housing will also spawn further activities, but whether this will amount to a nascent welfare pluralism it is as yet too early to tell. A multinational project in which the author is engaged aims to identify such new social movements over the period 1991–94.

Sixth, as was argued in the first point, 'democratic control' over policy and services is not readily apparent, and where it is increasing it is a market-based democracy which inevitably favours the already better-off.

Seventh, there is little evidence of any shift in the 'relationship of provider and user', to the extent that this means, for example, professional etiquette; otherwise the introduction of market mechanisms would, of course, substantially change this relationship.

Eighth, and very importantly, there is a growing tension between the 'distributive principles' of efficiency and equality, with many working people digging in for equality, while the advent of a market economy seems to imply the growth of inequality in the name of efficiency.

Ninth, there is as yet little discussion of changing 'family forms', beyond the occasional thoughtless remark about family and youth problems supposedly resulting from a mother's absence from the family (Gorbachev, 1987: 100). There is very little by way of an active women's movement, despite the clear evidence of gender inequalities discussed earlier. However, many commentators would for this very reason expect this situation to be ripe for change in the new era (Deacon and Szalai, 1990).

Finally, of course, the question of 'nationalism' is very pressing in the new republics, with a large number of lives already lost to interethnic disputes and little prospect for improvement in the inequalities felt to have been imposed by Russian domination. Indeed, with the erosion of central control, these conflicts are escalating, with the prospect of the repetition of Yugoslavia's experiences in some republics. As a specific issue in social policy this has only surfaced sporadically, in, for example, conflict over the control of jobs and houses in the Baltic republics, and over the place of Russian in the school curriculum.

While these ten areas raise a complex set of criteria for evaluating social policy, it is also instructive to summarize their implications for the dimensions used by Esping-Andersen (1990) to differentiate Western welfare states, discussed in general in Chapter 1. The three dimensions are the extent of commodification of goods and services, the nature and depth of social stratification, and the relationship between state and market. While as yet there is little evidence of marketization in traditional welfare state areas such as health care, education or housing, clearly the scale of price liberalization in January 1992 signals a significant change. Characterized earlier as sufficient to warrant the identification of a new phase of authoritarian populism, the conservative inertia of a corporatist welfare state is now challenged, but as yet there is no clearly articulated alternative model under construction; rather it seems likely that short term pragmatism in response to economic constraints and political tension will determine policy changes. Nevertheless even in the area most likely to move significantly towards commodification, housing, despite enabling legislation giving soviets the 'right to sell', little has changed except insofar as labour market performance can be seen to be a kind of proxy for this process. Rents, significantly, have not been raised. On the question of stratification, there have been repeated criticisms of 'levelling tendencies' which can only justify the growth of inequalities in the future as wages are adjusted differentially to compensate for inflation. Indeed this process has already begun, with the April 1991 and January 1992 price rises and the closer link between pay and productivity. Finally, the state/market mix has as yet altered little in terms of general privatization, although associate membership of the IMF will lead to change, and there are clearly signs that smaller enterprises, farms, shops and so on will very soon come under private ownership, even if only that of their employees.

Since housing has in principle become a potential private good, it is here if anywhere that we should look for nascent marketization; indeed we might even hazard a guess that what happens to rents, still very low, will stand as an indicator of the inroads of the market into welfare. In sum, while the conservative corporatist character of Soviet welfare has probably been given notice to quit, there is great uncertainty about the long term prospects of Yeltsin's authoritarian populism as an alternative.

Emerging strategies for welfare

Clearly the close link between occupation and welfare has emerged in the preceding discussion as one important model of Soviet welfare. This is very similar to the model of the 'organic labour state' outlined by Harding (1984). There are contradictory pressures between meeting needs, and hence severing this link, or motivating workers, and hence strengthening the link. But it is clear where Gorbachev's sympathies were. In *Perestroika* (1987: 100), he says, in a section entitled 'The Social Policy of Restructuring', that

> Intensification of social production suggests a new attitude to efficient employment and requires that the labour force must be regrouped. While working in this direction, we must thoroughly scrutinize how the principle of social justice is to be implemented . . . . This is how the 27th Congress of the CPSU formulated the problem of social justice: under socialism, work is the foundation for social justice. Only work determines a citizen's real place in society, his social status. And this precludes any manifestation of equalizing . . . . On this point we want to be perfectly clear: socialism has nothing to do with equalizing. Socialism cannot ensure conditions of life and consumption in accordance with the principle 'From each according to his ability, to each according to his needs'. This will be under communism.

There was and is a desire to re-establish the material bases of incentives to work. For example, there are numerous references to the desirability of 'economic-accountability' (this means fully priced) services in recent discussions, for which, no doubt, money will be earned in the more successful enterprises, and by the more senior staff. No wonder that management favoured perestroika, but workers did not: they had different interests in it!

Nevertheless, it is apparent that the economy of the region continues to decline. The shelving in 1990 of the Shatalin plan for rapid restructuring in favour of cautious price reform had left inflation rising past 18 per cent, production shrinking at 2 per cent, exports down by 14 per cent, and serious food shortages (Brasier,

1990); these figures were considerably worse for 1991, and the trend continues for 1992 (partly, of course, as a result of price reforms). Inevitably black marketeering is generated at points of acute shortage. Political legitimacy was shaken by the series of military interventions in the conservative build up to the August coup, including the invasion of key Baltic institutions early in 1991, demonstrations of protest in Moscow and executive permission for the military to patrol urban areas. The failure of the coup and Gorbachev's eventual resignation appears to have lanced this particular boil but, judging by other East/Central European countries such as Poland and Romania, conservative forces can still regroup to frustrate the plans of the new elites. How this will manifest itself in the new republics remains to be seen. Inevitably there has been a corresponding growth of social decay in terms of prostitution, crime and alcoholism, which are increasingly the subject of comment and analysis. If we are to make sense of this and to think about what strategies for social policy might be possible, it is essential to return to some theoretical explanations.

A traditional Marxist base–superstructure model of the kind adopted by Tatyana Zaslavskaya in her Novosibirsk 'Manifesto' (still a necessary code at the time it was written) would suggest that the traditional relations of production had become a hindrance to further growth. Modernization/convergence theory in a similar way might suggest that the technical logic of industrial development dictated a move to a more intensive stage of economic growth, often referred to now as post-Fordist. At the most general level, world systems theory would link these changes to the embeddedness of the Commonwealth of Independent States in an increasingly international economic context, symbolized most obviously by its new associate membership of the IMF.

However, as argued in the introduction to this chapter, these models are particularly based on economic factors, whereas the problems outlined above include important political and social dimensions. An alternative might be to look to political theory about democracy, and sociological theory about the nature of social integration. From the former, for example, we could draw out the nature of individual rights and freedoms and the conditions for their realization through democratic mechanisms, using these as a measure of the decay in political empowerment. For example, the new, and as yet current, administrative structure in Moscow city is in tension with the democratically elected Moscow Soviet: it is a new system of prefects and sub-prefects into which local citizens have very little input. From the latter we could set up models about the integration of individuals into society through family and school socialization, through the meeting of life-cycle dependencies, and opportunities for satisfactory engagement in the activities of production and reproduction. Again these could then provide us with indicators of the decline in opportunities for social integration which may underlie the development of social problems.

One particular model which has received much attention recently attempts to make links across the range of these concerns, and could consequently serve as an organizing model for identifying some strategy options – Marshall's (1950) theory of citizenship. This contains three elements. First is the legal constitution of citizens as of equal standing in relation to the law. Second is the access of all citizens to democratic apparatus for the exercise of political power over the state. Third is the provision of sufficient means for all people to engage in full social participation. The co-existence of these civil, political and social rights, it is argued, amounts to the conditions necessary for full citizenship. To Marshall they are both a historical description of the development of industrial societies, and the necessary precondition for their continued existence.

However, Marshall is at pains to point out that these rights do not exist without tension. Ironically the development of citizenship rights has occurred alongside capitalism and its associated inequalities. In particular the limitation of political rights to the formal exercise of voting rights results in the juxtaposition of multiple inequalities in the economy and in family life, with political interventions that attempt to mitigate these inequalities through social and other policies. Moreover, he argues that the best condition for the successful development of industrial societies is to maintain a balance between the economy and social rights. Too much economic freedom will undermine the long-term stability of the economy through the loss of political legitimacy and the breakdown of social reproduction. Too much political and social intervention, on the other hand, will stifle the dynamic growth of the economy, upon which everything else depends.

In sum, Marshall argues that a balance between economic growth via capitalism, political empowerment through democracy, and social integration/participation sustained through social policy is both historically and theoretically necessary for the sustained achievement of any one of these goals. Returning to the Soviet difficulties of recent years, we can see that the areas that Marshall discusses seem to be close to those of current concern: economic growth, democratic rights and social integration. To the extent that simultaneous shortcomings were perceived to have developed in these areas, it seems reasonable to characterize the situation as amounting to a crisis in citizenship.

The resolution of this crisis would therefore be via the mechanism that established those rights in the first place, namely social struggle and social movements (Turner, 1986). However, the review of social policy above shows little evidence of such mechanisms so far. Despite the repeated references to democratization that Gorbachev made, and hence, one would expect, the definition of social issues in popular terms, his specific social policy reforms were remarkable for their departure from public opinion. They were not handled simply in response to popular grievances percolating up through the political system. Politicization seemed to involve a campaign to change public opinion rather than to reflect it. The question therefore arises as to whose grievances or interests were being addressed in this process?

It is here that political science and the newer Marxist work get closest: the identification of interests in Soviet society, and the way those interests come to be disguised and presented as necessary in some sense for the nation/economy/socialism. It is clear from survey material that perestroika aroused scepticism amongst ordinary workers:

> While 20% of the enterprise executives, their deputies and the chief specialists think that restructuring is proceeding rather successfully at their enterprises, not one shop superintendent is of this opinion. (Ivanov, 1987)

> The greater part of managers are rather optimistic in assessing their own efforts and the level of their enterprises' successes in the first year of restructuring. The workers do not agree with them. In many cases they are inclined to think that management's words are often at variance with its deeds. The situation unquestionably bears the seeds of future conflicts. (Toshchenko, 1987)

> 45% of the enterprise directors and 35% of the superintendents of large shops are firmly convinced that the new economic conditions have significant advantages, while only 16% of the rank-and-file engineers, brigade leaders and workers are such determined optimists. (Chichkanov, 1987)

Among Soviet writers, Tatyana Zaslavskaya made the most extensive examination of the nature of social interests, not least in order to identify the sources of support for and opposition to perestroika. This survey evidence clearly supports her analysis, which is summarized in Figure 2.1, in which she specifically seeks to understand the place of social policy in perestroika, and the range of interests affecting its fate.

Much though one sympathized with the rhetoric of perestroika, and understood the sense of excitement that it generated amongst the intelligentsia, and even agreed that it could have led to greater economic growth, the social relations it sought to encourage were not progressive from the point of view of social need in the short term.

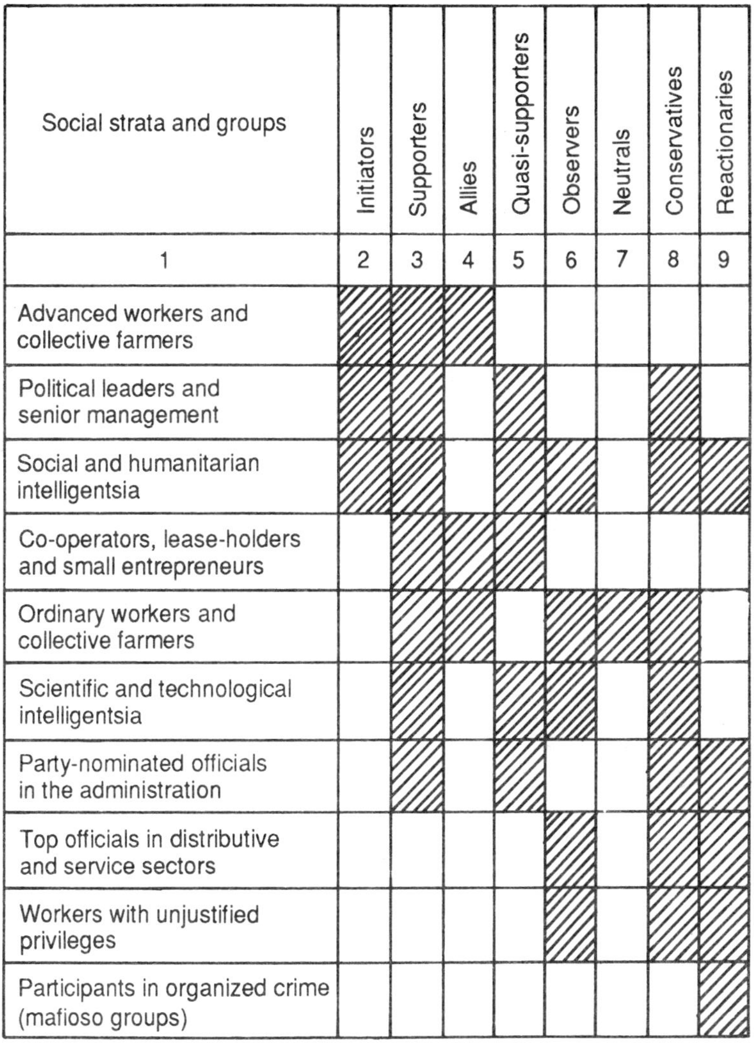

Social strata and groups	Initiators	Supporters	Allies	Quasi-supporters	Observers	Neutrals	Conservatives	Reactionaries
1	2	3	4	5	6	7	8	9
Advanced workers and collective farmers	▨	▨	▨					
Political leaders and senior management	▨	▨		▨			▨	
Social and humanitarian intelligentsia	▨	▨		▨	▨		▨	▨
Co-operators, lease-holders and small entrepreneurs		▨	▨	▨				
Ordinary workers and collective farmers		▨	▨		▨	▨		
Scientific and technological intelligentsia		▨		▨	▨	▨		
Party-nominated officials in the administration		▨		▨			▨	▨
Top officials in distributive and service sectors					▨		▨	▨
Workers with unjustified privileges					▨		▨	▨
Participants in organized crime (mafioso groups)								▨

Figure 2.1 *Typical positions of members of social strata and groups in relation to restructuring* (*Zaslavskaya, 1990: 186*)

On the contrary, the greater freedom for the intelligentsia to press its interests, on the one hand, combined with the inevitable erosion of subsidized social provision, on the other, would have squeezed ordinary workers.

This is a different conclusion to that offered by Szelenyi and Manchin (1987), who suggest that the evidence from Hungary is that a resurgence of market relations in the context of a dominant state redistributive system can lead to greater equality since it gives poor people an alternative source of power over the distributive system. This, it seems, begs the question of who has power in the first place, for those who are able to exercise influence in the administrative system, even if they are temporarily disadvantaged by a growth in the market, will without doubt soon come to exercise it again.

It is difficult not to conclude from this and the preceding section that in the immediate future there will be little substantial change in social policy, unless either there is a spectacular collapse in the economy, or Yeltsin's popularity begins to slip away. In the medium term, however, it will become apparent that a new era has developed. This may continue to be some kind of authoritarian populism; but it may be something rather different if there is a further popular ousting of the political elite or a successful counter-revolution by remnants of the party.

References

Adirim, I. (1989) 'A note on the current level, pattern and trends of unemployment in the USSR', *Soviet Studies*, XLI (3): 449–61.

Aganbegyan, A. (1988) *The Challenge: Economics of Perestroika*. London: Hutchinson.

Andrusz, G. (1984) *Housing and Urban Development in the USSR*. London: Macmillan.

Andrusz, G. (1990) 'A note on the finance of housing in the Soviet Union', *Soviet Studies*, XLII (3): 555–70.

Bettleheim, C. (1978) *Class Struggles in the USSR, 2nd Period 1923–1930*. Brighton: Harvester.

Brasier, M. (1990) 'Soviets hurtle towards abyss', *Guardian*, 6 November: 14.

Buckley, M. (1990) 'Social policies and new social issues', in S. White, A. Pravda and Z. Gitelman (eds), *Developments in Soviet Politics*. London: Macmillan. pp. 185–206.

Calnan, M. (1982) 'A review of government policies aimed at primary prevention', in M. Alderson (ed.), *The Prevention of Cancer*. London: Edward Arnold.

Chichkanov, V. (1987) *Izvestia*, 4 September: 2.

Chinn, J. (1977) *Manipulating Soviet Population Resources*. Oxford: Martin Robertson.

Connor, W.D. (1986) 'Social policy under Gorbachev', *Problems of Communism*, July–August: 31–46.

Davis, C. (1989) 'Priority and the shortage model: the medical system in the socialist economy', in C. Davis and W. Charemza (eds), *Models of Disequilibrium and Shortage in Centrally Planned Economies*. London: Chapman & Hall. pp. 427–59.

Davis, C. (1990) 'National health services, resource constraints and shortages: a comparison of Soviet and British experiences', in N. Manning and C.J. Ungerson (eds), *Social Policy Review 1989–90*. London: Longman. pp. 141–68.

Deacon, B. (1983) *Social Policy and Socialism*. London: Pluto.

Deacon, B. and Szalai, J. (eds) (1990) *The Social Policy of the New Eastern Europe*. Aldershot: Gower.

Dossett-Davies, J. (1988a) 'Where glasnost has not yet arrived', *Community Care*, 5 May: 19–20.

Dossett-Davies, J. (1988b) 'Glasnost and mental health', *Community Care*, 12 May: 27.

Economist (1990) 22 September: 25–8.

Ellman, M. (1989) *Socialist Planning*, 2nd edn. Cambridge: Cambridge University Press.

Ellman, M. (1990) 'A note on the distribution of income in the USSR under Gorbachev', *Soviet Studies*, XLII (1): 147–8.

Esping-Andersen, G. (1990) *The Three Worlds of Welfare Capitalism*. Cambridge: Polity.

Evans, A.B. (1986) 'The decline of developed socialism?', *Soviet Studies*, XXXVIII (1): 1–23.

Feher, F., Markus, G. and Heller, A. (1983) *Dictatorship over Needs*. Oxford: Basil Blackwell.

Ferge, Z. (1979) *A Society in the Making*. Harmondsworth: Penguin.

George, V. and Manning, N. (1980) *Socialism, Social Welfare and the Soviet Union*. London: Routledge and Kegan Paul.

Gilison, J.M. (1975) *The Soviet Image of Utopia*. Baltimore: Johns Hopkins University Press.

Gitelman, Z. (1990) 'The nationalities', in S. White, A. Pravda and Z. Gitelman (eds), *Developments in Soviet Politics*. London: Macmillan. pp. 137–55.

Goldfarb, J.C. (1989) *Beyond Glasnost*. Chicago, IL: University of Chicago Press.

Gorbachev, M. (1987) *Perestroika*. London: Collins.

Harding, N. (ed.) (1984) *The State in Socialist Society*. London: Macmillan.

Harwin, J. (1988) 'Glasnost children', *Guardian*, 6 April: 23.

Ivanov, V. (1987) *Izvestia*, 5 May: 2.

Kagarlitsky, B. (1990) *Farewell Perestroika*. London: Verso.

Keane, J. (1990) 'The politics of retreat', *Political Quarterly*, 61 (3): 340–52.

Kornai, J. (1980) *Economics of Shortage*. Amsterdam: North-Holland.

Lenin, V.I. (1965) *Collected Works*, vol. 30, London: Lawrence and Wishart.

Machover, M. and Fantham, J. (1979) *The Century of the Unexpected: a New Analysis of Soviet Type Societies*. London: Big Flame.

Mandel, E. (1989) *Beyond Perestroika*. London: Verso.

Manning, N. (1984) 'Social policy in the USSR and the nature of Soviet society', *Critical Social Policy*, 11 (Winter): 74–88.

Manning, N. (1985) 'Constructing social problems', in N. Manning (ed.), *Social Problems and Welfare Ideology*. Aldershot: Gower. pp. 1–28.

Marshall, T.H. (1950) *Citizenship and Social Class*. Cambridge: Cambridge University Press.

Mason, D.S. and Sydorenko, S. (forthcoming) 'Perestroika, social justice and public opinion', *World Politics*.

Matthews, M. (1986) *Poverty in the Soviet Union*. Cambridge: Cambridge University Press.

Melotti, U. (1977) *Marx and the Third World*. London: Macmillan.

Mezentseva, E. and Rimachevskaya, N. (1990) 'The Soviet country profile: health of the USSR population in the 70s and 80s – an approach to a comprehensive analysis', *Social Science and Medicine*, 31 (8): 867–77.

Navarro, V. (1977) *Social Security and Medicine in the USSR*. Lexington, MA: Lexington Books.

Niit, T. (1991) Unpublished paper given to the ESRC East–West Initiative Workshop . on Social Movements at the University of Kent, 2 October.

Perera, J. (1990) 'The shrivelled sea', *Guardian*, 9 November: 29.

Pierson, J. (1988) 'Back in the USSR', *Community Care*, 14 July: 22–4.

Pinkevitch, A.P. (1929) *The New Education and the Soviet Republic*. London: John Day.

Roberts, J. (1990) 'Winter in Leningrad', *The Health Services Journal*, 4 January: 18–19.

Rogovin, V.Z. and Ivanov, V.N. (1989) 'Social Policy in the USSR'. Unpubl. ms.

Shlapentokh, V. (1989) *Public and Private Life of the Soviet People*. Oxford: Oxford University Press.

Standing, G. (ed.) (1991) *In Search of Flexibility: the New Soviet Labour Market*. Geneva: International Labour Organization.

Steele, J. (1991) 'Soviet disabled struggle for political recognition', *Guardian*, 7 February: 12.

Steele, J. (1992) 'Fear and folly in Moscow', *Guardian*, 19 February.

Stetina, J. (1990) 'When hope hits zero', *Guardian*, 30 November: 28.

Szelenyi, I. and Manchin, R. (1987) 'Social policy under state socialism', in M. Rein, G. Esping-Andersen and L. Rainwater (eds), *Stagnation and Renewal in Social Policy*. Armonk, NY: M.E. Sharpe. pp. 102–39.

Toshchenko, Zh. (1987) *Izvestia*, 16 June: 2.

Trehub, A. (1987) 'Social and economic rights in the Soviet Union', *Survey*, 29 (4): 6–42.

Treml, V.G. (1982) 'Death from alcohol poisoning in the USSR', *Soviet Studies*, XXXIV (4): 487–505.

Tsivilev, R. and Rogogin, V. (1990) 'Social assistance for the elderly and the disabled in the USSR', *International Social Security Review*, XLIII (2): 180–8.

Turner, B. (1986) *Citizenship and Capitalism*. London: Allen and Unwin.

Urban, G.R. (1987) 'Introduction – social and economic rights in the Soviet bloc', *Survey*, 29 (4): 1–5.

White, S. and Nelson, D. (1986) *Communist Politics: a Reader*. London: Macmillan.

Yanowitch, M. (1977) *Social and Economic Inequality in the Soviet Union*. Oxford: Martin Robertson.

Zajda, J. (1984) 'Recent educational reforms in the USSR: their significance for policy development', *Comparative Education*, 20 (3): 405–20.

Zaslavskaya, T. (1984) 'The Novosibirsk Report', *Survey*, 28 (1): 83–108.

Zaslavskaya, T. (1990) *The Second Socialist Revolution*. London: I.B. Tauris.

3

Social Policy in Bulgaria

Bob Deacon and Anna Vidinova

To understand the social policy of Bulgaria both under the old regime before 1989 and under the emerging new regime since 1990 it is necessary to appreciate the special relationship between Bulgarian history and that of the Soviet Union. Unlike other East European countries, Bulgaria was not simply annexed by the Stalinist Soviet Union in 1948. The connection between the two countries stretches back to its liberation from the Turkish Empire in the nineteenth century. This goes some way to explaining the relative underdevelopment of a critical intellectual underground opposition in Bulgaria during the fifties, sixties, seventies and eighties. It also goes some way to explaining the divergent path that Bulgarian social policy initially took compared with countries like Hungary and Czechoslovakia. The establishment of a post-communist conservative corporatism within which Round Table deals are struck between the state and trade unions flows from this history. The future of Bulgarian social policy will have more in common with the future of Soviet social policy than with that of its northern and central European neighbours.

In this chapter we will first describe this special history and indeed the special nature of the 'overthrow' of communism within Bulgaria. Secondly, we will describe the achievements and limitations of 'communist' social policy in Bulgaria and emphasize the crisis points that the new regime will have to tackle. Thirdly, we will examine some of the new developments in social policy, particularly in the fields of employment, wages policy and social security. We will end with a critical comment on the problems associated with the broad strategy for welfare that was adopted during 1990 and 1991.

Historical context: the old regime and its collapse

Bulgaria has its own unique history as well as sharing the common fate of other East European countries after the Second World War. Both what it has in common with the rest of Eastern Europe and what is unique to Bulgarian history contribute to our understanding of the features of contemporary social policy (Staar, 1982; Lendvai, 1969; Harman, 1983). The unique history includes the liberation of the Bulgarian state from five hundred years of Turkish rule by the Russians in the late nineteenth century. The debt that the Bulgarian nation owes to Russia, echoed in all the speeches of the previous leader, Zhivkov, is therefore to be understood not just as acquiescence to the contemporary economic relationship of Bulgaria to the Soviet Union. Bulgarian nationalism owes its existence to Russia. Unique also is the fact that in the inter-war period Bulgaria was a relatively egalitarian peasant society. There were few large kulaks and almost half of the industrial capital was foreign. The almost complete eradication of the peasantry by the forced collectivization period of the 1950s under Chervenkov can be understood in the light of this. In place of private farms or even co-operatives, large agro-industrial complexes were developed.

The rapid industrialization and urbanization effected in Bulgaria after the Second World War was also unique. The country in Eastern Europe with proportionately one of the smallest urban populations (25.6 per cent in 1950) has changed in 35 years to the country that is second only to the former German Democratic Republic in terms of the proportion that is urban (68.6 per cent in 1985). Bulgaria has undergone in this period the biggest and most rapid transformation from a largely rural to an essentially urban society of all West, South and East European countries. This, as we shall see, has both led to major achievements in social policy and created in its turn new problems of social policy.

Not so unique has been the political history associated with the subordination of nascent Bulgarian socialism to the wider interests and control of the Soviet Union. Dimitrov founded the Bulgarian Communist Party (CP) in 1919. At this point one-fifth of the members of parliament were communist (Lendvai, 1969). The influence of the communists was to grow until they occupied a majority of the seats on the Sofia Council in 1931 (Lendvai, 1969). The unsuccessful fascist coup in 1923 led to the fleeing of Dimitrov to the Soviet Union, and the later successful fascist take-over in 1934 continued the crushing of the Bulgarian communist, socialist and trade union movements. It was with the experience of many years as General Secretary of the Comintern under Stalin (1939–43) that Dimitrov returned to Bulgaria in 1945 to assume the secretary-ship of the CP and the premiership. The active uprising by units of the Bulgarian soldiers to establish their own soldiers' councils was discouraged by Dimitrov. The democratic elections in 1945 that produced a massive victory for the alliance of the Communist Party

(277 seats) and other parties in the fatherland front (87 seats) over the anti-communists (101 seats) soon gave way to the outlawing of all opposition, and, subsequently, to rule by the Communist Party in association with the satellite Agrarian Party. Chervenkov, who was to succeed Dimitrov, successfully purged the CP of 100,000 members, including those with any trace of independence who were not associated with the Russian circle (Harman, 1983). Todor Zhivkov took over and consolidated power between 1956 and 1962 and remained Secretary-General until 1989. While this ended the overt Stalinist period, or 'period of the cult of the personality', it has not led Bulgarian communism on a path widely different from that of the Soviet Union.

In the 1970s, however, a new economic mechanism was introduced that had the aim of making enterprises more sensitive to the needs of consumers without resorting to the establishment of separate independent capitals not under the control of the central plan. This mechanism has been credited with the rapid rise in production and living standards that have characterized modern Bulgaria. Hella Pick (*Guardian*, 28 January 1985) was moved to write: 'It is as if the Bulgarian leadership have looked carefully round the Socialist camp, learning from the successes – and failures – of its friends, and is developing a model that even the Soviet leadership has come to admire, and perhaps even to emulate.' There was little evidence of an independent critical opposition movement in Bulgaria prior to 1989 that wished to press for a different form of Bulgarian socialism. The historical debt to the Soviet Union, the rapid urbanization and the continuing rise in living standards may have ensured this long period of legitimacy for the Zhivkov regime.

Despite the apparent stability of the Zhivkov years, changes came in 1989 even to Bulgaria. The process was different from that elsewhere in Eastern Europe. There was initially no popular uprising as in Czechoslovakia, although the Union of Democratic Forces was beginning to flex its muscles. There was no implosion led by convinced market reformers as in Hungary. Instead the scenario that Gorbachev worked for in much of Eastern Europe was played out here. Before it was too late, Zhivkov was overthrown in a coup by Mladenov and the party attempted to survive imminent developments by changing its name to the Socialist Party. It even won the first free elections in July 1990. Because its character had remained essentially unchanged, there was no reform in economic and social policy. The movement outside the party grew and a combination of trade union and student pressure finally forced the resignation of the 'socialist communists' and a coalition interim government was established in December 1990. This government subsequently began to take initiatives, but, as we shall describe, these were initially very much in the style of the past, with heavy involvement of trade union and other large interests.

In October 1991 new elections were held which for the first time gave rise to a non-communist government, under the leadership of the Union of Democratic Forces. This government, however, has a fragile majority of four seats over the ex-communist Socialist Party and depends on the support of the ethnic Turkish party, called the Movement for Rights and Freedoms (DPS), which has 24 seats. This fragile majority of the UDF was confirmed in January 1992 when Zhelyn Zhelev of the UDF was elected president with 53 per cent of the vote.

Social policy: past achievements and past shortcomings

Some of the key features of Bulgarian social policy before 1989 will now be described. The problematic aspects of these policies will be discussed after this account of the key features. We focus on issues of social security and medical care, rather than housing or education, because more information is systematically available in these areas.

Social security and family policy
The backcloth to earlier social security policy were the income differentials derived from work. An earlier commentator on Bulgarian society (Lendvai, 1969) described the Bulgarian wages policy as 'the most egalitarian of Eastern Europe'. A more exhaustive analysis by (Kyuranov 1984) seems to support this assertion.

The social security system, which provides incomes in all the usual contingencies, was based on the assumption of full employment and the guaranteed right to work of all citizens who were able. According to the spokesperson for the Giorgi Dimitrov Research Institute for Trade Union Studies, there were more workplaces than people who desired work: in 1986 there were between 20,000 and 30,000 vacancies. This context was used to justify the absence of any unemployment benefit and the very patchy and discretionary basis of the residual social aid scheme. Asked about whether any social experiments were undertaken to provide special working arrangements for Gypsies (who constitute 2.6 per cent of the population: Staar, 1982) whereby their casual relationship to employment could be acknowledged and compensated for, the trade union spokesperson informed us that no such experiments were carried out. The aim was to 'merge them with the labour collective, to assimilate them. To conserve the backwardness of a subculture would not be the best social policy, in my personal opinion.' Of the work-shy, and the problem that the work-related social security system did not seem to cater for their needs, it was commented by another member of the same institute that 'those who don't work shall not eat. We are not a Christian society. We do not tolerate such people.' Again it was stressed that the minimum wage for those who did work was high, 110 leva a month (1983 figure), just over 50 per cent of average wages.

For those, the vast majority, covered by the wage-based social security system, the provisions in terms of level of benefit compared very favourably with other countries and reflected the type of provision characteristic of other developed state socialist societies. The social security system was used as a weapon of labour discipline, particularly in relation to eligibility criteria for sick pay, and as an incentive to further work in the case of those eligible for retirement.

For those who fell foul of the work-based eligibility criteria of this comprehensive social security system, there was, as mentioned earlier, a patchy social aid provision. An important element of this affected those pregnant women who had not been receiving higher education, or had not been employed within the past six months. For them, a maternity allowance at the minimum wage rate was payable for 10 months in the case of the first child, 12 months in the case of the second child and 18 months in the case of the third, in addition to the usual child allowances. For lone mothers the payment was extended to two years. Social aid payments were administered by local councils and covered both regular payments and special payments to families with more than three children, the handicapped, mothers or pensioners who have not worked, lone parents and other categories. The system appeared to operate with deserving and undeserving categories of recipient. There were provisions for the aid to be given in kind rather than cash – for social workers to buy food and clothes on behalf of their clients, for alcoholics to accept a drying out period in return for aid. There was no right of appeal to an independent tribunal, but appeal could be made to a higher authority within the local council and ministerial system.

The official policy with regard to women's employment, the care of children and the relations between the sexes was much the same as that for other developed state socialist societies. Women's work was encouraged, indeed expected. Women were paid equal pay for equal work, but wage differences existed between the sexes because of differential qualifications and differential entitlement to enter certain trades. Disaggregation of incomes was presumed. Two incomes were generally required for the support of a family. The woman was regarded as worker, mother and citizen. The personal aspect of the relationship between the sexes was hardly problematized at all, although attention more recently was paid to encourage men to share in the caring of children.

We will discuss later whether women were able to combine their triple function adequately; the impact of their attempt to do so on the sexual division of labour in the home; the consequent strain on family life and divorce rates and birth rates, and the reaction of government to these pressures; and the possibility of the problematization of sexual relations and sexuality.

Medical care and health policy
Bulgaria has a national health service with medical services provided free at the point of use to all citizens. Private practice was abolished in 1972. Small charges are levied for medicines except those prescribed for children under the age of six. In 1944 Bulgaria had only 1.6 hospital beds per 1,000 population and an infant mortality rate of 120.6 per 1,000; it had progressed to being a country with 11.1 hospital beds per 1,000 and an infant mortality rate of 18.2 per 1,000 in 1982. In 1985 there were only 387 patients per physician, a ratio that was better than that in many West European countries. The distribution of health services in terms of doctors and nurses between different regions was claimed to be uniform, although very small rural settlements had to rely on visiting specialists. There were acknowledged differences in the quality of the services, however, and in particular a very wide disparity between the medical technology available in the best hospitals in Sofia (the Hospital of the Medical Academy and the Military Hospital) and that available in other parts of the capital and in the countryside. Over 60 per cent of beds in the two main Sofia hospitals were used by referrals from the country at large, leading to a crisis of adequate hospital provision in the capital. Given the comparatively low status of the medical profession, it has clearly not been able to mount a sufficient lobby to rectify the historical underinvestment in medical equipment. A further and emerging problem of distribution was that consequent upon the right of larger enterprises to provide their own polyclinics to supplement those of the councils.

The obverse of the under-investment in curative technology was the stress laid on the preventive aspects of Bulgarian socialist medical provision, in particular, the prophylactoria, which were regarded as an important innovation. Prophylactoria provide institutional accommodation for workers referred there for rest, dietary management, physiotherapy and various water and mud treatments. Workers may be referred for up to 30 days per year and stay overnight, but are bussed back to work during the day. They go home at weekends. Treatment is voluntary. In general the prophylactoria were provided by enterprises and managed by the trade unions in the workplace, with 'the trade union committee together with the doctor servicing the enterprise determining who should have priority by grading the seriousness of the individual cases and the applicant's qualities as workers' (Lissev et al., 1976).

Despite these concerns with prevention, however, it was clear from the latest available data that there was an emerging crisis of increased mortality in Bulgaria among the working population. In this respect, as for social security and family policy, the experience of Bulgaria was similar to that of other developed state-socialist societies. Later we will examine in more detail the evidence suggesting that life expectancy was falling in the 1980s and that the mortality rates for many groups of people of working age were increasing.

The undoubted achievements of post-war Bulgarian social policy were giving way by the 1980s to a series of emergent crises. In the following we shall outline some of the problems of policy faced in the areas of social security, family policy and medical care, before going on to describe the social policy priorities of the new post-1989 regime.

Work, need and the limitations of the orthodox socialist allocation principle

The incomes policy, social security system and associated education and training policy came under severe strain in the 1980's. While the socialist principle of allocation according to work has in theory operated for many years, it was increasingly felt by commentators that practice had actually erred *too much* in the direction of the communist principle of allocation according to need. A restoration of differentials and work incentives was called for. A spokesperson for the Giorgi Dimitrov Research Institute for Trade Union Studies claimed in 1987 that the present social security system was 'unfortunately more liberal than necessary'. One spokesperson argued by examples that the only cases in which sick pay could be docked were when the temporary incapacity for work was due to fighting following drinking or when the patient failed to follow a doctor's prescription. Even here, only the first three to five days' compensation could be lost. Or again it was argued that the 'size of pensions was influenced too much by the basic pay rather than the bonuses'. Reflecting on the degree of inequality in wages, the same spokesperson argued that 'from the viewpoint of encouraging work the differentials are not enough'.

Policy shifts that were discernible by the late 1980s suggested a more gradual move to increase differentials and increase work-based incentives. The new Labour Code approved by the National Assembly in 1985 made provision for workers to engage in regular 'extraordinary work', overtime work, on top of their basic job. A move toward a regulated second economy was suggested here. Additionally, small private enterprises of between four and seven people could be established and obtain government loans. These developed initially in the catering, dressmaking and handicrafts trades. There was also emphasis on enterprises now having more freedom to develop their own housing and welfare and medical services using the extra resources available to them if they were successful in selling their products under the new economic mechanism described earlier. These developments are set to expand within the context of the fuller marketization policy of the post-1989 government.

Sexual divisions and the limitations of orthodox socialist family ideology

The struggle to combine housework and child care with work and citizenship imposed immense strains on Bulgarian women and their families, notwithstanding the impressive range of services and benefits available to enable women to cope. The symptoms of these strains were a rising divorce rate and a declining birth rate. The state's reaction was to regulate further the lives of women and families in the interests of maintaining the family and the population. The possibility that a sounder resolution of these problems requires at least a re-division of labour between the sexes has only recently been articulated and is far from being realized in practice. The hidden world of women's sexual oppression in their relationships and the struggle of some of them to redefine their sexuality remains hidden.

A survey of the changing role of women in Bulgaria reported on by the then Vice-President of the Committee of the Bulgarian Women's Movement (Tropolova, 1979) concluded that: 'Society should take over what is needed for the rearing of children and other household work that *women* cannot successfully combine with social labour, or only at the price of additional physical and mental strain' (emphasis added). This, rather than the re-division of labour between men and women, remained the focus of family policy. The 'Communal Service' bureaux in towns provided, for example, 'the services of a *woman* for house-cleaning' (Vidova et al., 1983, emphasis added). While the new maternity law does provide for men to take paternity leave after six months, the expectation was that grandmothers were more likely to opt for it. These policies were supported by a clearly articulated rejection of 'Western' feminist concerns. 'Various feminist movements try in vain to solve this problem by "re-educating men" ' (Vidova et al., 1983).

The evidence pointed to the continued burden on women. A 1973 time-budget study reported that a woman spent 257 minutes per day in household chores compared to a man's 125 minutes. A later study in two Bulgarian communities (Whittaker, 1980) revealed the small proportion of men who took responsibility for household duties. They ranged from a low of 7 per cent responsible for repairing clothes to a high(!) of 28 per cent who decided on the menu (only 21 per cent cooking the meals).

It would be absurd to suggest that this uneven sexual division of labour was the only cause of the increased divorce rate, but a survey of divorced women concluded that the most important reason for first seriously contemplating divorce was the husband's 'rudeness' and hard drinking (Kyuranov, 1984). The New Family Code ratified by the National Assembly in May 1985 grappled with the divorce rate in a quite extraordinary way. Whereas divorce used to be possible by mutual consent after two years, it is now not possible until three years have elapsed. It seems that not only the rising divorce rate was a motivating factor in this apparently regressive development, but also the suspicion that marriages of convenience had been taking place to win some property benefits (housing loans/ furniture loans) or to ensure a move to another town for which permission would not otherwise be granted.

Some public political controversy surrounded this 1985 decision on divorce, which was debated in the party and in the press for nine months. One of those who opposed aspects of the policy, Chavdar Kyuranov, stresses the problems in marriage consequent upon the sexual division of labour:

> The question of redistribution of the workload in the household should become the concern of the entire society. It should become the concern not only of the Committee for the Movement of Bulgarian Women, but also of the public organizations, the Party and the Fatherland Front, because it is a question of the education of the entire nation . . . without this change the solemn claims that the family is built upon mutual respect and love will remain fine-sounding, but idle, words. (Kyuranov, 1984)

There is little evidence that changes in the direction called for by Kyuranov were taking place in the late 1980s and it has not surfaced as an import issue during or after the crisis of 1989.

The mortality crisis and the limitations of orthodox socialist medical care provision

Bulgaria, like other Eastern European countries, was by the 1980s confronted with a crisis of increased mortality. After many years of progress, life expectancy at birth began to decline, as indicated in Table 3.1. Eastern Europe, unlike the West and South (Table 3.2),

Table 3.1   *Life expectancy at birth in Bulgaria, 1965–80 (years of age)*

Year of birth	Men	Women	Overall
1965–7	68.81	72.67	70.66
1969–71	68.58	73.86	71.31
1974–6	68.68	73.91	71.31
1978–80	68.35	73.55	71.14

Source: Statistical Year Books of the People's Republic of Bulgaria (Sofia, 1977–1983)

Table 3.2   *Trends in life expectancy at birth in Europe, 1970–80 (years of age)*

Area	1970			1980		
	Men	Women	Overall	Men	Women	Overall
Western Europe	69.0	75.1	72.0	70.8	77.4	74.1
Southern Europe (including Albania and Yugoslavia	65.4	69.6	67.7	67.8	71.9	69.9
Eastern Europe	66.9	72.8	69.9	66.9	73.8	70.3
North America	68.2	75.4	71.8	70.6	77.9	73.9

Source: UNESCO Economic Commission for Europe, 1983

has shown no improvement in the life expectancy of men between 1970 and 1980. Cautiously, the United Nations report on this issue (UNESCO Economic Commission for Europe, 1983) suggested that it was too early to say if this was a long-term trend and proposed that it might have been a generational effect whereby men born 66 years before 1980 (1914) had been particularly exposed to health risks.

However, a closer examination of age-specific mortality rates for Bulgaria refutes the generational effect argument. It is evident from

Table 3.3 that the mortality rate worsened between 1976 and 1982 for men aged 20 to 24 and 40 to 44 years. Women aged 40 to 45 years were dying also at a higher rate in 1982. From this table it is clear that in the case of these selected ages only infant mortality rates and mortality rates of the elderly (60–4 years) continued to show improvements for both sexes between 1976 and 1982. Data in Table 3.4 suggests that between 1979 and 1982 the mortality rate for men and women of working age worsened at almost all ages.

Acknowledging this problem, one health policy analyst suggested in 1987 that this increased mortality rate amongst young people was a consequence of traffic accidents and the earlier onset of heart attacks and allied diseases which the young were less able to resist. More generally, the increased mortality was attributed to the pace of work associated with newer technologies and processes whereby an increased strain is put on both the physical and nervous system simultaneously. Changes in working practice and conditions seem to be suggested. A spokesperson for the Giorgi Dimitrov Research Institute for Trade Union Studies was more open minded, and, implying that the victims were somewhat to blame, suggested a combination of work stress and self-chosen diet and smoking habits. The official social policy textbook for the Institute comments rather obliquely:

> The socialist system is also confronted with some health problems proceeding from the scientific and technological revolution. They are a product of the intensive development of the economy or arise from the existing subjective factors – insufficient experience; nonutilization of the funds earmarked for prophylaxis; narrow institutional interests; and some difficulties of scientific, technological or economic nature which obstruct their full solution at the respective stage of development. (Dochev et al., 1984)

The crisis of work motivation, the crisis in family life and the crisis in mortality are some of the main social policy problems inherited by the new regime as a result of the policies of the past.

The new social policy

In Bulgaria today there are two views about the place of social policy and economic reform in the transition of society after the collapse of communism. Some think that the so-called 'shock therapy' is a panacea for everything. Others believe in a 'step by step' approach. But both groups share a vision of the future social order as a so-called 'social market economy' – a combination of a market economy with state welfare.

Table 3.3   *Bulgarian age-specific mortality rates per thousand,*
1976–82

Age group (yrs)	1976	1977	1978	1979	1980	1981	1982	Percentage change, 1976–82
Infants (<1)								
Male	24.6	27.2	27.0	22.3	23.1	21.1	20.5	−16.6
Female	19.7	20.6	19.7	17.2	17.2	16.6	15.8	−19.7
Youth (20–24)								
Male	1.19	1.25	1.30	1.24	1.34	1.18	1.36	+14.2
Female	0.59	0.58	0.59	0.57	0.53	0.52	0.48	−18.6
Middle-aged (40–44)								
Male	3.34	3.63	3.75	3.95	3.66	3.71	4.04	+20.9
Female	1.74	1.69	1.86	1.81	1.68	1.67	1.88	+8.0
Elderly (60–64)								
Male	22.0	25.2	23.4	24.0	23.5	24.1	21.5	−2.3
Female	13.5	14.7	13.6	13.2	12.7	12.5	11.7	−13.0

Source: Statistical Year Books of the People's Republic of Bulgaria (Sofia, 1977–1983)

Table 3.4   *Age-specific mortality rates per thousand for males*
and females in Bulgaria, 1979–82

Age group (yrs)	1979		1982	
	Men	Women	Men	Women
15–19	1.00	0.55	0.96	0.52
20–24	1.24	0.57	*1.36*	0.48
25–29	1.35	0.64	*1.41*	*0.66*
30–34	1.78	0.80	*1.94*	*0.83*
35–39	2.47	1.07	*2.61*	*1.19*
40–44	3.95	1.81	*4.04*	*1.88*
45–49	5.91	2.86	*6.59*	*2.95*
50–54	9.45	4.95	9.42	4.48
55–59	14.90	7.54	*15.82*	*7.72*
60–64	24.03	13.28	21.59	11.72

Increased mortality rates shown in *italics.*

Source: Compiled from mortality and demographic tables in *Statistical Year Books of the People's Republic of Bulgaria* (Sofia, 1977–1983)

Certainly, in the existing social and economic conditions in Bulgaria, shock therapy involves the highest possible social price for perestroika, because it stresses economic and not social problems.

Opponents of this policy say it reflects once again the privileging of the economic over the social sphere (expressed before as privileging of heavy industry over the production of consumers' goods).

Looking for the lesser of two evils, the first freely elected government formed in July 1990, by the ex-communists renamed Socialist Party, preferred a 'step by step' approach in introducing socio-economic reforms. In their election platform this approach was described as a 'guarantee against social uncertainty in market economy society and as a protection of human and labour rights'. Very soon after the elections it became clear that such guarantees could not be provided for every member of society in conditions of economic and social crisis. Bulgarians could 'stretch their arms no further than their sleeves would reach' so everybody would have to pay – one more, the other less – the social price of the transition period. Six months later, in December 1990, the coalition government was formed, led by adherents of 'shock therapy' policy. But its 'shock therapy' apears to have been considerably limited by the intervention of the two main trade unions, Podkrepa (which means 'support') and the Confederation of Independent Bulgarian Trade Unions. On 8 January 1991 the first agreement between the so-called 'social partners' – government and trade unions – was signed, concerning 'Implementing economic reform and maintaining social peace'. This agreement was revised and elaborated in more detail on 13 June 1991. Without these agreements trade unions would not guarantee social order. In practice this meant that no economic reform could take place before relevant social insurance and social protection measures were introduced. In the situation of economic crisis it was becoming an impossible policy, because it was not possible to realize benefits on the basis of distributing losses.

From 10 November 1989, when the previous regime was abolished, until November 1991 when, after new elections, the non-communist Union of Democratic Forces took power no political decision had been able to be made without considering the views of every participant in political life. There was no decision without discussion. There was no discussion without the Round Table. There was no Round Table without the participation of all political parties and trade union representatives. There was no trade union representation unless both trade and unions (one 'free' the other 'independent') were invited.

To all participants in the Round Table it must, however, have been clear that now was a time for accumulation and not for distribution: those who believe in capitalism knew that nothing can be done without primary capital, and Marxists believe that nothing can be built without a 'material' base. Given this implicit or explicit understanding of the need for accumulation, the usefulness of this long and complicated way of introducing new regulations came to be questioned. It reflected a struggle between differentiated social interests.

The process involved for some participants an attempt to re-interpret Marxist theory of social insurance and to incorporate it into a new welfare state. In the previous socialist society all social insurance contributions were socialized. The means, in other words, for health, education, social benefits, etc. were subtracted from the national product and allocated to the Social Insurance Fund before individual distribution in accordance with work done. This way no further deductions of work salary were required for social insurance.

As Penkov (1984) wrote, the 'Social Insurance Fund is the differentiated or socialized part of the surplus product allocated for people not involved in direct production'. Further, Penkov argued that social insurance relieves the active population from obligation to care about the non-active part of the population. Social insurance not only provides a living means for the non-active part of the population but it helps to smooth the differences in financial situation amongst economically active people caused by the need to care for different numbers of dependants. Therefore Penkov concluded that the part of the Consumption Fund which is distributed on insurance principles should grow faster than the part distributed according to the work contribution until it reaches the level at which the non-active part of the population will no longer need material support from the active members of their families. Only after this level is achieved should salary and insurance funds increase in parallel. This thinking is represented in Figure 3.1.

The initial thinking and policy of the 1990 coalition government was *not* to move away from this socialized conception of social insurance that sees the source of its income derived from *collectivities* of workers rather than deductions from *individual* wage packets. From 1 March 1991, for example, employers of state, co-operative or single-person firms had to pay to the Social Insurance Fund 35 per cent of their Work Salary Fund, instead of the previous level of 30 per cent. Where employees receive the right to retire five years before the standard date, a contribution of 45 per cent is required, and where the right to retire is ten years earlier than the norm, the employer contribution is 50 per cent of the Work Salary Fund.

We turn now to specific policy developments in the fields of employment and unemployment, price rise compensation and social security policy. Systematic material has not yet become available to

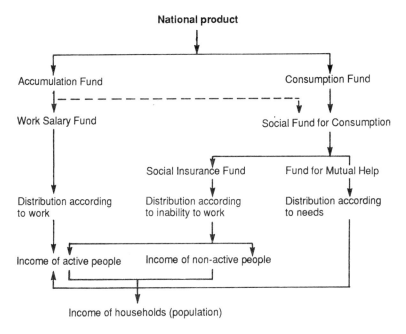

Figure 3.1   *Distribution of national product in socialist society*

enable us to describe parallel developments in housing, health and education policy.

In these sections we elaborate in more detail the policies emerging from the 'Round Table' politics of the coalition government up until October 1991. In November 1991, as we noted earlier, a new non-communist government was formed more committed to the 'shock therapy' strategy of paying a high social price, initially, for more effective market reforms. This new government will have less commitment to 'Round Table' politics. We comment on the implications of this development for the policies described below in the last section of the chapter.

Employment and unemployment policy

Bulgaria cannot make the transition to a market economy society without the existence of a real labour market. It is not enough to establish a market for goods or to increase insurance bonuses. Maintaining the priority of the social over the economic can only prolong the transition period which can only serve narrow political interests. In order to achieve both social and economic goals Bulgaria needs more value (for investment and for bonuses). As a step in this direction, in February 1991 the coalition government introduced a programme for de-centralization, de-monopolization and independence of business activities in state firms. This was in response also to the evident worsening of the economic situation. Production levels for January 1991 droppd by 24.7 per cent in comparison with January 1990. Net product fell by 28.8 per cent.

The 'socialist' state guaranteed a job for everybody and claimed that it paid according to the work done. Work was measured in units of time and production was measured by volume. The policy of full employment required everybody (except the ill) to be engaged 8.5 hours daily during the whole year. There was no grading based on hours of work (this changed in April 1991). If somebody worked only a thousand hours during the year he was still considered as fully employed. This was not economically efficient, and led to reduced social insurance potential. The longer the working time and the worse the working conditions, the more social benefits the worker got, a right protected by the state trade unions. If the same volume of production was produced in a shorter time, the worker lost. If working conditions improved they would also lose his supplementary allowance and right to early pension. Enterprises which overspent received more subsidies, the enterprises which produced more had higher income taxes and received less from the state. This remained until 1991 the basis of employment and production policy.

Now there is a serious intention to change some paragraphs of the Labour Code in order to establish a labour market, to activate its institutions and to develop re-qualification programmes. According to the Platform of the Independent Trade Union Confederation (ITC), however, the right of employment should be a 'sacred and immune right'. It should be protected and guaranteed. Nevertheless, although the Ministry of Labour and Social Care and the two trade union confederations may argue about the precise number of unemployed, no one denies their existence anymore. The Minister of Labour and Social Care's most pessimistic forecast was that there will be a 12.9 per cent unemployment rate at the end of 1991. Reports in early 1992 suggest a figure of 25 per cent is more accurate. Full employment is not actually defended any more. Policy has shifted from a policy of full employment to one of effective employment. The government is looking for a closer relationship between economic development and new jobs; between structural and technical changes and between the education and training systems. The bill for a New Employment Law was presented in 1991 for discussion to the Three-sided Round Table Committee. An Unemployment Fund would be established which would be financed by employers and from the state budget. The bill proposes the establishment of a National Employment Council with representatives of state organs, employers and trade unions. It will define the main direction of employment policy, will change and develop labour legislation, will control the use of the Unemployment Fund and the Fund for Professional Qualification and Re-employment.

Social policy-makers were therefore talking about the '*management*' of employment. Any management supposes comprehensive and sufficient data resources. However, the existing 120 employment bureaux have lost their administrative power. Their information about employment issues is no longer reliable, and they cannot respond to all existing, previous and newly emerging forms of firms and employment. They acted as a buffer to the first wave of unemployment but cannot withstand the pressure of a real labour market in which the unemployed are just a part. Together with the need for technological innovation, employment bureaux will need to change their methods of work. Bulgarian policy-makers understand that the new job centres will not only need to dispose of benefits but should also analyse the information about the conditions and trends of employment and foresee what any one of the interested parts of the labour market can expect in the future. They will need to act as mediators and also as consultants regarding the conditions of job contracts, explaining to employees details of living and work conditions, employment opportunities for their partners, school conditions for their children; and, to the employer, the quality of labour available, and whether it can be modified or provided at a certain time. Since September 1991 the British 'Know-How' fund has provided expertise to develop these services.

It is argued by some that the new management of the economy requires a new policy of employment, seen not as 'management' of employment, but as its 'regulation'. This means a transition from the administrative management of labour resources, seen as part of the management of material resources, towards economic methods for management of employment such as investments and technological innovation, finance regulators, re-employment and re-qualification programmes, labour market and social benefits. Little progress has been made in this direction.

A ministerial decision of June 1991 significantly extended the range of rights to unemployment benefit. Workers who have lost their jobs not because of unreasonable behaviour but because of employee initiative or because their contract has ended are now entitled to unemployment benefits. The duration of these benefits depends upon the length of qualifying period and the employee's age. Examples of benefit entitlement are shown in Table 3.5.

Table 3.5   *Bulgarian unemployment benefit provision: examples of entitlement*

Work experience (years)	Age (years)	Length of benefit payments (years)
≤5	≤40	6
5	≤40	7
5+	40+	8
10+	45+	9
20+	51+(men)	10
20+	51+(women)	12
25+	56+(men)	12

The period during which unemployment benefits are received is also considered as a qualifying period for pension. Only those unemployed who have been working at least five months by contract in the last twelve months are entitled to receive unemployment benefits. The level of benefit is set at 80 per cent of the previous salary paid during the past twelve months. The benefit level should not be less than the minimum wage and not more than four times this level.

We comment on the likely implementation of this policy in the light of the November 1991 government change at the end of the chapter.

Price rise compensation and social security policy

We now turn to recent developments under the 1990–91 coalition government in other aspects of income maintenance and social security policy. We begin this with a review of the discussion and policy concerned to compensate citizens for the price rises that have followed from the faster pace of economic reform and price liberalization initiated by the coalition government set up in December 1990. This discussion and policy clearly illustrates the point made in our opening remarks, and the one with which we shall conclude, that policy developments in this period are taking place in a corporatist mould whereby social protection is emphasized at the expense of economic growth and efficiency.

A new incomes policy was one of the main debates during 1990. Two methods were considered as most relevant for the protection of the buying power of the population likely to be faced with price liberalization. First was the agreement between participants in the Round Table (government, opposition party and trade unions) which was to introduce at the end of the year a centralized system for indexation of salaries. All conditions were negotiated, and first bonuses were indeed received for the last months of 1990. Full bonuses were given only to those on minimal salary, those with higher incomes were eligible only for partial bonuses or none at all. With a coefficient of 3 on salary differentiation (the lowest amongst East European countries) the full indexation for minimal wages helped delay the development of the labour market; helped level the incomes and thus reduce employee interest in increasing productivity; reproduced old centralized structures and preserved the old unified salary system; and, furthermore, increased inflation and did not help the competitiveness of the country. The indexation rate for 1990 was not accepted by the IMF, and from the beginning of 1991 it was to be changed to a system of compensation. This was meant to be a *decentralized* and *flexible* adaptation of salaries in different firms, institutions, etc. as a result of collective bargaining. According to this method, only a minimal salary should be determined centrally. The rate of compensation for other salaries was negotiable. Participants in the Round Table agreed, however, first on compensation by *centralized political* means. The aim was to keep income fixed over each 3- to 4-month period, and to ensure the standard of living did not drop more than 30 per cent. It could work only if the forecast of price rises was accurate. On 1 February 1991 the prices of all goods, except those of electricity, heating, gas butane propane and coal, were liberalized. Before price liberalization the conclusion of three independent research centres was that prices would increase by between 83 and 86 per cent; compensation would be at the 70 per cent level and therefore it would be necessary to increase salaries by between 56–60 per cent. After price liberalization prices actually went up by around 25 to 30 per cent higher than expected. Already negotiated compensations had to be revised after several months. Salaries and social bonuses could be renegotiated in this way and increased by further social pressure, but the Round Table did not seem to ask who was going to pay. Even the very first level of compensation proved to be unbearable for certain firms. Some trade unions discussed the acceptance of lower than official rate of compensation in order to save jobs. The state budget covers the sum of salary compensation only of the institutions subsidized by the state together with national insurance payments such as scholarships, pensions and child benefits. These expenses were provided in the new 1991 budget. Other firms and business organizations were obliged to provide money for salary compensations. If their Work Salary Fund was not sufficient they were allowed to transfer money from other funds, except from redemption funds and those provided for housing or money acquired by selling basic capital or raw materials. If even after this transfer the firm was still not able to pay off salary compensations, the only solution left was staff redundancy. Finance directors in budget-subsidized enterprises were therefore in a much better position than their colleagues in autonomous firms – they did not need to make any complicated calculations and to explain to the employees why there was no money to pay compensation. 'What kind of market economy is this?' – exclaimed one director – 'they do not give us any money, but require us to pay! The existing Labour Code does not allow redundancy so the only thing we can do is to close the enterprise.'

In fact, of course, one strategy for firms was the raising of prices, which then triggers a new series of Round Table agreements on next month's price rise compensation. In the summer and autumn of 1991 therefore the new Bulgarian political system of post-communist corporatism was running fast to catch up with the price rises occurring in its semi-liberalized economy. Thus in July 1991, as it was agreed, the level of compensation was re-negotiated. This agreement between the government and trade unions was announced by Ministry Council Letter N 110 on 13 July. It was accepted as two decrees, one concerning income compensation and the other concerning collective bargaining. The minimum income levels were as follows:

- minimum working salary – 620 leva;
- minimum wage level of collective bargaining – 652 leva;
- minimum level of wage compensation for June – 455 leva;
- unemployment benefits – 455 leva;
- minimum pension – 465 leva;
- minimum level of child benefit – 130 leva;
- benefits during pregnancy and child care period – 420 leva;
- scholarship for over 18s – 130 leva.

Some conditions for ensuring employment were also provided by this government decree. Firms and work organizations could use new forms of employment such as part-time work, division of work functions, work by the hour, shorter working week, work every second day, work on demand, etc. In the case of opening new jobs, firms were entitled to low-interest credit, and for those firms which provided full employment during 1991 for the staff that had been employed as of 1 May 1991, a tax relief of 50 per cent on their salary funds was provided.

Those who are registered as unemployed and want to start some private or collective business could be financially supported by the amount of benefits they were entitled to. Bureaux of employment were given a discretion to pay moving expenditure for those unemployed who sign a work contract for no less than 6 months with a firm at a distance of more than 100 km. Firms and organizations who employ more workers in addition to declared vacancies could receive a sum equal to the minimum salary for the new workers, which would last not more than 6 months for the employment of young specialists and not more than 3 months for young technicians.

New decrees, as all previously existing decrees, are only a partial solution of old problems. And these partial solutions may, in turn, provoke further problems.

In terms of other aspects of social security, the major development is the new bill on social secuirty, which, although tabled in 1991, is not due to become law until 1993 and its fate is in the hands of the new government elected in October 1991. In the meantime ministerial decrees enact parts of the policy. The Bill includes a modification to policy and provision in pensions and other insurance benefits such as sick pay and pregnancy. It has led one leader of the Social Insurance Office (Kostov) to comment, 'Bad economy and good insurance lead to worse economy and bad insurance, because it deepens the inflation process.'

There are also new approaches in the bill to pension insurance, such as 'flexible retirement'. The existing pension age is 55 years for women and 60 years for men. The new formula is: a right to receive a pension to be based on the sum of length of service and age – 95 years for men and 85 years for women, provided that they have at least 15 years' service. A pension increase of 1.5 per cent will be added for every year of service above 25 years for women and above 30 years for men. The existing regulations have a limit of 12 per cent in such cases. It is also proposed to provide a 5 per cent supplement for every year of work after achieving the right to pension. Men can retire at 57 if they have 30 years' service, and women at 52 if they have 25 years' service. There are four categories of work according to harmfulness and risk. Workers who have 1 or 2 work category can retire at 50 if they have 7 years' service. The level of pension in this case is reduced by 1.5 per cent for every year up to 95 for men and 85 for women. The aim of the new formula is to achieve a minimum pension level not lower than 75 per cent of minimum work salary and according to the insurance contribution paid during the working life of the retired person. The bill also provides for the separation of the Social Insurance Fund from the state budget. The state cannot divert money from this Fund but it must underwrite payments if the Fund is in deficit. The bill also provides for additional voluntary contributions to the national Fund.

In addition to the Social Insurance Fund, changes took place in 1991 to the system of income support. This is available to those without adequate means of income, with no savings and with no unoccupied property. Orphans, handicapped children, children with both parents unemployed, invalids, pensioners, single parents, families with several children, and unemployed who do not receive unemployment benefits can receive income support. For single people over 70 who have income below a specific level free lunches, half price water, electricity and heating are provided. Handicapped people who have no car are eligible for free travel cards; twice a year they can travel free by train or ship and once a year they can stay free in a sanatorium. Mothers with many children can also travel free once a year by bus, train or ship. The socially weak will receive help six times a year in buying expensive medicines, cleaning materials and clothes. Pension compensations and social bonuses for people living in homes for social care will be delivered to these institutions. According to the Ministry of Labour, a rough estimate of the number of people receiving income support in 1991 was 805,641, or 1 per cent of the population.

Emerging strategy for welfare

In response both to the legacy of social problems inherited from the past and in order to tackle the problems consequent upon market-ization and liberalization in ways that are least harmful in the short term to the population, the coalition Bulgarian government formed in 1990 embarked on a policy of government by consensus through Round Table negotiations in which the trade union movement had a significant influence. This could be regarded as a smooth passage from 'communism' to a social democratic capitalism. It is better regarded as the emergence of a post-communist conservatist corporatism within which major interests try to manage the economic changes in ways which actually prevent the real development of market economic mechanisms.

Indexation policies and compensation policies and the new social insurance and income support measures were an attempt to solve not only temporary social problems due to the transition period, but all those created during the previous social order. These new measures of social support have placed large burdens on the national insurance system, without increasing the work or financial obligations on its users. In the economic crisis now emerging this policy brought a deficit of one billion leva in the social insurance budget. At the end of December 1990 the Social Insurance Fund needed 300 million leva in order to cover its payments. The compensations and the budget itself had to be revised according to increases in the price index and the index of national work productivity. The level of compensation was set to increase continuously with rapid inflation and in the period of economic downturn. After the price liberalization employers were expected to pay an amount equal to almost 60 per cent of salary funds for social insurance. No real entrepreneur would have been willing or will be able to afford the money. The solution was initially once again seen as the state budget, but now this is coming under close scrutiny by the IMF. 'The most reasonable solution at this moment is to reduce some of the expenditure in order to cover at least those who are on the "bottom" . . . and to freeze all other payments for some time like they did in Germany after the Second World War', suggests Dr D. Ninov from the Institute of Labour Studies. He and we are sure that the coalition Bulgarian government would have found out very soon that such a desirable and extensive social policy is not yet economically viable. This is a result of the partial, economically unsustainable and distorted approach towards social policy developed since 1990. It served political aims and ambitions, the wish to attract more voters and achieve more publicity, and the protection of some nomenklatura and working-class interests. It smoothed problems for some time, but in fact only enhanced their causes. Thus ultimately Bulgaria is likely to face twice as many problems.

This period of coalition and Round Table post-communist conservatism may have come to an end with the election of the new non-communist government led by the Union of Democratic Forces in October 1991. This Union actually excludes smaller parties such as the social democrats and green parties that had played a large part in the initial overthrow of the freely elected ex-communist government in December 1990. These failed to secure enough votes for parliamentary representation. It is a centre-right union which includes the Podkrepa Labour Confederation which is committed to the 'shock therapy' of rapid marketization. It remains to be seen whether this minority government, dependent on the party of the ethnic Turks for support, will be able to proceed with rapid marketization or whether it will find itself having to compromise with social measures the economy cannot afford because of the extra-parliamentary power of the larger, non-Podkrepa, trade union movement and the substantial presence of the ex-communist Socialist Party inside parliament. While the essential political issue will be the balancing of moves towards an efficient economy while placating those who wish to retain the new social agreements on welfare measures, the underlying danger in the situation is that the ex-communists could draw on Bulgarian national sentiments against the increasing political power of the Turkish minority to re-establish a post-communist conservatism wearing nationalist colours, as in neighbouring Serbia and Romania.

References

Dochev, I. et al. (1984) *Social Policy*. Sofia: Giorgi Dimitrov Research Institute for Trade Union Studies.

Harman, C. (1983) *Class Struggles in Eastern Europe*. London: Pluto.

Kyuranov, C. (1984) *The Bulgarian Family Today*. Sofia: Sofia Press.

Lendvai, P. (1969) *Eagles in Cobwebs*. London: Macdonald.

Lissev, G. et al. (1976) *Social Security in Bulgaria*. Sofia: Sofia Press.

Penkov, P. (1984) *Basis of Social Insurance*. Sofia: Giorgi Dimitrov Research Institute for Trade Union Studies.

Staar, R. (1982) *Communist Regimes in Eastern Europe*. Stanford, CA: Hoover Institute Press.

Statistical Year Books of the Peoples Republic of Bulgaria (1977–1983) Sofia.

Tropolova, Y. (1979) 'Changing roles of sex and Bulgaria's social policy', *Bulgarian Journal of Sociology*, 2 (1): 97–100.

Tryd [Truth] (1991), 57 and 58. Sofia: Confederation of Independent Bulgarian Trade Unions.

UNESCO Economic Commission for Europe (1983) Paper for meeting on population. October, Sofia.

Vidova, M. et al. (1983) *100 Questions and Answers concerning Bulgarian Women*. Sofia: Sofia Press.

Whittaker, R. (1980) 'Continuity and change in two Bulgarian communities', *Bulgarian Journal of Sociology*, 3 (1).

4

Social Policy in Czechoslovakia

Mita Castle-Kanerova

The current debate about social policy in Czechoslovakia (since 1990 formally the Czech and Slovak Federative Republic, CSFR) reflects the forty-year-old conundrum facing the countries of Eastern Europe – was the state's involvement in social welfare beneficial or not? How much of the state's responsibility should be retained and how much should be handed over to market forces or anyone else? Democratization is the buzz word, yet no one quite knows what that means. It is clear that social policy, despite its growing prominence, has so far been introduced only in its narrow sense; it responds to the economic reform. So far, only 15 per cent of policy changes have been innovative. This is an admission made at a public meeting in November 1991.

The ensuing discussion does not, however, constitute a mere theoretical pastime for those who have been through it all before. What distinguishes Czechoslovakia is that a discussion about policy issues constitutes a fiercely political battle between emergent rival governmental factions. With Czechoslovakia embarking on its transition towards a market democracy (as it likes to call it), albeit more slowly than some of its neighbours, there is now a clear political divide over the issues of what is best described as the new 'social morality'.

Civic Forum, the leading force behind the ousting of the communist regime in Czechoslovakia in 1989, has split under the chairmanship of Vaclav Klaus, the Finance Minister. He now leads the Civic Democratic Party and openly talks about a need for 'our new party' that would stand to the 'right of an imaginary centre' (Janyska, 1991). His views have been described as straight monetarist, and he himself likes to be known as more Friedmanite than Friedman. Various rumours have circulated around Prague that his attitude, for example, to unemployment is unflinching: 'If it takes 2 million unemployed to make our transition to a market society, so be it' is one such statement attributed to him.

But the Finance Minister must at some stage meet with the Labour Minister. Here lies the interesting tension, as the Labour Ministry of Czechoslovakia does not share Klaus's sentiments. Peter Miller's Ministry of Labour and Social Affairs has been publishing a whole series of governmental discussion papers raising the spectre of 'social justice and social solidarity'. Confused as some of the arguments in these papers are, particularly about retaining or dropping the old 'socialist' terminology, nevertheless, the battle over private or collective morality has been joined. The social reforms envisaged by the Ministry of Labour and Social Affairs are in effect a significant political statement and represent a challenge to hard-line monetarism.

The situation in mid-1991, was further complicated by a shift in the predictions about the impact of marketization. The cautious headlines in 1990 about unemployment not being a problem at all have gone. The Labour Minister, Miller, broadcast the possibility of 1 million unemployed before the end of 1991. Currently, at the beginning of 1992 unemployment stands at 3.8 per cent, with monthly increase of 20 per cent, and predicted 6–8 per cent unemployment by the end of the year. The Labour Ministry advocates an 'active employment' policy as part of the social policy strategy, yet the population seems to have little faith in social policy reform so far. It appears that the traditions of egalitarianism have not disappeared. In fact, a public opinion poll from the end of 1990 suggests that marketization and privatization are viewed with apprehension. 'The opportunity to become rich is mostly seen as something improper', and the fear of growing social inequalities is greater than the fear of losing one's job (Konopasek, 1991: 13). The Ministry, however, suffers by not opening its documents to wider discussion, and leaving the public largely uninformed. In the meantime, the Finance Minister commands greater respect among the international business community, which is the source of his influence.

Public opinion in Czechoslovakia at the time of writing is divided. On the one hand, the economic reform is seen as a necessity. It is argued that Czechoslovakia cannot stand apart from wider European developments, and that it has to adopt the market in order to become an equal partner. It is believed that in the long run this will enable the country to choose its own brand of political development and will spare it from dependency. Moreover, it is argued that marketization is the only way to break down monopolistic structures, the bureaucratic mentality and the population's indifference – Czechoslovakia, wants to avoid the 'short, sharp shock' approach, previously advocated in Poland, and find its own way out of the long years of imposed statism. There had been no scope for self-activity, critical thinking or innovation. Thus the past has created a sense of an arrested, paralysed, anaesthetized society. The other opinion prevalent in Czechoslovakia is of a society threatened by uncaring monetarist reductionists who are merely pursuing their self-interest. 'KLAUS EQUALS HUNGER', written on a Prague wall, is typical. In response to the question 'There must be absolute freedom for private business', Czechoslovak respondents have slowly moderated their opinion from May 1990 when 15.7 per cent responded definitely not or rather not to June 1991 when 26.1 per cent responded in this way (Vecernik, 1991a).

This duality of thinking, that sees the economic reforms as both necessary and a threat, is accompanied by a further duality of debate on the issue of family policy. On the one hand, the Family Policy document of February 1989 emphasizes the 'equal rights of all citizens' (*Family Policy Conception*, 1989: 5), but, on the other hand, it argues that the family is a 'fundamental link between the private and public spheres'. The liberal concept of equality of citizenship is 'creatively' blended with the old Stalinist concept of the family with its more traditional role. It is noted elsewhere that there is an 'excessive employment burden of women that the economy will not be able to sustain in the future' (*Zasady Strategie*, 1990: 12), implying that the family will resume some of the welfare functions previously undertaken by the state.

It is clear that the centrality of social policy to the societal changes taking place has its roots in Czechoslovak history. Czechoslovakia's pre-war past has invariably been described as the most democratic of all East and Central European nations, with a strong liberal, reformist and somewhat egalitarian bent. The Czechoslovak Republic of 1918 was among the first European countries to legislate for a minimum wage in 1919 (Tomes, 1990b).

What I argue in this chapter is that neither 1968 nor 1989 brought a full-scale democratic revolution. As a result there are a number of contradictions in current social policies. However, for the first time in forty years social and economic issues are not being dealt with in isolation from each other. Neither is it universally presumed that economic policy will automatically solve all social questions. There are indeed optimists who say that whilst 'the whole economic reform contains a strongly right-wing element, the political spectrum is in reality tipping over to the left' (Konopasek, 1991: 12).

Czechoslovak social policy under the old regime: from pre-war to post-war

The governmental declaration that the 'system of social guarantees under the communist regime proved to be wholly illusory' (Navrh, 1990a: 3) is not unique to Czechoslovakia. Such revelations are now commonplace in East Central Europe. What *is* unique, however, is the current search for a blend of pre-war social democratic social policy and the remnants of some of the principles espoused under 'idealistic socialism'. A majority of the discussion papers that have been prepared by the Ministry of Labour and Social Affairs, where the legislation on social security and social welfare is prepared, start from a critique of the shortcomings of the past monopolistic tendencies of the communist/totalitarian regime. At the same time they make references to establishing a 'legal state' which would oversee a 'universal and uniform system of social security' (Navrh, 1990a: 1 and 1990b). What is interesting is the combination of an attack on a centralist state whilst at the same time wanting to retain some of its roles. Although this may be interpreted as a confusion, a full appreciation of the seeming conflict and the already referred to conundrum in Czechoslovakia cannot be made without a closer look at the country's past.

Otto Ulc (1974: 45) makes a reference to the fact that Czechoslovakia

> before 1938 . . . was the sixth largest industrial nation in Europe . . . Its foreign trade was four to five times that of any of the fourteen countries of East Central Europe – Finland, Greece, and Turkey included . . . The land reform of 1919 fixed the maximum amount of arable land which could be owned by an individual at 150 hectares. Compulsory social insurance covered all wage earners. Differences in levels of wealth were much smaller than, for example, in neighboring Hungary or Poland.

All in all, the 'twenty years (1918–1938) of Czechoslovak independence furthered the development of a pluralistic society while avoiding the extremes of social polarization'. He adds that by 1945: 'The capitalist sector was weak and unimportant, owing to the gradual process of liquidation since 1939' under the Nazi occupation. 'By the end of 1945, about 65 percent of all industry (in terms of manpower and output) was owned by the state' (Ulc, 1974: 4).

The establishment of the first independent Czechoslovak state in 1918 is therefore associated with a highly progressive development, particularly in the sphere of social policy. A textbook on aspects of social development in pre-war Czechoslovakia published in Prague in 1985 curiously refers to the impact of the Bolshevik Revolution in the Soviet Union as the main factor triggering the welfare legislation in the Czechoslovak 'first republic'. It notes that the Versailles peace treaty of 1919 included elements of social policy as far as improving working conditions and working hours, the recruitment of labour, the fight against unemployment, health insurance and insurance for industrial injuries, pensions, invalidity, etc. were concerned (Deyl, 1985: 21). This, the textbook stresses, was mainly due to the bourgeoisie 'needing to prove that we were entering the "epoch of social consensus" ' and that 'social problems that were being addressed by the Soviet power were also solveable within the confines of bourgeois systems' (Deyl, 1985: 21). The impression one is supposed to get from reading this textbook is that, were it not for the Russian Revolution, Czechoslovakia and the rest of the world's working classes would be living under much harsher conditions. Though a wider world perspective and particularly the globalization of capital is important to take into account when assessing the evolution of social welfare in industrialized societies, this old line elevating the liberatory influence of the Russian Revolution above everything else is now seen as idolatory and outmoded. What remains to be undertaken is a full analysis of the conditions and the legislation originating in Czechoslovakia in the 1920s.

Previously an adviser to the Labour Minister, Igor Tomes, has publicly stated that the new Czechoslovak social insurance legislation should return to some of the principles of universality and adequate coverage first developed in the 1920s and then codified in 1948 post-war legislation that predated that of the communist coup (Tomes, 1990a). The fact that present-day legislators, whose real political identification is with 1968 and 'socialism with a human face', can combine pre-war concepts of social justice with the reform-minded humanitarian yet still deeply socialist approach of the communist era of the late sixties is another historical curiosity unique to Czechoslovakia. The Action Programme of the Czechoslovak Communist Party in 1968 was perhaps, a statement of those who were longing to return to the democratic roots of the independent Czechoslovakia before the war. Stalinization in the 1950s in Czechoslovakia took off with a fierceness not seen elsewhere in the Eastern bloc, but the political education of many of the Czechoslovak reformers participating in 1968 – and who have now returned – predated the imposition of the Soviet model of politics.

The blend of political thinking that seems to be emerging today, that is, the combination of democracy (by which is meant individual freedoms of self-expression and action not stifled by a pseudo-authority of the state) and an adherence to the idea of social justice mirroring some of the ideals of classless society, is an evolutionary product of the two liberal periods, the twenties and the sixties.

What remains to be seen is to what extent the younger generation that now speaks of a new 'nomenklatura' of the original liberal Civic Forum personnel will retain some of its critical stand or transfer its sympathies to the pro-market lobby.

The older generation of Czechoslovak intelligentsia has a reputation as suffering from a certain form of idealism, not altogether appropriate for the tasks of the day. It is said to look longingly to the past, feeling moral indignation, opting for politics of the 'middle ground' and being unprepared for practical politics at hand, the 'real politics of today' (Pithart, 1990). Here, the battle with hardline monetarism is yet to prove decisive – first, because idealism and monetarism clearly clash, and secondly, because the younger generation has not yet gained too many seats in the decision making structures.

Also, the legacy left to social policy from the 1920s may not be as unproblematic as it looks. Leaving aside the cruder interpretations of Deyl (1985), the 1920s were years of high unemployment and consequently of high state involvement in policy. Unemployment among industrial workers in 1919 was 20 per cent, it fell to 8 per cent in 1920 but went up again in 1922–3. In the twenty years of independent Czechoslovakia, Deyl claims, the reserve army of labour was on average 14 per cent of the total industrial work force. Among the 'interventionist' state policies was the implementation of an eight-hour working day at the end of 1918, abolition of small insurance companies in 1919 and, most significant, the comprehensive social insurance legislation of 1924 (Deyl, 1985: 30–84). The industrial workers' insurance scheme was based on joint contributions, half payable by the employer and half by the insured. It was founded on the principle of equivalence between wages and expenditure, which, as Deyl is quick to add, 'didn't form a firm support in times of economic crisis' (Deyl, 1985: 90). He also claims that it was a piece of 'class legislation', favouring in some cases the state employees over the industrial working class. And though it was hailed as a piece of consensus legislation, it was a 'compromise between bourgeois and reformist coalition, without taking any of the then objections of the newly established Czechoslovak Communist Party into account. . . . It was cheap insurance . . . transferring the financial burden from the present on to the future generation' (Deyl, 1985: 88). Nevertheless, it covered basic risks, such as old age, invalidity, widowhood, orphanage, ill health and injury. It was followed by several amendments, completed in 1928, some of which were seen as negative, such as exclusion of workers under the age of 16. Despite such reforms, however, Czechoslovakia at that time ranked only between seventh and tenth place in

Europe as far as its welfare provisions were concerned (Deyl, 1985: 102).

The 1930s were times of serious economic crisis with high unemployment and concomitant lowering of wages. The average daily wage of an industrial worker in 1935 fell to between 83.3 and 85.5 per cent of the wage in 1929. By 1935 the yearly nominal pension payable through the Central Social Insurance Company was down to 63.8 per cent of the 1929 level (Deyl, 1985: 130, 132). The 1930s were generally perceived as a mixed blessing. They saw a dramatic increase of state subsidies of unemployment benefit, creation of investment for retraining, lowering of weekly working hours to five working days without reduction in living standards, but also an establishment of 'work camps' and 'workhouses' for the unemployed. One may, however, get a certain sense of a caring society that struggled with its newly found independence in the midst of a European crisis. A more comprehensive national insurance was being prepared in the underground even during the war, according to Karel Pinc (1989: 73). This became the basis for the universalistic and uniform national insurance system in 1948.

The prospects for further progressive legislation were radically altered with the imposition of the Stalinist model of economic and political structure in the 1950s. The Czechoslovak economy was restructured from its foundations. From a balanced economy it became the 'machine tool workshop' of Eastern Europe. 'The emphasis on quantitative expansion of the national economy resulted in 75% of investment being allocated to production, and a mere 25% to service industries' (Ulc, 1974: 48). The same ratio, incidentally, as in the Soviet Union. Krejci adds that: 'The second wave of nationalization, declared after February 1948 [the communist coup], extended nationalization to all enterprises with more than fifty employees or fifty hectares of land' (Krejci, 1972: 16). There was also confiscation of property, and a second monetary reform in 1953, 'performed according to Soviet experts', that established a

> conversion ratio of 5 crowns of the old for 1 crown of the new currency . . . for all claims from employment including pensions and other social benefits – . . . [however] for all other private cash balances and all other claims of individuals . . . the conversion ratio was stated as 50:1, which meant 90% confiscation . . . Savings deposits in pre-1945 currency were completely annihilated. (Krejci, 1972: 18)

This process of 'homogenization' of Czechoslovak society, as Krejci calls it, had its new inverted class bias. Ulc refers to it as 'social pseudo-security', and argues that 'socialism of the Stalinist variety is bound to be insensitive to the poor and needy' (Ulc, 1974: 49). It began with labour-intensive industrial production, which, rather than modernizing itself, added 'women and the aged to the labour force' (Ulc, 1974: 48). It has now been recognized that this system created a 'feminization of poverty' and pauperization of old-age pensioners (Pinc, 1990). Social policy legislation, however, according to Pinc, was out of tune with this development. He claims that the national insurance reforms of 1951–2 brought in a comprehensive free state medical care and that even during the fifties on paper Czechoslovakia ranked among the world's top welfare states (Pinc, 1989: 74).

It seems that, above all, it was the principle 'each according to his merit' that represented the new Stalinist 'class approach' to social policy. Ulc paraphrases Igor Tomes, pointing out that the result of this system 'was political aristocracy at one end and political outcasts at the other . . . Social security was degraded from a legal right to a political award, subject to ex post facto whims of the state' (Ulc, 1974: 50). A similar analysis is presented by both Mishra (1977) and McAuley (in Godson and Schapiro, 1981) when referring to the Soviet Union. Ulc is uncompromising when he says that:

> As the construction of socialism proceeded, social insecurity increased. In 1956 a principle was openly promulgated relating one's retirement benefits to his record of contribution to the socialist cause. A further step was taken in 1958 when local people's committees were authorized to cut a recipient's social benefits if they felt that he had committed political sins. Benefits for orphans of politically suspect parentage were also subject to reexamination. These prerogatives of local committees remained in force until 1967. (Ulc, 1974: 50)

Here lies one of the contradictions of the old system of welfare – generous on the one hand, but politically discriminating on the other. The Stalinist social policy appeared to be generous to only certain selected categories of the population. The main weakness of that period was the almost total substitution of ideology for theory. According to Pinc, the dominant opinion from the 1950s onwards was that as 'socialism' in Czechoslovakia matures, 'there will no longer be any need for social policy as a distinct and relatively separate sphere of social activity' (Pinc, 1989: 76). The poverty of theory is reflected in the rigid adherence to Marxism-Leninism. As Pinc points out, one of the authoritative statements on social policy became a comment in one of Engels's letters where he offers his view that the 'theoretical solution of the so-called "social question" lies in the liquidation of capitalism' (Pinc, 1989: 76). Social problems had clearly been pushed to the periphery of social concern, and any conceptualization of social policy under Stalinism had 'withered away'.

This was officially justified by pointing out that the socialist economy was thriving and thus the 'traditional social problems' (such as poverty and unemployment, and social ills like prostitution) were on the way out. As Pinc also says, the new 'socialist arrangements would automatically bring about a situation where there would no longer be problems to be solved by social policy'. Equally, it was mentioned that social policy in the past, under capitalism, had pejorative, 'policing' connotations, tinged with 'philanthropic superiority and an undignified approach to the disadvantaged' (Pinc, 1989: 77).

Ulc sums this up by saying that, after 1948, a primitive glorification of the proletariat was pursued. He gives an example of a steel mill where '93% of each worker's wage was fixed and secured by his mere physical presence at the plant'. The situation, however, produced a rather idiosyncratic, and for post-Stalinist development, a somewhat favourable situation. As members of working-class origins were elevated in the political and economic hierarchy, as Ulc says, thus

> leaving their former jobs to be filled by their class enemies, who as casualties of the revolution were assigned to manual labour [there was] a weakening of Party spirit at the point of production. Along with the demoted bourgeois elements, the working class was augmented by recruits from a politically harmless but non-proletarian milieu, in particular by housewives and rural people. (Ulc, 1974: 51)

Thus, unwittingly, the communist regime reinforced some latent egalitarian tendencies in Czechoslovak society. This egalitarianism was later coupled with some overtly anti-regime attitudes. As Holubenko points out with reference to the Soviet Union, the inefficient and unenthusiastic performance of the Soviet worker reflects the fact that 'the right not to work hard at the factory is one of the few remaining rights which the Soviet worker holds . . . the worker (in effect) carries on a clandestine economic struggle' (Holubenko, 1975: 22). Conversely, an efficient work performance was associated with supporting the communist regime.

There were some obvious casualties of the period of Stalinism in Czechoslovakia in the fifties and sixties. Paramount among these, according to Machonin et al. (1969: 236), authors of one of the most comprehensive sociological study of the Czechoslovak social structure, was the 'destruction of the civil society and atomization of individuals . . . together with a reduction of legitimate power to a mere state power'. As far as the general living standard was concerned, the levelling of incomes among the substantial 'middle strata' became one of the main characteristics: whereas, for example, the percentage of average earnings received by those working in education, culture, health and social welfare was 120 per cent or more in 1948, it had been reduced to around 90 per cent by 1953 (Vecernik, 1991b). This was accompanied, by the existence of a 'large lower category of the poor'. Thus pauperization has been a fact since the late 1960s. Machonin et al.'s study found that the main groups falling into the category of the poor were the 'economically inactive', such as pensioners, women (with 66 per cent of the average male earnings) and rural workers.

However, one of the interesting conclusions of the study was that 'only 11% of those questioned say that they are worse off than their parents (16% as the same, 63% as better off), and 42% of those questioned feel that they would have been better off 30 to 40 years ago (23% as the same, 35% worse off)' (Machonin et al., 1969: 318). The study refers to this as 'opinion schizophrenia', and indeed concludes that the differentiation of life styles in Czechoslovakia was far greater than anticipated by the researchers themselves.

Despite the attempt to reverse the traditional pattern of social stratification in industrial societies, what Stalinism achieved was undoubtedly a severe disruption of social life, with political insecurity for many, purges for some and rewards for others, but the final effect was a freezing rather than transforming of society as a whole. The dislocation between private and public life only served to preserve the dominance of the private over the public. This point is echoed, for example, in a new family policy from February 1989, which states that: 'Young people are products more of familial . . . behaviour than of the intentions expressed in the ideology of education' (*Family Policy Conception*, 1989: 8). A similar point is made by Western writers who comment on the failure of Soviet ideology to re-socialize its population. However, this argument should not be used too readily to support some recent views in the Western media that East/Central Europe and the Soviet Union are thus favourably receptive to the ideas and ideologies of the West. Although there was widespread poverty under the old regime in Czechoslovakia, its pre-war history of relative prosperity and emphasis on moral politics of justice provide the specific ingredients for the present changes.

The past twenty years in Czechoslovakia: the 1970s and their policy problems

As with other East European societies which experienced an imposed shift towards heavy industry, Czechoslovakia suffered from pollution and shortages. One of the most damning records has been its health policy.

Health

Life expectancy among Czechoslovakian men, is one of the lowest among today's industrialized societies, at 67.7 years in 1988, with infant mortality at 11.3 per 1,000 (*Statisticka Rocenka*, 1991). The main problem is mapping out the exact state of affairs, due to the inaccuracy and inadequacy of much of the official information in the past. The official policy under socialism was to claim that all was well. Thus, it has only recently emerged that in Prague 25 per cent of hospital buildings are more than 100 years old and that only 8 of the 115 hospitals have been built since 1948 (*Svobodne Slovo*, 1988). Some aspects of medical care policy, such as immunization schemes for infants, were efficient, but were undermined by the effects of disastrous environmental pollution. It is now reported that many children have completely lost their immunity, and the percentage of still births is high. Every fourth pregnancy in North Bohemia is a risk pregnancy and the level of premature births for Czechoslovakia as a whole is 6 per cent. The main infant complaint twenty years ago was skin disease, whereas the most com-mon ailments now are kidney infections and respiratory diseases. Bureaucratization has created incredible inconsistencies; the health of the patient meanwhile is pushed into the background. Under the previous regime, hospitals had to fill a quota of beds, otherwise they would not qualify for bonuses. This situation was apparently exploited by those who came to have a 'rest'. Some of the spas, officially described as a service to the convalescing worker, were taken over by members of the elite and their families. The bonus system also forced numerous workers working in hazardous con-ditions not to report the lack of safety because they would be disqualified from higher pay and pension schemes.

Health care in the past was generally viewed as an unproductive sector, and was thus resourced only in those areas that were seen as prestigious or contributing to the production process. Shutting away mentally and physically handicapped in poorly resourced institu-tions, and clearly hiding the extent of the problem, was symptom-atic of that approach. The effect of these policies, of outdated equipment and of a non-existent environmental policy are to some extent visible on the streets of Prague, where a high ratio of people have minor handicaps whose conditions have environmental and dietary causes. Prevention has never been a strong point of health policy in Eastern Europe generally. It was not only prevention that was a myth, so also was the concept of equal treatment. This can be gleaned from the condition of the Gypsy population. Their infant mortality rate was four times the national average at between 40 and 50 deaths per 1,000 live births. In addition, 20 per cent of Gypsies born in Czechoslovakia are mentally retarded (Kostelancik, 1989).

Unequal treatment of ethnic minorities has never been directly addressed. A government publication from 1986 talks of the 'Gypsy population enjoying excellent social conditions', yet 'a dictionary of the Czech language gives a definition of the Gypsies with a small "g" as a "member of a wandering nation, a symbol of mendacity, theft, wandering, . . . jokers, liars, impostors, and cheaters" ' (Kostelancik, 1989: 320). Gypsies were also excluded from the official census between 1948 and 1965. The Stalinist method of dealing with minorities was to re-define them, to disperse them and to strip them of political and national identity.

Housing
Ulc comments that in Czechoslovakia in the seventies 'there were less than ten square metres of living space per person [and] only 10% of all apartments were centrally heated' (1974: 56). However, he refers to a Czechoslovak source quoting that in 1970 'the number of households with electricity reached 98.6%, with gas 30.3%, running water 76.7%, private baths 57.2% and central heating 29.4%. The average apartment consisted of 2.1 rooms with 3.4 occupants' (Ulc, 1974: 160). Thus, according to official sources, the situation was improving. This is not entirely false, as post-1968 Czechoslovakia had experienced a short-lived boost in its living standards as compensation for the military clampdown by the Warsaw Pact forces.

Housing, as a social service, played its political role. It is reported that, in common with other East European societies, population policy, for example, was being 'solved' through housing policy. A newly-wed couple, on promising to start a family of two or more children, could not only jump the housing queue, but also got favourable terms on state loans and a substantial reduction in loan repayments. It is now known that forceful resettlement policies were imposed on the Gypsies since the late 1950s to implement half-baked integration policies. Housing of Gypsies in Czech lands was made available for those taking up employment in areas where unskilled labour was needed. These were jobs that the local Czech or Slovak population did not want (Kostelancik, 1989).

Social security
What distinguished the seventies from the sixties in Czechoslovak social policy was the shift in the income/price relationship. Living

standards in the fifties and sixties were maintained through 'slow growth in wages accompanied by slow reduction in prices . . . this form of social economic policy in the seventies was replaced by a model more common in more dynamic industrialized societies where faster growth in wages is followed by faster price increases' (*Informacni Zpravodaj*, 1990: 93). This sparked off a greater emphasis on social welfare for a wider network of citizens, particularly among the lower earners. One-off cash benefits became the dominant form, according to the Report from the Research Institute of Social Development and Labour. The benefit system quite clearly could not cope with the increasing poverty, particularly among the elderly. Furthermore, the unco-ordinated nature of *ad hoc* benefits put further stress on the economy. Whilst in 1970 the number of people who received cash benefits was 195,000, by 1988 this had grown to 365,900. As the number of recipients increased 1.9 times, the sums paid out increased 4.2 times.

> In 1970 welfare service in the form of care was provided to 14,600 old people, and in 1988 to over 87,000. This represents a six-fold increase. The number of professional care workers has increased 2.8 times . . . The number of places in the old people's homes has increased 1.2 times; however, a considerable problem arises because 70% of these homes are in unsuitable buildings, and 50% of them were built before 1900.

It is acknowledged that so far the 'most widely used form of care for the elderly was care within the family, and this was seen by them as the most suitable'. At the same time, the demographic pattern is such, that between 1990 and 2000 'among those over 70 years of age, 64% will be women, and women will constitute more than 70% of those above 80 years of age' (*Informacni Zpravodaj*, 1990: 9–98). This phenomenon is debated in today's Czechoslovakia only as an issue of pensions and old age insurance schemes, rather than of care and who 'cares for the carers'.

A change in thinking has yet to come. In the 1970s the social security system and its administration became much more remote and the thinking behind these services did not change in any significant way. The separate Ministry of Labour and Social Affairs was in fact abolished, and the number of specialist workers, particularly among those dealing with cases such as the handicapped, were being reduced. It was also reported that 'social care belongs to one of the smallest branches of the tertiary sector of our national economy' (*Informacni Zpravodaj*, 1990: 86). The paradox is that, despite the fact that it never commanded great resources, the actual institutional infrastructure grew. The main preoccupation was the aged. Here, as in the other sectors, however, the lack of quality care is widely known. Thus quantity rather than quality, and 'extreme feminization of certain branches of care', became characteristic of the 1970s.

Whether in the field of health policy, housing policy or social security provision, the old regime bequeathed numerous problems to the new government of 1990 and 1991.

Current social policy in the Czech and Slovak Federative Republic

What then are the main concerns of Czechoslovak social policy in the 1990s? All of the documents now in preparation take as their starting point a critique of the past. Pinc says that not only did the economy suffer under the old regime, but 'many serious deformations of the concept of social guarantees were committed' (Pinc, 1989: 115). He follows this by an argument, expanded recently at a conference in Prague, that economic stagnation was not and is not caused by paying attention to social welfare. What is important is to 'overcome the previously vulgarized, deformed aspects of social welfare . . . and to distinguish between legitimate social policy and "crypto-social policy" ' (Pinc, 1989: 126). Social welfare is not to be seen as handicapping economic growth.

Quite clearly, the main theme that is emerging in Czechoslovakia now is the future role of the state. It is intended that the old state bureaucratic monopoly of power be dismantled. Its heritage is seen as overtly negative. The dismantling of old structures of administration is seen somewhat idealistically as representing the opening up of new opportunities for the individual. Emphasis is placed on unleashing 'creative potential'. Thus, the state should not stand in the path of individual's initiatives. Though such comments to a Western ear sound like a direct reference to Thatcherism, one must look at them in the context of Czechoslovak experience. It is also argued that the processes of marketization, such as price liberalization, convertibility of currency and the new taxation system, are not goals in themselves. The main aim is the 'privatization/de-nationalization of state ownership', the symbol of an excessively top heavy concentration of power. Without this new forms of thinking will not be able to emerge.

Another element of the debate is a critique of monetarism and neo-liberalism. How well co-ordinated these discussions are is difficult to tell at this stage, yet it has been openly declared at a conference sponsored by the Ministry of Labour and Social Affairs that neo-liberalism needs to be viewed as representing another form of narrow economism, with a 'nihilistic approach to social needs', similar to the economism of the past (Pinc, 1990).

Particular attention in the new government's documents is paid to de-nationalization of national insurance. State domination of the system of social insurance is seen as originating from the policies of the fifties and the first half of the sixties. 'It was fully in accordance with the then predominant system of extensive growth of the national economy and central planning' (Navrh, 1990c: 1). Social policy, the document continues, was then based on the assumption that an 'increase in living standards can be achieved by reducing of prices and keeping wage stability'. This is now considered to have led to a static system of social security and illusory social guarantees. Such a system not only failed to solve the problems of the past, in fact it also created pauperization, the 'perpetuation of a de-humanizing and humiliating practice that instills a sense of subjugation' (Tomes, 1990a). As such it is unable to offer any help today. What the Czechoslovak policy-makers suggest instead is a new dynamic concept of social policy.

In the initial phase, the phase of transition, social policy will play a defensive role. What is envisaged by the policy-makers is not just the cushioning of citizens from the worst effects of inflation and unemployment. Social policy is also conceived as playing a constructive role in the process of 'democratization'. Here, the contradictory approach to the role of the state is evident. New social theory is necessary but, equally, old concepts of social solidarity and social justice that have emerged in the 'humanitarian phase of Czechoslovak development in 1944–8' (Tomes, 1990a), and later in 1968, must be upheld. Thus the association with the old state forms remains, at least as far as the state's guarantees of the basic types of social welfare to citizens are concerned. The citizenry, however, is to become gradually autonomous. Social policy is to promote 'active subjectivity'. However, the consequences of the transition to a market economy are uncertain, and there are some very pessimistic predictions that living standards will fall below the official poverty line. Thus the state is called upon not only to protect the most vulnerable, but also to go on the offensive: 'The gravity of the social consequences of liberalization of prices and other effects of economic reform demand an offensive approach by the state' (*Zachranna Socialni Sit*, 1990: 2). The two seemingly contradictory views, one of the minimal state with the maximum of 'active democratic' participation by the individuals themselves, and the other with the state as a dominant institution in the economic lives of the people, are resolved in the light of the ultimate goal, which is a 'legal state', not the arbitrary administrative system of the past.

A more interesting and telling subtext to this is that the present government is under mounting pressure from the international community, particularly the IMF, to control the transition while allowing the 'free market' to develop; a situation not unknown in the majority of developing countries as well as Western societies that had to start implementing programmes of cutbacks in public expenditure as a way of increasing their competitiveness. Thus the duality of the state's role in Czechoslovakia is by no means unique. The Czechoslovak state is being told in particular to hold down wage demands during the crucial period of price reforms that would lead up to convertibility of their currencies, if it wants to qualify for foreign investment. Its success in marketizing, the necessity of which seems to be agreed upon across the political spectrum in Czechoslovakia, is therefore directly dependent on the role of the central authorities. The paradox of marketization with the state's help is in this case linked with identifying two of Czechoslovakia's distinct pasts – the authoritarian/monopolistic and the social democratic.

The social democratic past is now clearly resurrected. The 'legal state' is conceptualized as distinct from the arbitrary state of the 'communist' era. This state is expected to have fresh and honorable responsibilities. Its role is to 'help the citizens to realize their rights to be economically active and to come to their assistance if they find themselves without employment' (Navrh, 1990a: 7). In the past, work was not only a right but also an obligation. The state criminalized non-work. The role of social policy is to break those old connections. It is believed that by freeing the subject from state control a co-operative, humanitarian relationship between the new state and the individual, will be enabled to develop.

In the first phase of the transition, social policy is to have an instrumental and 'reactive' character, assigning the state perhaps more than just a caretaker role. 'The state will ward off any social demagogy that calls for resources above our means. For the time being, social policy will be conceptualized not as a purposeful sphere of social development but as providing a basic life-line during the economic transition of our society' (Navrh, 1990a: 7). The text, in the same breath, qualifies this by stating the need for a more 'proactive' social policy in a market economy, justifying its offensive approach.

> If there is to be a successful radical economic reform, then this must not be hampered by social tensions. Unemployment and inflation may create undesirable conflicts. That is why the government prefers for the next two years to create an institutional system of employment strategies and

a means of reducing the effects of inflation, particularly for the socially vulnerable, such as children, the infirm and the old.

From the ministerial documents a vision emerges of an active social policy with a new theoretical framework and a new institutional base. The basic principles are said to be (1) the principle of social guarantee, (2) the principle of social solidarity and (3) the principle of participation (Navrh, 1990c: 3). In addition, social policy is not to lose its political character. It is envisaged that it will contribute to (1)democratization, (2) liberalization and (3) privatization. These entail (1) democratic control from below, (2) plurality of forms of satisfaction of social needs and (3) citizens' initiatives (Tomes, 1990). There is to be a three-fold relationship between the state and the citizen: (1) the state will guarantee the basic minimum and protect against poverty; (2) the citizens will co-operate and communicate with the state (choosing from what is available); and (3) citizens themselves will engage in self-help initiatives. The state will be responsible for the administrative framework and also oversee that no unjust gains are being made.

With these kinds of intentions, it comes as no surprise that the Czechoslovak model of welfare rather closely approximates the corporatist/social democratic model. Principles of democratic control and social justice are not to remain mere ideals. Instead, it is envisaged, again, that a tri-partite structure will support the new social welfare system. A new kind of relationship between the state, the employers and the trade unions is being encouraged, as well as the creation of a social fund, separate from the state budget. However, on reviewing some specific policy proposals, one can see that many dilemmas and contradictions remain.

Employment and social security
The ministerial documents talk of the old system of over-employment stemming from the 'politics of directed employment policy'. More than 48 per cent of the population in Czechoslovakia was in employment (Navrh, 1990a: 1) under the communist regime. This meant, according to the debate, that 'cheap labour supported technical backwardness . . . as well as the expansion of a wasteful administrative system. On the other hand, poor utilization of labour potential meant low productivity, with the productivity of labour [in Czechoslovakia] not reaching even half of the level of developed countries' (Navrh, 1990a: 1). The new labour market policy is to alter this and 'limit the ineffective, purposeless employment policy'.

These comments, however, precede the emergence of unemployment in 1991. Apart from calls for greater creative activity and entrepreneurship, the envisaged employment policy is deeply conservative, one might say reactionary, especially as far as its static concept of the sexual division of labour is concerned. The old system, it is argued, brought about 'a devaluation of labour', 'devaluation of the family income', because all families had to rely on two wages, and 'devaluation of childbearing', by not paying enough and allowing child benefits to fall against average monthly incomes (Navrh, 1990a: 8). The attitude to the family and to women in the current documents reflects a state of non-debate and non-involvement of women in policy-making. Whilst it is argued that the previous regime overstepped its boundaries by issuing a heavily pro-natalist population policy, thus 'not appreciating other life and cultural functions of the family', the state monopoly over employment and remuneration 'crippled the family by the high employment of women' (Navrh, 1990a: 2). As can therefore be expected from these references, the new employment policy will attempt to redress the balance.

In a statement from the end of September 1990, a ministerial document claims that 'Czechoslovakia has at its disposal a high labour potential'. It ranks 'among the world's highest', in terms of employment of relatively well-qualified labour. When it comes to female employment, however, it is argued that this 'has over-reached its optimal level' (Navrh, 1990a: 3). The risk of expected large-scale unemployment between 1990 and 1992 can, in the eyes of the policy-makers, be slowed down or arrested by 'gaining new employment posts through the freeing of a section of working old age pensioners (estimated at 70,000 – 140,000 posts), and through the exit of women taking up maternity leave (estimated at 30,000 posts)' (*Zasady Strategie*, 1990: 1).

The document reveals that this may be helpful, but creates its own problems, since the previous regime enabled the 'creation of feminized branches of employment, such as textiles, the food industry, transport, retail, education and health. These, as well as potentially some branches of engineering, electrotechnical industry and agriculture, could seriously suffer from the exit of the youngest female workers' (*Zasady Strategie*, 1990: 15). Virtually the whole of the economy will be affected if the envisaged so-called progressive legislation proposing to bridge the gap financially between women's child-caring activities and employment is put into effect. The female labour force is here treated as dispensable in the interest of 'marketization', but it is also openly admitted that the 'wage prospects in the freed posts will not be very interesting for men since female wages are on average lower by 1,500 crowns per month' (*Zasady Strategie*, 1990: 13).

It is only the rising women's movement that openly questions the rationality guiding these decisions. It points out that the state plans to waste the resources of a vast part of the female labour force in Czechoslovakia, which is highly qualified, and remove it into the home. The possibility of hearing these extra-parliamentary voices (women currently have only 10 per cent representation in the parliament) coming from women themselves, at a time when in men's eyes, there are so many other 'interesting and important issues on the agenda', is yet to be realized (Valterova, 1990).

The politics of employment during the transition period until 1992 is to consist of:

• the creation of the labour market;
• efforts to maintain the balance between supply and demand;
• a minimizing of the extent of unemployment;
• the creation of conditions for future effectiveness of the Czecho-slovak economy. (*Zasady Strategie*, 1990: 1)

This strategy will be supported by new labour exchanges and employment funds. The employment funds are to be resourced from state/republic budgets, the employers and the employees. The funds will provide contributions to those who are embarking on self-employment, to new job creation, to re-qualification programmes and (here an interesting euphemism for unemployment benefit is used) to cover those who are prior to entry into employment (*Zasady Strategie*, 1990: 3).

Unemployment, which is mostly talked about only as a temporary phenomenon, is 'not expected to go beyond the economically and socially acceptable level'. The current recorded unemployment in the first quarter of 1991 was 3 per cent, with female unemployment not significantly higher than male unemployment. The federal government allocated financial reserves of 9.535 billion crowns to cover unemployment benefits at a predicted 4.2 per cent. A recent article suggested that these reserves will not be able to meet the need. A conservative estimate for unemployment in 1991 was 6 per cent compared with the actually recorded 3.8–4 per cent. It is also reported that unemployment among school-leavers, women and Gypsies is rising faster than among the population as a whole. 'Among the working population, there is about ¼ who are below 30 but they represent 48 per cent among the unemployed' (*Hospodarske Noviny*, 1991c). Equally, regional differences are significant, with unemployment in Slovakia being at 54 per cent of the total in May 1991.

Unemployment benefit now runs at 60 per cent of the unem-ployed person's previous monthly earnings for the first six months

(65 per cent in Slovakia). If the benefit falls below the accepted poverty line, additional money is available. The entitlement requires an 'exit' certificate from the employer together with a certificate of the average net monthly earnings. One's identity card has to be also presented at the labour exchange. An application is filed for new employment, which, if not found within seven days, turns into an automatic entitlement to unemployment benefit. An additional condition is that the person has to have been in gainful employment in the past three years for at least twelve months (*Hospodarske Noviny*, 1991b). If the person registers for re-qualification, the benefit could rise to 75 per cent of average wage. This applies for up to a year, after which time a different form of state support is available, the precise mechanism of which has not still been worked out. Those on unemployment benefit may earn small additional sums.

There is emphasis in all of the documents on preventive measures, which in this case means keeping the unemployment period to a minimum. Suggestions range from re-qualification to restricting employment opportunities for pensioners, as well as greater international mobility of labour (*Hospodarske Noviny*, 1991a). Support for private enterprise and new educational programmes, together with the above-mentioned policy on pensioners and women with children, is optimistically expected to slow down the growth of unemployment. It is also expected that women will take up more part-time jobs, particularly with the expansion of services, but the status and remuneration of these jobs is not mentioned. Other possibilities are in extending educational requirements for school-leavers, offering specialized training and study, as well as study abroad. It is also argued that: 'The common goal of the state, the employers and the trade unions should be a general reduction in the labour time (shorter working time, longer holidays) . . . The result does not have to be new labour opportunities, but a lowering of tension within the labour market, as well as a greater opportunity of qualitatively better reproduction of the labour power' (*Zasady Strategie*, 1990: 7).

Considerable discussion in the ministerial documents is devoted to the minimum wage and its protection. At present the minimum wage applies to only 3 per cent of the employed in the national economy (approximately 200,000 people). However, 80 per cent of these are women (*Zachranna Socialni Sit*, 1990: 4). Czechoslovakia is aiming to adhere to the guidelines of the International Labour Organization, thus defining minimum wage as serving the needs of an individual and not his/her family needs. It is generally felt that the economic reform will lead to a lowering of people's living standards. The governmental documentation suggests that

> the population will be able to respond by tolerating restricted consumption, by a qualitative change in the structure of their demand, or by postponing the purchase of goods of long-term value. This, however, will work with only a limited success. The anticipated level of social tolerance can be expected with the lowering of living standards by an estimated 15–20% a year. (*Zachranna Socialni Sit*, 1990: 2)

However, it is mentioned in the same document that there are social groups whose 'limit of social tolerance is practically zero because they are already partly or wholly dependent on social benefits'. Here, the state still hopes to play the role of the social guarantor, protecting the socially weak and not allowing them to fall below the poverty level.

One specific policy change that can be evaluated in terms of whether the most needy are being protected is the introduction in July 1990 of the 'equal benefit for all' worth 140 crowns (£3) a month per person to compensate for the removal of food subsidies. Vecernik (1991c) has estimated that whereas the main beneficiaries of food subsidies were single people, pensioners, families with many children and low-income families, those benefiting most from the new universal benefit are the better-off and young people. The techniques of a compensatory social policy have clearly yet to be refined if they are to accomplish the stated goal of protecting the weakest.

A major issue in social security is the indexation and valorization of pensions to prevent the impoverishment of the past being repeated. Preservation of the real value of old age pensions, particularly for those whose pension is the only income, is stressed. However, it is also said that the ratio of the old age pension to the average income will not change. In the current situation the basic pension is estimated to be between 20 and 25 per cent of the national average income (Navrh, 1990c: 14). The pensionable age for men will remain 60 years, possibly raised to 62, and for women it is expected to go up from 57 to 60. The anticipated numbers of individuals of pensionable age proportionate to active working population remains favourable until the year 2000, after which the gap starts to widen. Policy planners talk of the present situation providing the much-needed 'financial reserves for the future' (Klimentova, 1990).

Overall, in relation to social security a view is presented to the public that the social and economic transition will involve costs which will not be fully compensated for by government policy or by new benefits. To offset this, the social security system will permit additional insurance schemes in the form of voluntary, private or co-operative initiatives. How far this mixed form of welfare will work and be accepted remains to be seen, particularly if one takes into account the continuing egalitarian expectations of the population, mentioned earlier.

Housing

The area of policy and provision that will most likely suffer in the · transition period is housing. The planned adjustments of the rent system are envisaged to have far-reaching consequences. In many cases this may mean a 100 per cent increase on current rent. What complicates the housing situation is the legislation passed by the parliament early in 1991 enabling property confiscated by the state after 1948 to be reclaimed. Many original owners, some exiled in the West since 1948, are returning, destabilizing the housing market and placing many sitting tenants in an insecure position. Many talk about the emerging negative social consequences, particularly as the cost of living rises simultaneously with the cost of housing. It is felt that the 'temporary lowering of people's legal and social guarantees is most probably an unavoidable expression of the new conditions in the sphere of housing policy' (*Zachranna Socialni Sit*, 1990: 18). A system of supplementary benefits will attempt to avoid situations in which individuals would 'have to leave their dwellings for financial reasons'.

It is estimated that there will be a category of people who now live on average income, but whose increased outgoings will push them down to a position just above the poverty line, yet they will not fall to a level where they could qualify for social assistance. This situation may affect roughly 1.5 million individuals, particularly families with children and old age pensioners (*Zachranna Socialni Sit*, 1990: 19). One may therefore ask, how will the emerging situation actually differ from the old one, which has been so vigorously criticized for its 'pauperization' of these same two categories? The government response to this emerging crisis has so far been to propose a new tax reform, which will not take effect until 1992.

Family policy

A certain form of financial generosity was already evident in the area of family and child benefits. This has, to some extent, its own tradition in Eastern Europe. There is now a reluctance to depart from this established framework of thinking.

The family is seen as an important social unit. The outlines of the new family policy take as their starting point a critique of the previous 'mutual alienation between the state and the family that led to a loss of the ability to solve one's own problems and to a crisis of the family' (Navrh, 1990a, Appendix: 1). The document then proceeds to follow a clearly economic form of argument that is, and indeed was, so common (in a different form, of course) during the years of the former socialist regime. 'The current family lives without reserves, and even with the utmost effort vast numbers of households do not manage their economic situation.' The 'spiritual function of the family' is seen to have suffered, and the outcome is family 'instability'. 'The one-sided and disproportionate burden by existential worries that the family had to face created a breakdown of its educational and socialization functions, which are irreplaceable' (Navrh, 1990a, Appendix: 2). A very detailed and deeply conservative discussion follows. There is to be a revival of the 'primary mutual solidarity', of family 'sovereignty', of expanding the space for 'family creativity', etc. The existential burden is to be removed in order to allow the family to flourish. As if economic freedom was the key to solving all other problems. Gender politics is conspicuously absent.

As in the past, women continue to be subsumed under 'humankind'; the family policy does not change this. The nuclear family is also still the norm. However, a more progressive element of the new policy is the introduction of parental benefit. It is to be paid 'to a parent who cares for a child under three years of age. The aim is to provide conditions for all parents so that one of them will be able to decide whether to care for the child at home or to entrust the care to a nursery and return to work. . . . This is a specific social wage, replacing earned income' (Navrh, 1990a, Appendix: 8). This 'social wage', which is a fixed uniform sum of 900 crowns per month, equates child care with employment outside the home. The fact that the sum is below the minimum old age pension is not discussed, and it is hard to envisage men wanting to stay at home on that kind of money. In another document it is revealed that, although the benefit will replace a wage, it is estimated to cover 'approximately 320,000 *women*' (*Zachranna Socialni Sit.* 1990: 10; my emphasis). Thus the fact that it is a parental benefit is seriously brought into question. There will, however, be tax reliefs, additional benefits according to the number of children, and special assistance for disabled and children with learning difficulties or children with special dietary requirements.

Health

The government documents on health insurance stress that health policy will be guided by the same principle of indexation as pension policy. Health insurance is to cover:

• periods of ill health;
• support for those caring for an ill member of the family;
• cash maternity benefit;
• additional benefit during pregnancy and maternity;
• burial costs (Navrh, 1990b: 4).

All the above are to be related to wage levels, with the exception of burial costs. A proposed indexation and valorization of benefits is to be implemented. Some of the benefits are to be paid from the new independent social fund. Parental benefit, additional child benefits and maternity benefit on the birth of the child, etc. will still be payable by the state, which will determine the level by assessing the general rise in the cost of living.

The social fund will be resourced by:

• the employer's contributions;
• the employee's contributions;
• the self-employed's contributions;
• contributions from individually insured persons (Navrh, 1990b: 5).

Health is seen as an area where mixed forms of provision would be easy to achieve. The fact that there is no Federal Ministry of Health (just as there is no Federal Ministry of Education) seems to suggest that regionalized decisions with 'opting out' may be encouraged.

In terms of the environmental pollution and high morbidity and mortality mentioned earlier, it will be a long time before changes in production techniques and living conditions will be sufficient to allow improvements in health to be registered.

Conclusions

Czechoslovak social policy is undoubtedly undergoing important changes. Social justice and social solidarity emerge as the key concepts. However, the very same concepts have been used before by Beveridge, Titmuss and the Czechoslovak social democrats of the twenties and forties as well as by some more ideologically inclined orthodox Marxist-Leninists. Thus the present planners are trying to bridge an enormous gap. It is of interest, however, that some of their debate is in open opposition to the theorization of a free market economy.

Social policy-making in Czechoslovakia is in this sense profoundly political. Social reform has set itself in opposition to purely economic reform. Will it merely mitigate the effects of the latter or will it set a new political agenda? The current situation is such that social policy remains, despite the arguments to the contrary, a system of paternalistic and patriarchal proposals. The weakening of women's bargaining power in the labour market alongside renewed support for the family leave us with a contradictory package. The confusion over the way forward is reflected in the current practice whereby, according to some Czechoslovak observers, social policy is merely a matter of grafting money benefits on to the old system.

The example of Eastern Europe shows that economic processes are fundamentally social processes. Some talk of a 'complex social reform with a deep incision into the institutional fabric of contemporary social reality'. It is argued that a shift away from the false protectionist tendencies of the past will lead to 'respect for the rights of individuals and lead to humanization of the whole system' (Navrh, 1990a, Appendix: 1). Perhaps we shall have to accept that ideas such as these only have meaning when located in context. Therefore it is yet to be seen how the ideals of justice and active citizenship will be translated into everyday reality. It would be easy to comment in a critical way on the proto-Thatcherite line of argument of 'taking one's fate into one's own hands', but, at the same time, I feel we need to be careful not to fall into 'conceptual ghettoization', and rather should allow the unfolding of a new social reality, that has its own unique past, to go unhindered by judgements based on Western experience.

The Czechoslovak social policy planners are themselves talking of a reform that will take 15 to 20 years. Thus a long-term rather than 'quick fix' approach is proposed. Undoubtedly, one of their main problems remains the lack of real experience with decentralized forms of social organization. This fuels the ambiguity about the precise nature of the state's involvement. Opening up of new individual initiatives is thus debated alongside notions of 'active state policy', be it employment or welfare. The state remains a double-edged instrument: one for implementation of humanitarian as opposed to crude market values, yet one that can step in to impose control mechanisms under the guise of 'good intentions', such as the proposed exclusion of women from the labour market or restrictive wage policy. What is missing so far is a system of citizen's participation. It has been suggested that a democratic infrastructure, even in Czechoslovakia, with its democratic tradition, is less than embryonic. On the other hand, regional policy is taken very seriously. What we are left with, therefore, is the first phase of the dismantling of the past patterns and structures, and an attack on the monopoly of power.

There is a great likelihood that economic decisions will predominate, particularly as Eastern Europe moves away from central planning and adopts a form of market economy. Its absorption into the Western world is possible but not a foregone conclusion. One must give credit to the populations of these countries, who have suffered economic 'one-dimensionalism' for some time, and whose patience with the slogan 'affluence comes at a price' has been tested before. One of the tensions emerging now is around the acceptable level of unemployment. As it is already clear that the government's predictions have been wrong and the financial reserves depleted, people's views on the benefits of the market are changing. What is also changing is their view of the government's and the parliament's competence. There has been a drop in real income by 3.1 per cent in the first quarter of 1991, with prices up by 31.3 per cent between December 1990 and February 1991, alongside a drop in industrial production by 3.7 per cent. There is a visible differentiation of incomes, with 6 per cent below the minimum wage level. Crime increased by 63.8 per cent between 1989 and 1990 (*Hospodarske Noviny*, 1991c). In the past pauperization was a consequence of generally low wages. In the future it might be a consequence of social exclusion and widening inequality. Czechoslovakia is at a crossroads, which partly accounts for the presence of highly contradictory policy statements and developments. In my view, Eastern Europe in the next decade will remain a test case for conceptualization of the role of social policy in the broadest sense.

References

Deyl, Z. (1985) *Socialni Vyvoj Cekoslovenska 1918–1938* [Social Development in Czechoslovakia 1918–1938]. Prague: Academia.
Family Policy Conception (1989) Prague: Research Institute for Social Development and Labour, Bratislava, Prague Branch. [Published in English.]
Godson, J. and Schapiro, L. (eds) (1981) *The Soviet Worker*. London: Macmillan.
Holubenko, M. (1975) 'The Soviet working class', *Critique*, 5.
Hospodarske Noviny (1991a) 12 March. Prague.
Hospodarske Noviny (1991b) 9 April. Prague.
Hospodarske Noviny (1991c) 30 April. Prague.
Informacni Zpravodaj (1990) [Information Bulletin]. Prague: Research Institute for Social Development.
Janyska, P. (1991) 'Budujeme stranu' [We are building a party], *Respekt*, 18 December.

Klimentova, J. (1990) Paper presented to the Conference on Social Security, its Development and Perspectives, 19–22 November, Prague.

Konopasek, Z. (1991) 'From reform to rescue: social policy in Czechoslovakia, 1990'. Unpublished manuscript, Charles University, Prague.

Kostelancik, D.J. (1989) 'The Gypsies of Czechoslovakia: political and ideological considerations in the development of policy', *Studies in Comparative Communism*, 22 (Winter): 307–21.

Krejci, J. (1972) *Social Change and Stratification in Postwar Czechoslovakia*. London: Macmillan.

Machonin, P. et al. (1969) *Cekoslovenska Spolecnost*. Prague: Epocha.

Mishra, R. (1977) *Society and Social Policy*. London: Macmillan.

Navrh (1990a) Material pro schuzi vlady CSFR [Briefing paper. Information for a meeting of the government of CSFR]. Prague: Federal Ministry of Labour and Social Affairs.

Navrh (1990b) Hlavnich zasad noveho systemu financovani socialniho zabezpeceni [Briefing paper. Key principles of the new system of social security financing]. Prague: Federal Ministry of Labour and Social Affairs.

Navrh (1990c) Koncepce socialniho zabezpeceni [Briefing paper. Social security proposal]. Prague: Federal Ministry of Labour and Social Affairs.

Pinc, K. (1989) *Nastin teorie socialni politiky*. Obecna Cast [Theoretical overview of social policy. Introductory part]. Prague.

Pinc, K. (1990) Paper presented to the Conference on Social Security, its Development and Perspectives, 19–22 November, Prague.

Pithart, P. (1990) *Osmasedesaty* [The year '68]. Prague: Rozmluvy.

Statisticka Rocenka (1991) [Statistical Yearbook] Prague.

Svobodne Slovo (1988) 14 May. Prague.

Tomes, I. (1990a) Paper presented to the Conference on Social Security, its Development and Perspectives, 19–22 November, Prague.

Tomes, I. (1990b) Interview with the author, 14 November (personal communication).

Ulc, O. (1974) *Politics in Czechoslovakia*. New York: W.H. Freeman.

Valterova, A. (1990) 'Nechteji zustat Popelkami' [They don't want to remain Cinderellas], *Sondy*, 28 October.

Vecernik, J. (1991a) 'The labour market in Czechoslovakia: problems and prospects', paper presented to the conference on 'Le Capital humain à l'aube du 21e siècle', Luxembourg, 27–9 November.

Vecernik, J. (1991b) 'Earnings distribution in Czechoslovakia: intertemporal changes and international comparison', *European Sociological Review*, 7 (3).

Vecernik, J. (1991c) 'Income distribution in Czechoslovakia', *Bulletin of the Basic Income Group*, 13.

Zachranna Socialni Sit (1990) [Social Safety Net] (intended for a meeting of the government of CSFR). Prague: Federal Ministry of Labour and Social Affairs.

Zasady Strategie (1990) *Zasady Strategie Zamestnanosti 1990–1992* [Basic principles of employment strategy 1990–1992]. Prague: Federal Ministry of Labour and Social Affairs.

5

Social Policy in Poland

Frances Millard

Few mourn the passing of the communist system in Poland; it left a legacy of bitterness and political, social, economic and moral failure, more stark in the light of its ideological promise of social justice and individual liberation. The new Solidarity governments had the unenviable task not only of picking up the pieces, but also of dealing with problems arising from or exacerbated by their programme of transition to a market economy and a democratic polity. Poland was the first country in Eastern Europe to break with communist monopoly rule; in September 1989 Tadeusz Mazowiecki became the first non-communist prime minister since the war. Poland also moved the most rapidly of all in the direction of a capitalist market economy. At the same time Poland was the last to experience the process of free, competitive parliamentary elections, which did not take place until autumn 1991. The first period of the intended transition to capitalist liberal democracy has thus been one of political and economic discontinuity, with major consequences for the sphere of social policy.

The aim of this chapter is three-fold. First, it seeks to explain the nature of communist social policy and how and why it failed. Second, it will examine the implications of this failure for the two Solidarity governments of 1989–91. Third, it aims to explain the social policy of the early post-communist period, indicating the extent and reasons for change. The problems encountered provide us with the basis for an assessment of future prospects for the survival of a Polish welfare state; these prospects are not encouraging.

The evolution of communist social policy

The salient feature of communist social policy in Poland was – as elsewhere – the virtual monopoly of the state in determining social need and in establishing bureaucratic mechanisms to implement policy. Voluntary organizations and social groups played a very restricted role, always under the direction of the Communist Party (PZPR, literally the Polish United Workers' Party). When the communists came to power in the aftermath of the Second World War, they largely ignored the Polish experience of the inter-war period, although protective legislation had been quite extensive (Zweig, 1944: 140–5). Instead they adopted Soviet institutions and processes. Their ability to do this was assisted by two major factors.

First, the war had destroyed the socio-economic infrastructure. A high proportion of the population had perished, including much of the intelligentsia. People were exhausted from the privations of war and occupation. The communists, with Soviet assistance, controlled the means of coercion and used them unhesitatingly against opponents of the new order. Second, the country's boundaries were shifted westward to incorporate previously German territories (the 'recovered lands') and relinquish territory in the eastern borderlands. Since the eastern areas of inter-war Poland had been ethnically diverse, this shift meant that the population was now ethnically and religiously homogeneous, that is, Polish and Catholic. Internal migration was extensive. The division of the western lands and the allocation of scarce goods and services became both a source of patronage for the new elite and a mechanism of social control. Coercion was effective where persuasion failed.

The adoption of Soviet views was as notable in the social policy sphere as elsewhere. The state, as the major employer, would provide security of employment and beneficial working conditions. All the essentials of life – food, shelter, warmth, culture – would be available at prices guaranteeing their accessibility to all. The state would provide facilities for health care, education and leisure pursuits. The working class would be particularly favoured; now liberated from its previous exploitation, it had become the leading force in society, under the guidance of the Communist Party.

At first, policy took the form of *ad hoc* remedial action to deal with the pressing problems of wartime devastation, notably in health, housing and education. Public health was a priority, for example, because of the danger of epidemics. Shelter was another urgent need. Powerful local government housing bureaux (the *kwaterunek*) took control of the remaining housing stock and distributed it. Education was clearly urgent since the communist government's primary development aim was the transition from a rural economy to an industrial one. Policy was two-dimensional: a mass, basic education programme aimed at eliminating illiteracy and providing vocational education, with higher education also concentrating on producing technically skilled cadres in subjects like engineering and medicine. At the same time, the socializing role of education was stressed, giving it an overtly ideological content to counter a political culture characterized by high levels of religiosity and anti-Russian and anti-Soviet sentiments.

Despite their *ad hoc*, fragmented and often unplanned nature, quantitative achievements in these and other areas were impressive, though never enough to meet public expectations. Moreover, social policy was subordinated to economic policy, especially in regard to investment. A short-sighted and narrow view of industrial development prevailed up to the late 1960s. This treated health, education and housing as 'unproductive' sectors. Agriculture, too, was suspect because of the 'petit bourgeois mentality' of the individual peasant farmer. Collectivization had failed in Poland in 1956; but private agriculture did not receive government support. The private sector was also excluded from many benefits, including health care and pensions, until the 1970s. Neglect of the social infrastructure and agriculture both resulted in unfulfilled individual needs and generated barriers to future economic development.

At the same time, the emphasis on the needs of the skilled working class did provide some mechanisms for their protection (for example, through protective labour legislation and occupational health care); advancement (through increased access to education and emphasis on adult education for new jobs in industry and in the party apparat); alleviation (through social welfare benefits); security (of housing tenure and employment); and well-being (through food subsidies, payments in kind, and workplace and cultural benefits). None of these worked very well, for a variety of reasons, not least the lack of sufficient funding to keep pace with the development of heavy industry and the problems generated by the neglect of agriculture and consumer goods. Chronic shortages created social discontent, first manifest in overt working-class protest in 1956. They also undermined the redistributive tendencies of working-class 'privilege', as the intelligentsia, though often more poorly paid, proved better able to manipulate official systems of access: better utilizing cumbersome bureaucratic procedures and maintaining networks of informal contacts. Some employees, notably the military and the police, acquired protected status. Atop the pyramid were the upper echelons of the party-state elite, whose privileged access to scarce goods and services was legion.

There were other specific and systemic causes of failure. The planning process emphasized quantity at the expense of quality and innovation. Protective labour legislation was often ignored due to pressures to fulfil the production plan. Occupational health services duplicated scarce resources and competed for equipment with residentially based care. Social security and welfare payments were very low and benefits often failed to reach the most needy. Housing was poorly designed and badly built; moreover there was not enough of it. Thus up to the late 1960s both the identification of and provision for 'needs' proved problematic, while the primacy of industrial development created an enormous lag in social provision.

The turn of the decade between the 1960s and 1970s brought fresh political upheaval and renewed promises of change, along with recognition of past failures. There would be more balanced economic development, greater emphasis on social services, more responsiveness and accountability. Social policy gained respectability; it became a recognized academic discipline. Social and economic development were now conceived as reciprocal and interrelated: economic policy provides the resources for social reproduction and social policy; social policy allocates these resources and in meeting social needs increases labour productivity and thus economic output. Theorists stressed the 'planned development of social relations' to improve the material, environmental, cultural and spiritual conditions of the population; to protect the vulnerable and disadvantaged; and to eliminate social inequalities, thus contributing to the emergence of the classless society (Szubert, 1979: 30–6). They identified certain policy areas as crucial to one or more of these elements: labour policy (employment, wages, working conditions); housing, health, education, culture, social security, environmental protection; and the prevention of and battle against social deviance (Czajka, 1986: 15).

The new concern with social theory was in part a response to failures which were becoming increasingly apparent. But the gap between theory and practice remained as wide as ever. When Edward Gierek succeeded Władysław Gomułka as leader of the Communist Party in December 1970, he confronted angry strikers responding to sudden, dramatic increases in the prices of fuel and basic foodstuffs. The period of open debate inaugurated in the press revealed a minefield of discontent, not only because of shortages of basic goods, but also over housing and health. The regime had been trying to increase the contribution made by individuals by reducing subsidies on foodstuffs and rents; and by encouraging private and co-operative housing. Suddenly it found itself promising an *enhanced* state contribution. As the Gierek programme unfolded, it offered all things to all people. Health would get more money. More housing would be built. Prices would be frozen. Managers would be accountable to their work force. Local government would be streamlined, making it more efficient and more responsive. Expert commissions would advise on educational reform. More consumer goods would be produced and more imported. The urban–rural divide would be addressed by new investment and by incorporating the private peasantry into the system of social provision. Old age pensions would be raised. Thus was the jam today. The jam tomorrow would be generated by the Second Modernization, based on the introduction of new technology from the West. The New Poland would generate sufficient exports to repay the debts incurred and to continue to improve the standard of living.

The economic failures of the old regime are well known. After a period of growth in the early 1970s, the economy began its rapid downhill course. The emergence of Solidarity in 1980 meant increased political, social and economic demands in a context of economic decline. The Communist Party losts its ability to control the situation, and in December 1981 the military declared martial law, banning Solidarity and imprisoning its leaders. Despite attempts to regenerate the party, it never regained its former position. Dedicated to reform and promising a new 'social contract', but beset by internal conflicts, membership decline and increasingly devoid of authority, the party/military complex for nine years tried to manoeuvre a course between the Scylla of its international creditors and the Charybdis of a resentful population. A new wave of strikes in 1988 pushed it into a last-ditch attempt to salvage its position by dialogue with Solidarity, still an illegal organization. Then, following its disastrous performance in the 1989 elections (see Lewis, 1990), it quietly transferred lawful authority to a new Solidarity-led coalition government of Tadeusz Mazowiecki in September 1989. Just over a year later Lech Wałęsa won the presidential election. In January 1991 a new government took office under Jan Krzysztof Bielecki. Fully free parliamentary elections in October 1991 marked the final stage in the transition to non-communist rule.

The legacy of communist social policy

We have identified sources of failure in communist social policy: in theory it was the centrepiece of policy, in practice it was always subordinate to economic policy. It was beset by the internal contradictions of central planning and yet it generated high social expectations. At the same time the failures of the communist regime provided the legacy and the starting point for the new initiatives of the post-communist regime. In this section we shall examine features of this legacy in the key areas of housing, education, health and welfare benefits.

Housing
Housing was long regarded by many as 'social problem No. 1' (Experience and the Future Discussion Group, 1981: 145), a view shared by Prime Minister Bielecki in 1991. The communist regime failed to meet its promise of decent housing for all; indeed, from about 1957 it tried unsuccessfully to shift a greater burden of provision on to the individual. The chosen vehicle for this shift, the co-operative, was rightly deemed an agency of the state and its failures were seen as failures of the state. Nor did the population come to see housing provision as an area of personal responsibility. Indeed, as expectations rose, the failure of the state loomed larger.

The most glaring aspect of the housing problem was its chronic shortage. Underinvestment and the inefficiency of the centralized construction firms meant that building did not keep pace with rising demand, resulting from a high birth rate, continuing rural–urban migration, the decline of the extended family, a rising divorce rate and higher expectations. Increasingly, the distribution of housing shifted from the state to co-operatives and industrial enterprises. After 1965 local government formally assumed direct responsibility only for the 'most needy'. State policies encouraged the co-operatives and gradually removed many obstacles to private construction. State housing construction ceased in 1976, after which the co-operatives had to turn over a proportion of new dwellings to local government and factories. This share was reduced in the 1980s, along with further concessions to the private housing market.

The cumulative impact of shortage meant lengthening waiting lists for co-operative housing. Twenty-four years was reported to be the national average waiting time in 1988, with higher figures for major cities (Zięba, 1988). Homelessness made its first visible appearance. More than 30 per cent of families did not have independent accommodation of their own.

Housing was also of poor quality. Many rural homes still lack basic amenities such as running water and indoor lavatories; even in urban areas 22 per cent lack bathrooms (all figures come from the annual 'Polish Statistical Yearbooks' (*Rocznik Statystyczny*) unless otherwise stated). Flats are generally small and poorly designed. Inadequate maintenance and repair were a characteristic feature, so post-war housing deteriorated rapidly, due to poor-quality building materials, cost-cutting design and sloppy workmanship. Furthermore, the tendency to build large housing estates without nearby schools, health centres, shops and services, as well as ill-considered transport links between home and workplace, exacerbated the time-consuming, frustrating and demoralizing problems of satisfying essential needs in an economy beset by shortages.

The advantages of low rents and secure tenure were largely unappreciated by a population whose high expectations were not being met. Poor quality and long waiting lists made housing a persistent unresolved issue of Polish social policy.

Education

Education also suffered intense criticism, though it never had the political resonance of housing or health. By the late 1980s the teaching profession was shrinking, demoralized and poorly qualified; and pupils' aspirations were declining (Kozakiewicz, 1987; Wójtowicz, 1988). The quality of education was suspect, even disregarding distortions caused by rigid ideological regulation. Shortcomings were identified in the structure, content, physical plant and personnel of the system, not least by the authoritative report of a team of government experts in 1973 (*Raport*, 1973); but to little practical effect. An equivalent report reached similar conclusions in 1987, confirming the 'catastrophic' state of education (Sarzyński, 1990).

The system provided non-compulsory pre-school facilities; however, less than half of urban and about one-fifth of rural children benefited. The 1973 report urged expansion of pre-school education; it identified the shortage of rural pre-schools as a source of persistent systemic inequality (*Raport*, 1973: 115–19). Yet expansion of places remained slow or static, while the mid-1980s saw a new demographic bulge reaching the schools.

From age seven followed eight classes of compulsory primary education, with a rigid, centrally determined curriculum, criticized as placing little emphasis on creativity, reasoning and subject integration (*Raport*, 1973: 120–3; Sarzyński, 1990). Schools were physically inadequate and poorly equipped. Parents experienced chronic problems in providing textbooks. A shortage of places forced many children to attend school according to a two- or three-shift system.

Secondary schooling took place primarily in a variety of vocational schools or in the general lyceum. Despite the stress on vocational education, these schools often lacked necessary equipment and were poorly co-ordinated with industry (Kaczór, 1987). Greater support for expanding general education followed the 1973 report; this was also an urgent recommendation of the 1987 expert group; yet in Warsaw in June 1988 there was a shortage of 2,000 places. Vocational education was often linked to a particular factory or sector of the economy, with the expectation that pupils would take up employment there. The lyceum has always been the main route to higher education.

Tuition was free for higher education, and almost three-quarters of students benefited from grants. From the late 1960s until 1986 a points system gave extra credits to compensate for weaker entrance examination performance, especially for those from manual worker and peasant backgrounds; but the compensation was not weighty enough to make a substantial difference; the system was replaced by a less precise system of allocating places to 'worthy' candidates. Higher education came to be dominated by children of the intelligentsia; it was also characterized by a high proportion of women. The attraction of higher education to men was reduced by wages policies which paid scant heed to educational qualifications, due primarily to the shortage of semi-skilled labour in the economy.

Organizationally, the tendency in the 1980s (c. 1982–8) was for increased centralization in higher education to reverse the gains in autonomy achieved by pressure from Solidarity in 1980–1 (see Tomiak, 1982: 162–3). Numerous personnel changes ensued from 1982, the independent students' union was prohibited, and the Minister gained the power to overrule virtually every decision taken by a college, polytechnic or university. Increased political control, the drop in educational aspirations, and centrally fixed ceilings for particular disciplines led to a fall in the number of students; by 1986–7 it had declined by one-quarter in comparison with 1980.

At no level, then, did education achieve the social aims of reducing inequality, the political aims of integrating and socializing young people, the cultural aims of self-fulfilment and breadth of outlook, or the economic aims of an educated labour force utilizing its skills to the full. Indeed, its effects often appeared counter-productive.

Health care
The health of the Polish population deteriorated over the last two decades as a result of a confluence of factors, including alarming levels of pollution, poor working and housing conditions, unhygienic methods of producing and distributing foodstuffs, and negative behavioural patterns (diet, exercise, use of tobacco and alcohol, personal hygiene). All these variables deteriorated from the late 1970s, though with certain regional differences.

The worsening of conditions conducive to health and the perennial problems besetting the system of health care delivery (Millard, 1982) were reflected in major indices such as reduced life expectancy and increased death rates for all age groups, especially adult males. Most of the increase in adult mortality since 1965 is accounted for by cardiovascular diseases, violent causes (mainly accidents and poisoning) and malignant neoplasms. Morbidity figures also became worrying, particularly for long-term debilitating diseases such as hepatitis.

Like housing and education, health suffered from underfunding, such that many problems have been cumulative, for example, the physical deterioration of hospitals, where overcrowded and un-hygienic facilities predominate. Malfunctions of the system pro-longed the length of hospital stays: for example, shortages or failure of equipment lengthened the time needed for diagnostic tests; endemic shortages of drugs and equipment also had an effect. Poor housing conditions meant that some patients, especially elderly ones, remained in hospital longer than medically necessary.

At the same time, inadequate primary care increased pressure on hospitals and specialists. Work in primary health clinics became very unpopular; clinics suffered extensive turnover and shortages of personnel, despite the fact that Poland has more doctors per head of population than Britain, Australia or Japan (20.8 per 10,000). Primary care doctors referred their patients to specialists almost as a matter of course. In theory people were assigned to a primary clinic at their place of residence, with sectors of heavy industry providing additional care at the workplace, where it was easier to receive attention. Yet local clinics were often closed or fully booked or lacked equipment, forcing patients to seek help elsewhere, some-times in the co-operative or private sector. The main obstacle to medical consultation was the sheer length of time involved in getting to a doctor (Rychard, 1980: 766).

Health personnel were traditionally poorly paid; indeed, with teachers, they found themselves at the bottom of the wages table. One result was an acute shortage of ancillary personnel, especially cleaners. Like teachers, medical staff often took on extra jobs, including onerous night duties. They became tired, demoralized and susceptible to corruption. Doctors were criticized for their brusque and hurried manner, their receptiveness to bribes, and for their notion of medical practice as either à referral agency or a repair service. This led to patient choice of primary care doctor in some areas; but although the principle of choice was accepted by the mid-1980s, there were serious practical limitations.

Obtaining drugs and medication was an ordeal. Shortages were acute, with no continuity of stock even for fundamental life-saving drugs such as insulin. The population filled prescriptions by stalking the network of pharmacies or mobilizing informal contacts; a substantial black market developed in pharmaceuticals. It was often remarked that only the healthy were fit to use the Polish health service.

Health care, in principle the most egalitarian of all social services, itself became a source of inequalities. Provinces with a more developed social infrastructure received more resources than poorer ones. The geographical distribution of specialists reflected neither the age composition nor the spatial distribution of the population nor the incidence of disease. Rural–urban disparities also remained salient, with urban areas highly favoured in the distribution of resources. As with housing and education, the communist regime left an unenviable legacy. The population's health was deteriorating, while the health care system seemed on the verge of disintegration.

Social benefits and the problem of poverty

Most monetary entitlements were provided in communist Poland through a social insurance system operated by the Institute of Social Insurance (Zakład Ubezpieczeń Społecznych, or ZUS), which received funds calculated as a proportion of the enterprise or institution's wage fund (38 per cent in 1989) or contributions from the self-employed. (On the evolution of ZUS, see Szubert, 1987.) ZUS provided about sixteen different types of individual and family benefit, with entitlement usually dependent on years of employment.

Retirement and invalidity pensions constituted the largest single category of expenditure (about 40 per cent) on social provision. The retirement age was 65 for men and 60 for women, but numerous exceptions permitted early retirement. Both types of pension depended on length and sector of employment. Sickness benefits were related to earnings and tenure: 100 per cent of earnings for those employed for more than eight years.

Maternity and child care benefits improved steadily from the 1970s (Kurzynowski, 1988: 169–88). Maternity leave rose from 12 weeks to 16–18 weeks on full pay, supplemented by up to three years' unpaid parental leave with no interruption of seniority. There was also provision for maternal paid leave to care for a sick child. Family allowances depended on the number of children and their continuing full-time education, related to per capita family income.

In addition to ZUS provision, there were numerous benefits financed from the state budget: heavy subsidies on basic foodstuffs, rents, heating, newspapers, books, theatres, sport and entertainment; as well as spending on health and education. Unemployment benefit did exist but was unimportant because of the general labour shortage (Muszalski, 1987: 261). From 1960 the Ministry of Health was responsible for social care for those lacking insurance entitlement. As well as orphanages, homes for the elderly and the like, there was a benefit system operated by a network of social workers. The situation was legally confusing, as the system functioned on the basis of a 1923 law, altered over the years by administrative regulations. Social workers in effect had discretion over benefits provided to the needy and/or the disabled as long-term, temporary or one-off cash payments or as benefits in kind or services, such as food vouchers or cleaning. Provision in kind was administered by social workers acting through social organizations such as the Polish Committee for Social Assistance. Enterprise social funds also provided help to needy employees and pensioners, but their social functions declined in the 1980s (Frączkiewicz and Frączkiewicz-Wronka, 1989: 260–1). Local government also had a role in providing benefits for the needy.

During the 1980s prolonged economic crisis reduced the population's standard of living and increased poverty. The term poverty was avoided; 'social minimum' became the preferred (if controversial) phrase, that is, the amount in money needed to purchase the goods and services to satisfy minimum biological, social and cultural needs (Rajkiewicz, 1988: 24). Official calculations by the Central Statistical Office in the early 1980s suggested that 19 per cent of families were impoverished, but this probably underestimated the extent of genuine deprivation.

The most disadvantaged groups were the elderly, the disabled, single-parent families and families with large numbers of children (see *Warunki życia ludności w 1987 r.*, 1988, and *Warunki życia ludności w 1989 r.*, 1990). State benefits were low, and although index-linking began in 1986, to take account of price increases, it did not eliminate hardship. Retirement pensions were set at about half the average wage, and many pensioners continued with some form of employment, made possible due to persistent labour shortage. Invalids with partial disability also worked, giving rise to allegations that many were not genuinely disabled.

Despite the growth of poverty, the proliferation of social benefits and a more relaxed attitude to private enterprise contributed to the emergence of a view among a section of the intelligentsia that the communist state had become 'over-protective' of its citizens, who thus lost the capacity for individual self-reliance. This view had much in common with (and was influenced by) right-wing attacks on the so-called dependency culture of the European welfare state. It was a view which would gain adherents among the new entrepreneurs of the post-communist period.

The problems of transition

We see, then, that Solidarity inherited a system beset by economic crisis and profound dislocations in key areas of social policy. The increasing strain caused by rapid price rises and declining service provision became palpably evident by 1989. However, Solidarity did not take office with an alternative vision of social policy. Indeed, many seemed to share the unstated assumption that the removal of communist power would itself resolve a considerable part of society's problems: with the cancer cut out, the organism would heal itself. Of course, this would also require the removal of some blatant economic irrationalities, such as the absence of a meaningful pricing system and absurd levels of government subsidy. The patronage system of the nomenklatura would give way to a merit system of appointment. The state would encourage private enterprise, while state enterprises would respond to the new requirements of competition. Lifting the burden of central control would release civic initiative and imagination.

These issues were not debated publicly. Gradually, however, a new agenda emerged and was strengthened by the personnel changes of the Bielecki government. The economic agenda – in large measure a liberal, laisser-faire one, concerned above all with the development of a capitalist market economy – generated a new social agenda. Increasingly, social policy came to be viewed as a political necessity rather than an aspect of good government. Given the history of explosive social protest, it would have to be taken seriously; however, its scope would be reduced. This represented the partial triumph of the view that the state was over-protective and discouraging of individual effort.

We shall show how this view affected various aspects of social policy. First, however, it seems pertinent to sketch the developments in the political sphere and the genesis of an economic programme which has proved vital for social policy developments.

The political context
Despite the social calm of the first months of the new Solidarity-led coalition government of Tadeusz Mazowiecki, the period of transition has been one of considerable political discontinuity. In the short term, disruptions came firstly from the transition from communist to non-communist government. Mazowiecki's cabinet reshuffles had removed most non-Solidarity ministers by the autumn of 1990; but by then Solidarity itself had split into two main camps, the pro-Wałęsa Centrum and the pro-Mazowiecki ROAD (Ruch Obywatelski Akcji Demokratycznej: the Citizens' Movement for Democratic Action). This split generated increasing

pressure for an early election to replace the Communist President, General Jaruzelski. Mazowiecki lost the presidential election to Lech Wałęsa largely because of disillusion with his government's economic policy. Wałęsa's election to the presidency in December 1990 led to the appointment of a new government in January followed by increasing political, economic and social tensions throughout the year. Finally, in October 1991, the first fully competitive parliamentary elections were held.

These elections produced an inconclusive result, with twenty-seven different parties and groups attaining parliamentary represen-tation. The two largest parties were the Democratic Union of Tadeusz Mazowiecki and the ex-communist Democratic Left Alliance, both with just over 12 per cent of the vote. The process of government formation took two months, with Prime Minister Jan Olszewski's new coalition resting on fragile foundations. Tensions between Olszewski and President Wałęsa, coupled with the large number of parliamentary parties and lack of party discipline, set the scene for a further period of unstable institutional relationships.

Mazowiecki began his government with great popular consensus and tolerance of economic hardship. It was short-lived, however, and President Wałęsa's own disparate constituency soon began to pull in different directions. The reaction against the incompetence, corruption and inefficiency of the *ancien régime* stimulated an anti-state ethos and a rejection of many social functions of the allegedly 'over-protective state' by a highly influential element of the liberal intelligentsia, now represented in government. A number of them are typical of the emerging entrepreneur, with vested interests in a reduction of the role of the state. Such attitudes are reinforced by the widely shared view that economic crisis prohibits large-scale intervention in the social sphere: Poland cannot afford extensive social policy expenditures.

At the same time, the population expects a high level of social protection guaranteed by the state. Numerous signs of growing social unrest emerged in the autumn of 1990, gaining momentum throughout 1991. The problem for Wałęsa is that his main constitu-ency is the working class, particularly in the old bastions of heavy industry, that is, precisely the sectors least likely to prove competit-ive in the world capitalist market. He also had considerable peasant support, which eroded as peasant hatred of Finance Minister Balcerowicz intensified. Wałęsa's popularity declined rapidly in the first months of his presidency. His government, under the self-styled Thatcherite Prime Minister Bielecki, pursued policies which were largely a continuation of those of the Mazowiecki government, but which led to progressively deeper economic recession. In the first instance Wałęsa tried to deflect blame for the situation on to the *Sejm* on the grounds that it was behaving obstructively because of continuing communist influence. A manifestation of this tension was Wałęsa's battle with the *Sejm* over the electoral system in June 1991, when a political crisis was narrowly averted by his unwilling signature on the new electoral law. Wałęsa also failed to convince the *Sejm* to grant the government special powers. The public mood at the time of the October elections was sombre, disillusioned and uncomprehending. Nor did the election result offer any hope of resolving this collective social frustration.

Government economic policy and its consequences
Economic policy was the primary concern of both the Mazowiecki and Bielecki governments. It would be misleading, however, to see the Mazowiecki government as providing a decisive break with the past. Some policies, notably the elimination of subsidies, were also part of the economic strategy of the communist regime (see Clarke, 1989, on the abortive reforms of the 1980s). The Bielecki government, too, – preparing for a short term of office before parliamentary elections – took continuity as its watchword.

The short, sharp shock of the Balcerowicz programme accelerated the removal of subsidies, thus generating a series of massive price increases to add to those implemented in the 1980s. The programme also included mechanisms to keep wages down, so that the standard of living was bound to fall further and faster. In the abstract the population supported this programme, and in the short term they remained stoically accepting. By 1988 the failure of the socialist state coupled with widespread knowledge of Western consumerism had already generated the 'myth of the market . . . as a universal cure for all the shortcomings of the Polish economy' (Kolarska-Bobińska, 1990: 163). Positive attitudes to the market, private ownership, competition and wage differentiation were strengthened in 1989–90. Respect for Tadeusz Mazowiecki, endorsement of the principles of the market economy and relief at the ejection of the Communist Party provided a strong basis of consensus and legitimacy. Severe price rises, which had generated waves of social protest under communist rule, were initially borne passively. Wałęsa's own attacks on the government contributed to undoing this consensus, however. In November 1990 Mazowiecki was humiliated in the first round of the presidential election in favour of Wałęsa and the eccentric ex-patriate Stan Tymiński, both of whom promised an easier transition to the market.

Mazowiecki was brought down by growing unemployment and a rapid fall in the standard of living. Full employment was touted as the greatest achievement of the socialist system; however, the system never achieved the *rational* deployment of labour. Artificial labour shortages and subsidies inhibited the development of new sectors of the economy. The whole system became locked in a time warp, where modernization was equated with the development of heavy industry. No one doubts the need for economic modernization. However, the price of economic restructuring is unemployment. The question therefore is how healthy elements of the economy can be supported and new sectors stimulated. These questions have been little addressed by members of the government, who have often assumed that the process of economic regeneration would occur spontaneously. The Olszewski government was more sympathetic to state intervention but found it difficult to generate a coherent policy towards the state sector of the economy.

In the first year of (virtually) free market pricing and international competition, Polish enterprises showed little sign of adaptation but there were also relatively few bankruptcies. Cost-cutting, cutbacks in production, the using of existing reserves, and mutual credit arrangements were the prime response in the short term. Already by spring 1990 large numbers of workers were on short time or enforced holidays, while unemployment reached 400,000. As the short-term responses were exhausted, unemployment began to climb, reaching about 1.2 million by the end of 1990 (excluding worker-peasants who had lost their industrial jobs) and 1.5 million in June 1991. The collapse of trade with the important Soviet market in 1991 added to the recession.

The combined effects of price rises, deepening recession and unemployment were great hardship and deprivation. In 1990 there was a decline of about 30 per cent (this figure remains controversial) in the standard of living. By the latter part of 1990 about 44 per cent of employee households and over half of pensioners' households were said to be on or below the poverty line (Kordos, 1990). The situation will worsen as unemployment increases; indeed, the government became more sensitive to social policy issues as it became clear that unemployment was rising faster than anticipated. The small group of Solidarity social democrats associated with Zbigniew Bujak and Ryszard Bugaj began to plead more loudly for an industrial policy. However, the Bielecki government faced a severe budget deficit as the recession deepened and the tax base shrunk. Its determination to balance the budget through deep cuts in social services entailed the deterioration of an already dreadful situation.

Olszewski's successor government formed in December 1991 under Prime Minister Jan Olszewski faced enormous economic, social and political problems in attempting to devise a new strategy. The dramatic resignation of the Finance Minister in February 1992 illustrates internal conflicts within the weak coalition government.

New developments in social policy

There was no articulation of a coherent social policy and little sign of a social policy debate in Poland between 1989 and 1991. The scope of social policy automatically narrowed through the removal of price subsidies on food, shelter, leisure and cultural resources. It is economic changes rather than social policy choices which have proved to be the major source of recent developments. Ameliorative policies have not been absent, to provide sufficient social protection to prevent social disorder. However, there is little talk these days of redistributive measures. We can illuminate these points by looking at recent developments in the social services, housing, education and health.

Social services and the benefit system
Some alleviative mechanisms were put in place quite quickly. However, there has been no macro-economic strategy for employment and investment. Planning and temporary job creation schemes have largely been left to provincial authorities. The two areas of emphasis thus far concern the unemployed and those suffering the worst economic hardship. In a departure from his original non-interventionist strategy, Minister of Labour Jacek Kuroń introduced initiatives to promote youth employment and the revival of small towns facing large-scale unemployment due to the threat of closure of their single, dominant employer. His successor, Michał Boni, previously Solidarity's chief negotiator with Kuroń, followed this with plans for 'enterprise zones' in areas hardest hit by unemployment. These limited positive measures have had no notable impact.

The extension of unemployment benefit was achieved easily, given the small numbers registering. Unemployment policy and benefits are paid for by the Employment Fund, financed by the state and by a 2 per cent payroll tax. At first benefits were very generous and continued throughout the period of unemployment. Gradually, however, a more restrictive view of entitlement was introduced, along with reductions in the period of eligibility. This has been a result of the mounting costs of unemployment; the view that unemployment benefit can operate as a 'demotivating factor' in the search for jobs; and the difficulties of policing benefit claims by those working in the thriving second economy.

Start-up loans and tax concessions were also introduced for new businesses. Local job centres would provide information and participate in retraining programmes; in theory each unemployed person would be offered retraining. The early obstacles quickly became apparent. Job centres lacked offices, equipment, personnel and information about vacancies. Retraining, like job creation, was largely left to local initiatives. Some help was forthcoming in 1991: a World Bank loan of 100 million dollars over five years, to support small businesses and to improve the efficiency of job centres. However, the deepening recession did not appear to dent the government's basic assumption that the release of entrepreneurial initiative would result in rapid, spontaneous economic regeneration.

Protection of existing levels of pensions and most benefits was assured; the employer contribution was raised to 43 per cent of the total wage fund. Yet the quarterly index-linking of pensions and cash benefits to wages created hardship due to the fall in real wages. In 1991 pensioners made some gains relative to workers, but the attempt to claw back these gains was declared unconstitutional and triggered a major crisis for the Olszewski government. There were serious worries about the implementation of Kuroń's 1990 law on social care, providing that local authorities would be financed from the state budget to provide extra funds, shelter, food and/or essential clothing for families and individuals whose per capita income fell below the level of the lowest retirement pension. The homeless, the unemployed, the chronically or mentally ill and those suffering from drug or alcohol abuse are some of the categories identified as potentially qualifying for assistance. Advice and counselling are to help them to help themselves.

Certainly the general confusion in local government is such as to cast doubt on its ability to carry out these statutory requirements. It has acquired increased responsibilities but lacks the resources to cope with them. Early reports to the *Sejm* noted that lack of money and inadequate training of social workers were proving major obstacles to providing the envisaged individualized care-mix.

Kuroń himself had high hopes for the development of independent social initiatives. His own major charity appeal, the SOS Fund, has proved very successful. The government is understandably anxious to encourage community initiative and voluntary activities, and notions of participation and user involvement are gaining currency. But the response has been limited, except for the increase in charitable work by the Catholic Church (e.g. soup kitchens and hostels). Indeed, voluntary associations which functioned under the communist regime – like the Polish Committee for Social Assistance – are struggling to cope with the loss of their state subsidies. Moreover, it is not surprising in the circumstances that the poor and unemployed are demoralized or that generally people's energies are largely devoted to their own family affairs.

Housing

Mazowiecki's minister of housing, Aleksander Paszyński, was in favour of the state's withdrawal from the housing sector; his successor, Adam Glapiński, was a fervent free market liberal who stressed this aspect even more. In the short term the population must meet the real costs of its housing. The medium- and longer-term goal is that people should buy or rent their own accommodation. This is to be facilitated by the privatization of the construction industry; it is hoped that increasing supply through the stimulation of greater efficiency by means of competition will reduce costs. When income tax is brought in in 1992, subsidies will be provided through a system of tax relief. The state will retain a minimal role as provider. Basically, however, the government wishes to disabuse the population of any notion of a 'right' to housing. Housing should be seen as a commodity (Paszyński, quoted in *Zycie Gospodarcze*, 38, 23 September 1990).

There are currently two key dimensions to the housing problem. First are the financial difficulties arising from massive increases in rents, maintenance charges and utilities. Housing subsidies are being phased out gradually, with the first big increase in charges in January 1990. In the autumn rents and charges were raised again so as to cover the cost of current exploitation and repairs. By 1993 full-cost charges are to be introduced, extending to the costs of capital renovation. Increased housing costs are a major contributor to the decline in the standard of living.

The government did respond with some temporary ameliorative measures. Upper limits were established for rents in local-government-controlled housing. Housing benefit helped with housing costs (rent or service charges, central heating, electricity, gas) and there was some provision for help with interest payments. Initial take-up was low, since the administrative mechanisms were incomplete. The rules were complex, with the level of benefit depending on income and on certain norms for floor space. However, it was estimated that in September 1990 in the public sector (the old *kwaterunek*) about 20 per cent of households with earned income and 60 per cent of households of retired people were already eligible. The figure for the co-operative sector was thought to be even higher (Kulesza, 1990: 18). Fears were expressed that local government would be unable to cope with the administration, and that the strain on the state budget would be intense. Indeed, the rules for housing benefit were tightened for the period March to June 1991 (thereafter to be reviewed).

The second major dimension of the housing problem is the situation of those without their own accommodation. Supply has also been affected by price increases. Rocketing building costs left half a million uncompleted housing units by mid-1990, and 1990 saw fewer completions (132,500) than 1989 (150,200). Banks refused credit to the co-operatives because repayment could not be guaranteed, while few private borrowers could afford the astronomical interest rates.

Improving housing supply presents a number of legal and administrative problems. The situation regarding legal title to building land is a Gordian knot of tangles. Second, local government has been given many new responsibilities, including the administration of housing benefit, while its revenues and budgeting powers remain totally obscure. Third, communist law is ill suited to the new environment. Thus the draft bill on housing law (in full in *Rzeczpospolita*, 111, 14 May 1991) envisaged change in a number of respects. Broadly, contracts are to replace administrative regulations, and many restrictions are to be removed, such as the limits on density of occupation for rented accommodation. Eviction is to be facilitated, removing the present obligation to provide alternative accommodation. The bill also removes the limit of one per person on housing ownership, in order to encourage investment in housing offered for rent. All these measures mean reduced protection for tenants and they have been controversial for precisely this reason. Other facilitating measures were proposed in a separate draft bill on housing construction (*Rzeczpospolita*, 110, 13 May 1991), giving the commune or district more control over local land use, with subsidies to support infrastructural development of housing sites.

The Ministry's longer-term aims for housing ownership envisage differentiation according to income. The prosperous would be left to provide their own housing. The middle group would have a choice of various types of preferential mortgage credit, subsidized and/or guaranteed by the state. The poorest would have a low standard of housing provided by the state, through the agency of local government. None of these arrangements will come into operation for some time.

Meanwhile, the plight of the homeless and those living in overcrowded or inadequate accommodation continues, while the government's proposals have generated an atmosphere of insecurity regarding rented accommodation. Some two million waiting members are furious at the inadequate revaluation of their co-operative savings and their lack of housing prospects. Many are young people, least equipped with the necessary financial resources and most vulnerable to unemployment. Modern flats are too small for the immediate expansion of rented lodgings or bed-sitters. The spectre of homeless people on city streets is already generating anxieties regarding links between homelessness or poor housing and ill health and unemployment; and a myriad of social problems, including alcoholism and crime. Furthermore, lack of housing is a major obstacle to the creation of a mobile labour force. Housing has always been politically sensitive and there is no reason to assume that it will become less so.

Education
Education is one sphere where one might expect little change in the central role of the state. There is general acceptance of the view that education is a social investment as well as a means of individual development. Private schools do acquire legal sanction under new legislation; a few began to operate in 1990, with a small state subsidy. Yet financial stringencies and lack of accommodation make large-scale expansion of the private sector unlikely in the short term. State education will not increase its share of resources, however. Indeed, the government proposed severe cuts in educa-tion funding in the budgetary crisis of summer 1991. Thus the problems of inadequate accommodation, overcrowding and lack of books and equipment will continue.

A changing structure of provision is certainly likely. Vocational schools linked directly to industry are already closing to save enterprise costs. This would have happened in any case, but its unplanned nature is causing disruption. The vocational–lyceum division will remain, though clearly vocational education must become more flexible. Higher education is expected to expand as wage structures begin to favour those with more advanced qualifica-tions. Some future fee structure is likely, but currently the old system of free tuition and student stipends still operates. The present level of support is inadequate, with the result that student numbers are falling, student poverty is pronounced and more students are taking sabbatical leave. In consequence, universities eased entry requirements for 1991/2.

A redistribution of functions is taking place, with decentralization from the Ministry to schools and institutions of higher education, which are being exhorted to 'greater pluralism'. The Ministry aims to increase the role of parents, not least as a way of overcoming the conservatism of the teaching profession. Indeed, the new law on education envisages a hierarchy of educational councils (*rady*) at school, provincial and national level, with a tripartite membership of teachers, parents and pupils; these councils must be consulted regarding school programmes and personnel. It looks a cumbersome, unworkable system.

Of course, some content has changed radically, especially for history, while teachers of Marxism-Leninism and Russian language have moved to other subjects. Retraining of teachers and the provision of new text books are intended, but there are neither the resources nor the facilities for this to occur quickly. The most dramatic curriculum change came shortly before the new school year 1990–1, with the introduction of the Catholic religion, taught by priests, into the schools. Although children may opt out, over 90 per cent now attend religious classes. Surprisingly, the new law on education makes no reference to religious instruction, though it removes the 1961 requirement of a lay curriculum.

Other changes are unintended consequences of policy decisions taken elsewhere. There is already anxiety at the closure of pre-school facilities, especially in the countryside. By late 1990 90,000 places had been lost in comparison with 1989 (*Rzeczpospolita*, 107, 7 May 1991). The enterprises and state farms are no longer subsidized to maintain their pre-school provision, and their attempts to transfer it to local government have met resistance: local authorities are reluctant to assume extra responsibilities without guaranteed funding. Raising direct charges has not resolved the difficulty because the fall in real incomes and fears of unemployment have led to parents' withdrawing their children; high costs have thus led to closures on grounds of 'lack of demand'.

Health

Reform of the system of health care has been on the political agenda for almost a decade, but it remains controversial (see, e.g. Millard, 1989: 204–40). Some would like a rapid shift to market dominance, with the state functioning as a provider of last resort. For the present, 'marketization' or 'commercialization' approaches have been rejected, partly because of the short-term problems engendered by the Balcerowicz programme. However, the determination to reduce the scope of state health provision and to increase direct charges is clear. The Deputy Minister responsible for reform, Piotr Mierzewski, has stated baldly that Poland cannot afford modern medicine, arguing that 'solidarity between patient and doctor must be temporarily replaced by a higher solidarity with . . . society, which cannot be permitted to go bankrupt because of health expenditure' (*Rzeczpospolita*, 45, 22 February 1990).

The radical reduction of subsidies hit the beleaguered health service exceptionally hard. The 1989 budget envisaged price rises of between 40 and 60 per cent; at the end of 1989 the inflation rate was edging towards 900 per cent. Piecemeal extra budget allocations did not keep pace. The problems of drug supply were particularly acute. Pharmaceuticals' prices remain fixed by the government. While they were increased considerably in October 1989, February 1990 and May 1991, the producers continue to maintain that many prices still do not reflect production costs. Prescriptions remained heavily subsidized, but because subsidies were calculated as a proportion of retail price (100 per cent or 70 per cent), increased prices hit both the Ministry of Health's budget and the patient's pocket. A vicious circle began when the Ministry lacked the money to pay Cefarm, the monopoly controller of pharmaceutical supply (also responsible for the retail network), so Cefarm could not pay the producers. Hospitals also reduced their drug orders. Cezal, the medical equipment monopoly, found itself in a similar predicament. Inventories piled up as the health service cancelled or reduced orders and failed to pay its debts. In September 1991 a new law on prescription charges removed all rights to free prescriptions but maintained a subsidized flat rate for so-called basic drugs.

By autumn 1989 hospital wards and clinics were closing because of lack of funds. The Ministry of Health started the new financial year with a major debt and a budget allocation which again underestimated price increases. The experience of 1989 was repeated in 1990 and again early in 1991, with clinics and hospitals staggering under the pressures of shortage of funds. Periodic emergency injections of finance have enabled the system to stagger along, but only just.

Some *ad hoc* proposals for change were taking shape, as well as a longer-term reform strategy regarding the priorities, finance and organization of health care. Some short-term steps pre-empted or undermined longer-term strategy. For example, the Ministry tried to ease its budgetary plight by the rapid, uncontrolled (and often procedurally illegal) privatization of pharmacies and by encouraging hospitals to deal directly with suppliers. Privatization has led to allegations of corruption and excessive price increases, as well as the development of a black market among private pharmacies and enterprises importing drugs. Some pharmacies refuse (illegally) to fill subsidized prescriptions. A number of small rural pharmacies have been closed.

The longer-term approach has been developing gradually. Initially a widely held view, which the Ministry itself came to support, favoured the establishment of a basic comprehensive state service based on compulsory health insurance contributions, with the opportunity to purchase additional services from the public sector or privately. However, after almost a year of working to this brief, the Ministry accepted the World Bank's reservations: the Bank's experts argued that the move to an insurance-based system should be a longer-term aim, given the projected rise in unemployment, continuing inflation and the existence of a deeply rooted second economy.

Thus for the next few years the major source of finance will be the state budget, though direct charges are to be introduced along with some private tendering. Charges are anticipated for sanatoria, unwarranted use of the ambulance service and self-referrals to specialists. The World Bank has warned that co-payments and direct charges should be closely monitored to assess their impact 'on utilization patterns and equity in order to avoid perverse effects from being introduced into health care financing. The latter would undermine care for the vulnerable part of the population and the advantages of pre-payment financing for health care' (World Bank, 1990: 26–7). There are already reports that increased costs are deterring patients from filling prescriptions.

The major substantive aspect of the Ministry of Health's proposed organizational changes is a shift of emphasis to primary care and health promotion, with the training of genuine general practitioners, rather than primary care specialists in internal medicine, gynaecology and paediatrics, as hitherto. This has also been previous policy, without notable impact; but the fact that primary care is cheaper than specialist care does appear to be acting as an incentive for change. This shift also entails proposals to eliminate duplicate services provided by other ministries and the system of occupational medicine, with the latter to be limited to prevention. However, health promotion and preventive medicine are likely to remain mere slogans in the near future. Much that is needed is beyond the province of the Ministry (housing, sports facilities) or requires co-operation with the Ministry of Finance (over alcohol and tobacco) or others (reduction of other ministerial health provision). Mounting political campaigns fostered by the powerful Catholic Church against abortion and contraception, public ignorance and intolerance of AIDS, new problems of child prostitution and increasing drug abuse – such developments imply increasing demands on the health service as well as requiring co-ordination with other spheres.

In the meantime the situation continues to deteriorate. Shortages persist, now dictated by financial constraints. Health workers saw only a temporary improvement in their remuneration and they continue to be overworked, demoralized and over-concentrated in the hospital sector. Capital investment is at a standstill. The outlook seems less than optimistic.

Welfare strategies for the future

The most obvious direct consequences of new policies are the growth of poverty and deprivation, one aspect of which is the deterioration in social provision. Certain groups, notably the elderly, are particularly disadvantaged; for them, this is a reinforcement of previous patterns of inequality. New patterns of inequality are also emerging, not only between the employed and unemployed but because of greater income differentials within the working class and between the working class and the intelligentsia. There are indications that women will suffer particularly from unemployment, as well as from the consequences of expected anti-abortion legislation and the erosion of pre-school child care provision. Inequalities will develop with changes in class structure and the policy decisions of the new government. These in turn will be affected by the dynamics of social values and attitudes. There is little doubt that people did not comprehend in advance the extent and scope of the price rises entailed in the removal of subsidies. Shortages have disappeared, and with them the queues and the illegal market in hard currency. But if goods are now available, it is only to those who can afford them. This commodification has brought a new consciousness of what the state had previously provided (not always efficiently or continuously): not only cheap food, housing and energy, but also books, cinemas, children's summer camps – and, of course, jobs. The clash between the abstract, idealized market and its harsh reality has yet to be played out. The Polish tradition of political combativeness had begun to reassert itself by autumn 1990. Yet it is also possible that unemployment and increasing hardship will lead to apathy and inaction, as has often been the case with recession in capitalist countries. Political alienation is one sign of this.

It would be misleading to refer to social policy debates in this context. The governmental response thus far appears *ad hoc*, based on an implicit view of social policy as a means of alleviating the social problems arising from the economy. Social policy appears as a de-motivating factor, a burden on the economy, rather than as an integral part of the economic system. Therefore the state should withdraw as far as possible, while encouraging social participation and voluntary and charitable activity. Ironically this neo-liberal view has much in common with the old Stalinist notion that social investment was 'unproductive' and secondary (cf. Księżopolski, 1992). It took until the 1960s for the communist government to recognize that social investment, especially in health, housing and education, can improve economic efficiency; though this view was never reflected in practice, while clearly the policy of ever-increasing levels of price subsidy did lead to massive distortions.

The use of Western expertise is likely to reinforce a liberal strategy for Polish social policy. At the same time, political pressures may well pull in a different direction. The concern to foster social participation and voluntary activity has met little response thus far. Despite the proliferation of new groups and organizations, they lack funds, organizational resources and expertise. The state may be forced to retain many of its functions as the limitations of the market and the community become apparent. The trade unions, both Solidarity and the OPZZ, are raising social policy issues more insistently. Limits to the erosion of the welfare state are unlikely to result from coherent academic or political debates about social policy but rather from assessments of the political feasibility of dismantling social provision. At the end of 1991 major social disruption was being taken seriously, as respect for major institutions (government, parliament, the president, the church, Solidarity) declined, while insecurity in regard to employment and law and order issues increased. Protests by miners, pensioners, teachers, peasants and health workers underlined the sense of crisis. Certainly the period of transition will last far longer than the initial optimistic projections of two years.

References

Clarke, R. (1989) *Poland: the Economy in the 1980s*. London: Longman.

Czajka, S. (ed.) (1986) *Zarys Polityki Społecznej* [An Outline of Social Policy]. Warsaw: Państwowe Wydawnictwo Ekonomiczne.

Experience and the Future Discussion Group (1981) *Poland: The State of the Republic*, translated from the Polish. London: Pluto.

Frączkiewicz, L. and Frączkiewicz-Wronka, A. (1989) 'Social care in Poland: the direction of change', in F. Millard (ed.), *Social Welfare and the Market*. London: London School of Economics. pp. 241–70.

Kaczór, S. (1987), 'Aktualne problemy szkolnictwa zawodowego w Polsce' [Current problems of vocational education in Poland], *Kwartalnik Pedagogiczny*, 32 (3): 71–80.

Kolarska-Bobińska, L. (1990) 'The myth of the market and the reality of reform', in S. Gomulka and A. Polonsky (eds), *Polish Paradoxes*. London: Routledge. pp. 160–79.

Kordos, J. (1990) 'Some aspects of living conditions of households of retired persons and pensioners in Poland'. Paper presented to the Third Polish–British Seminar on Social Policy, Warsaw, October; and subsequent discussion.

Kozakiewiczs, M. (1987) 'Kryzys gospodarczy i kryzys szkolnictwa w Polsce' [Economic crisis and the crisis of the school system in Poland], *Kwartalnik Pedagogiczny*, 32 (4): 17–27.

Księżopolski, M. (1992) 'Prospects for social policy development in Poland for the coming years', in Bob Deacon (ed.), *Social Policy, Social Justice and Citizenship in Eastern Europe*. Aldershot: Gower.

Kulesza, H. (1990) 'Źle sytuowani' [The Badly Off], *Polityka*, 49, 8 December, p. 18.

Kurzynowski, A. (1988) 'Social benefits connected with the maternity of working women in Poland in the years 1960–85', in J. LeGrand and W. Okrasa (eds), *Social Welfare in Poland and Britain*. London: London School of Economics. pp. 169–87.

Lewis, P.G. (1990) 'Non-competitive elections and regime change: Poland 1989', *Parliamentary Affairs*, 43 (1): 90–107.

Millard, L.F. (1982) 'Health care in Poland: from crisis to crisis', *International Journal of Health Services*, 12 (3): 497–515.

Millard, F. (1989) 'The Polish health service: the current debate' in F. Millard (ed.), *Social Welfare and the Market*. London: London School of Economics. pp. 204–40.

Muszalski, W. (1987) *Ubezpieczenia społeczne* [Social Insurance]. Warsaw: Państwowe Wydawnictwo Ekonomiczne.

Rajkiewicz, A. (1988) 'Niektóre dylematy polityki społecznej' [Some dilemmas of social policy], *Nowe Drogi*, 4: 28–35.

Raport o Stanie Oświaty w PRL (1973) [Report on the State of Education in the P(eople's) R(epublic of) P(oland)]. Warsaw: Państwowe Wydawnictwo Naukowe.

Rychard, A. (1980), 'Opieka zdrowotna w regionie Łodzi w latach 1967–69 na tle jedenastu wybranych regionów zagranicznych' [Health care in the Łódź region compared with eleven selected regions abroad]. *Zdrowie publiczne*, 12: 757–71.

Sarzyński, P. (1990) 'Reforma między ławkami' [Reform among the Benches], *Polityka*, 6, 10 February, p. 5.

Szubert, W. (1979) 'Przedmiot, geneza i zakres socjalistycznej polityki społecznej' [The subject, genesis and scope of socialist social policy], in, A. Rajkiewicz (ed.), *Polityka społeczna* [Social Policy]. Warsaw: Państwowe Wydawnictwo Ekonomiczne.

Szubert, W. (1987) *Ubezpieczenie Społeczne* [Social Insurance]. Warsaw: Państwowe Wydawnictwo Naukowe.

Tomiak, J. (1982) 'Educational policy and educational reform in the 1970s', in Jean Woodall (ed.), *Policy and Politics in Contemporary Poland*. London: Frances Pinter.

Warunki życia ludności w 1987 r. (1988) [Conditions of the Population in 1987]. Warsaw: Główny Urząd Statystyczny.

Warunki życia ludności w 1989 r. (1990) [Conditions of the Population in 1989]. Warsaw: Główny Urząd Statystyczny.

Wójtowicz, D. (1988) 'Pięć minut po dzwonku' [Five minutes after the bell], *Przegląd Tygodniowy*, 22, 29 May, p. 3.

World Bank (1990) *Poland. Health System Reform: Meeting the Challenge*, Working Draft, 13 September (unpublished).

Zięba, A. (1988) 'Pociekalnia marzeń' [The waiting room of dreams], *Przegląd Tygodniowy*, 3, 17 January, pp. 4–5.

Zweig, F. (1944) *Poland between Two Wars*. London: Secker and Warburg.

6

Social Policy in Hungary

Julia Szalai and Eva Orosz

This chapter on Hungarian social policy adopts a format that is rather different from those on the former Soviet Union, Poland and Czechoslovakia. It does not claim to be a comprehensive review of past problems and current developments in all aspects of social policy. Instead it focuses on social security policy and medical care policy. It does this in ways which reinforce a point about Hungarian exceptionalism which is developed in Chapter 7.

The major part, by Julia Szalai, is an analysis of the way in which developments in social security policy in the years before 1989 underpinned the organic development of a second economy which in turn facilitated the growth of a hidden civil society in Hungary. It was this organic development of bourgeois activity that ensured, in the case of Hungary, such a smooth transition from the old order to the emerging new. The contribution does, however, strike a note of caution, pointing out that there remains a second half of Hungarian society who were dependent only on the official state economy. The urgent task of social security and other social policy is now to integrate this lost half. The story of the more recent development of Hungarian social security policy and provision is taken up in Chapter 7, where additional information is provided.

The final section (starting on p. 159) is the contribution by Eva Orosz, in which the focus is the current proposals by the Ministry of Welfare to overcome the legacy of morbidity and mortality problems bequeathed to it by the previous inefficient and under-funded state medical care service. Just as in the case of social security and income maintenance, the operation of the official and unofficial economy gave birth to a section of society able to operate in the emerging market economy. In the case of health care the unofficial practice of paying gratitude money for officially free services seems to have laid the foundation for the call by the new government to abolish the right of citizens to health care and the overt development of an insurance-based system. A note of warning is again sounded in terms of the possible negative consequences of this emerging policy for a section of society.

What the chapter loses in comprehensiveness (there is little here on housing and education policy) we believe it gains in immediacy and in terms of bringing sharply into focus the rather exceptional nature of the Hungarian past and transition which we believe underpins the argument in Chapter 7 that the future for Hungarian social policy is rather different from the other East European countries. It also underlines the point that even two years into the reform process very little has yet been settled by way of the new institutional mechanisms to implement a new social policy.

The Hungarian transition and social policy

Some months after the free parliamentary elections of April 1990, the new government announced its comprehensive and ambitious programme for the first (three-year) phase of the 'transition'. The introductory words set out the priorities, as follows:

> The fundamental and all-embracing endeavour of the government is to carry out the systemic changes of the economy. Thus the programme envisages the creation of a new, viable, market-regulated economy. It should replace the malfunctioning order of the last forty years, which has been based on administrative interventions and repressive care of the state, accompanied by external isolation. The experiences of the successful West European countries should be utilized in the process of creating the new economy, suitably adapting the lessons to the existing Hungarian conditions. This new order will be an up-to-date European *social market economy*, based on the primacy of private property, and be integrated into the world-market. (Programme of the Government, 1990)

The term social market economy, at first sight, is identical with the notion of the 'Soziale Marktwirtschaft' in German economic literature. It must be noted, however, that the concept denoted by the attribute 'social' is unclear and much disputed. 'Social' has several – partly contrasting – meanings and connotations in Hungarian. It either might refer to the notion of the (classical) welfare state, implying universal rights, a wide range of well-developed social services, extended entitlements for a number of decent benefits, a significant share of public (neither state, nor private) properties and control, etc. Or, it might equally mean the opposite, since the term 'social' has also a 'welfare' connotation in the Hungarian language. In that reading, the programme of a 'social' market economy means the drive to create a free market (with the minimum possible presence of and intervention by any 'external' agents), where it is emphasized that any help following non-market rules should be targeted only to the poor, and such help should be offered on the fringes of the system. Finally, it also might point to the frequently emphasized peaceful character of the transition. Namely, that the transformation will not be too rapid, some 'social'-ism will be preserved. In that reading the message is a compromise between the former and the present rulers; although the necessity to reduce the burden of the state budget is unanimously acknow-ledged. The 'socialist' responsibilities will be kept in the hands of the state, with all the resulting implications for the relative stability of the given positions in the state bureaucracy and in public administration. (The latter interpretation is reinforced by the fact that the former ruling party, i.e. the Hungarian Socialist Party, also gives outstanding priority to the 'social' aspect of marketization in its programme.)

The central importance of social welfare in the marketization process is underlined in several chapters of the above-cited pro-gramme, and it is repeatedly emphasized by the new politicians of the governing parties[1] in their public speeches and writings. How-ever, the notion of social policy has remained hazy until now. There seems to be practically no intention of going beyond the mere rhetorical advocacy of a social welfare programme. In fact, it has been a striking feature of the period since the elections that the actual steps taken in the name of the transformation have been restricted exclusively to the narrowly defined 'productive' spheres of the economy.

This failure to go beyond rhetoric is even more marked in relation to the core issue of the transition, namely, in the new (though hesitant) regulations on the conversion of the existing property-relations. The recently published numerous official and semi-official programmes on 'privatization'[2] have one characteristic in common. When speaking about the transformation of 'socialist' ownership, they hardly ever go beyond the proposals to change the owners of state-dominated enterprises in industry, in agriculture, in trans-portation, in trading, etc.

Social services, institutions and organizations of the so-called public infrastructure seems to be 'forgotten', both in the discourses and in the crisis-management programmes of the various agencies and responsible government bodies. Only some vague and unelucid-ated ideas have been formulated on the desirable future distribution of the wealth of the institutions administered by the former local councils or by the faceless 'state' in health care, in education, in services for children or for the elderly. Their omission from the practical considerations concerning the changes of property rela-tions is all the more surprising, since they represent (according to some expert estimations) at least 40–50 per cent of the national wealth.

Does this mean that there are to be no changes in the spheres of 'public consumption'[3] at all? Or does it indicate that the relevant processes are less controlled and that there are no social-political forces aspiring to become the ultimate owners of the wealth in question? Or are the actual processes anarchic, spontaneous, unregulated and chaotic? Or, on the contrary, does the 'silence' perhaps show that they have already been drawn under more state control than before? These questions seem to be crucial, even if they are not very frequently raised.

The detailed answer has yet to be provided. It will involve research into the interrelations, tensions, controversies and potential intermeshing of the changes of ownership in both the 'productive' and 'non-productive' spheres of the economy.

This part of the chapter aims to outline some of the antecedents, historical processes and evolving interests that might influence (or even determine) the yet unclear future property relations of the 'public' spheres.

It will be argued that the 'de-nationalization' of the institutions and services in question had already started considerably before the overt collapse of 'socialism'. Their quasi-marketization was an organic part of the slow erosion, making the Hungarian case quite peculiar in the recent history of the East Central European region.

One can state in general that it is quite difficult to tell precisely when Hungarian society began its move from classical 'socialism' towards a market-regulated socio-economic order. This ambiguity was a decisive feature of the transition in the recent past and will continue to be so in the years to come. The so-called 'systemic changes' of 1988–90 were the completion of a previous long-term gradual erosion of the 'old rule' and of all of its institutions rather than the revolutionary beginning of potential radical social and economic changes of the future.

The slow decomposition holds true as much for the macro-economy (including the institutions and services of social policy) as for the hidden marketization process that was taking place in the micro-organizations of families, which was due to the independent and non-state-regulated economic activities of thousands of private households (Vajda, 1991).

This part of the chapter will try to demonstrate the participation and the role of the social security system in the erosion. It will be argued that the most important development in this respect has been the multiplication (and the accompanying duality) of its functions during the last 10 to 20 years which served both the preservation of the state-socialist order and its simultaneous gradual decomposition.

That peculiar role has developed in close relation to the dual project of the post-1956 regime of Kádárism, which was to reconstruct the totalitarian post-Stalinist order after the defeat of the revolution, and to find a viable compromise between the (oppressive) rulers and the (oppressed) ruled.

This part of the chapter will also demonstrate how the services of social security came to be used in the interests of the central state power, of the state-run (though slowly and partially emancipating) firms and of the employees in their activities outside the direct control of the state. The typical conflicts between the partially coinciding and concurrently contrasting interests of the users and controllers of the services will also be analysed in the light of the final outcome, which was a serious and overall crisis of the institutions of social policy.

It will also argue that the multiplication of the social security system's functions led to increasing dysfunctions with regard to the initial purposes of its services. The consequences in terms of increasing inequalities in access, in the uneven (and unjust) shifting of the burdens to the most defenceless social groups, in the ultimate open exclusion of the weakest clients, and the contribution of those developments to the recent expansion of poverty will be illustrated in the context of the most dramatic socio-political tensions of the present phase of the transition.

The interpretation that the processes of erosion of state-socialist social policy were a prefiguration of the potential changes of property relations will be supported by some recent examples of the sharpening conflicts around the 'redefinitions' of social security. This will complete the picture of the emerging struggles for power and control over the property changes in public services.

The multiplication of functions and the duality of Kádárist social policy

As was mentioned above, the gradual erosion of the 'classical' system of social policy, the slow evolution of new 'quasi-owners' of the social services beneath the unchanged surface and within the existing framework of 'socialism', was closely associated with the political characteristics of the post-1956 era.

The continuous attempt of the party politics of the Kádárist period (1957–88) can be summed up as an ongoing search for the delicate compromises between full rehabilitation of ('human-faced') totalitarian rule and the striving of society for individual autonomy and freedom. In other words, the basic features of the 'socialist' system were preserved but they simultaneously went through significant reinterpretations during the last three decades. The organization of affairs in a top-down way, the existence of centralized authority, the direct administration of social life and the economy, and the implications of this for the continuing extensive industrialization, for compulsory full employment, for the directives for the daily management of the economic organizations, were not changed. What was new about them related to the development of restricted freedoms of *individuals* within a very limited scope of choices. If people successfully conformed to the conditions dictated from the top, they 'deserved the right' to back-door entry into educational institutions, to change their jobs, to make (partial) use of their firms' equipment 'at home', in their private economies, to move to more urbanized settlements utilizing their private resources, added to by subsidized loans from the state which were awarded only to the 'most deserving' employees on the basis of the recommendations of their workplaces.

In accordance with the Janus-faced character of the regime, social policy also gained some 'new' features in addition to its old classical 'socialist' ones. To make clear my arguments below, let me briefly recall those 'classical' characteristics.

As it is commonly known, in the period of building the socialist planned economy the new system abolished social policy in general. All of its traditional institutions were cast away as the requisites of overthrown capitalism. At the same time – and it was the essence of its self-contradiction – the 'socialist' planned economy was regarded as the main trustee of social rationality and the social good. It followed that each and every segment of economy and society, of private and public life, became imbued with 'social' considerations as the central intention. In this sense we can say that the elimination of social policy was accompanied by 'injecting social policy' into the entire system. All this happened not as an ideological mistake or because of the 'encroachment' of Stalinist voluntarism, but because it was inherent in the totalitarian system.

The cessation of social policy and its identification with the centralized planned economy remained the unchanged and inbuilt element of the system even after 1956. The planned method of economic control, the associated political processes, full employment forced by the devaluation of the labour force and – in parallel with this – the redefinition of social membership by binding it to employment, quantitatively satisfactory health services defined as 'allowances in addition to wages' and the established system of social security degraded to a 'budgetary branch' and subordinated to the current political objectives, have all been meshing as inseparable gears and have been serving the social transformation programme intended and controlled by the central power.

The political aim of forced economic development had reduced the satisfaction of social needs to simply a means, that is, to the means of maintaining the artificially low level of wages which represented the most important and most durable source of centralized surplus.

The residualization of social objectives which continuously accompanied the forty-years history of socialism stemmed from this fact. It directly followed from the logic of the centrally controlled planned economy that it seemed sufficient merely to decree administratively the equality of access to the social remunerations. In the system of all-embracing 'planned control', the declaration of rights seemed to be identical with the automatic guarantees for their realization. The most important argument used to counteract the still artificially depressed wages were the so-called free social benefits in kind and the central redistribution system of social security benefits in cash, covering the entire 'socialist' workforce.

The most important function of the machinery of centralized redistribution in everyday reality was, however, not the provision of adequate benefits and social services but the operation and financing of the economy, because of the serious dependency of its institutions on the state budget. Some 80 per cent of the yearly Gross Domestic Product (GDP) was concentrated in the hands of the state, and nearly 60 per cent of that huge sum has repeatedly flown through the productive sector of the economy – in the form of donations, subsidies and support to firms – to keep it alive. In this way it becomes understandable why the 'social budget' (the source of health services, culture, education, etc. defined as 'free' statutory benefits and the source of the entire social security system) was repeatedly in a hopeless, impoverished and residual position. In such a situation the functioning of the social sphere was shaped not by needs but by scarcity: the limited available money, means, investment and labour force had to be concentrated where they were needed most.

Nevertheless, some important shifts within the unchanged structure of residual social policy did slowly emerge from the early seventies as it became a means of helping the Kádárist regime to find a compromise with the society which continued to be in silent opposition to it.

The direct antecedents of this development are to be found in the worsening economic conditions around the late sixties, which gave rise to the introduction of quite significant (though ambiguous) reforms of economic administration in 1968.[4]

As is already well known from the vast literature on the successes and failures of the policy of 'new economic management', the reform was aimed at loosening the rigidity of the central directives and control of production by giving more space to the spontaneous drives, diverse moves and motivations of the economic actors. The role of 'particular' (as opposed to 'all-societal') interests was gradually acknowledged both on the ideological and on the more practical level. The accompanying socio-economic element of the programme was the recognition of 'individualism' as the main incentive of the producers for better economic achievements. Thus the newly introduced measures deliberately attempted to give a more pronounced role to material stimuli in the name of 'differentiating earnings according to performances'.

However, the actual rise of earnings was seriously limited by the centrally defined and strictly controlled wages policy. In other words, there was a permanent (and irresolvable) clash between 'marketism' and 'planning'. Though economic growth and better productivity were desired political goals of the regime, the 'old' regulations on depressing personal incomes could not be abandoned . for the structural reasons previously outlined. The state budget did not have the funds available to pay higher wages.

The day-by-day resolutions (or, more accurately, mitigations) of the conflicts and clashes were found in two 'innovations' of the system, namely:

1 in the gradual acceptance of the second (informal) economy based on people's work on top of their regular participation in the formal, state-controlled sphere of production; and
2 in allowing the social security scheme to be regarded as an additional resource of personal disposable income. Institutions and workplaces could resolve the emerging tensions by this 'multifunctional' use of the social security funds.

Before turning to a more detailed description of the latter developments, it has to be noted that those innovations also served the search for compromises of a more general political character. They fitted into the socio-political programme of 'raising living standards', declared by the central party organs as the fundamental commitment of the socialist regime toward its citizens.

As was pointed out earlier, however, the realization of this much emphasized goal did not imply the liberalization of the cash-flow of the first economy. Instead, a marked shift between the 'targets' of social spendings had been introduced. In concrete terms, the expenditures of the state budget on in-cash benefits of social security were increased, while the aggregate share of funds for the whole of 'public consumption' remained in its previously described residual position. Some significant data on these shifts can be presented here: while spending on the social security 'branch' of the state budget represented 11 per cent in 1963, its share had already increased to 15 per cent by 1980. It is even more informative that the ratio of in-cash benefits within the expenditures on public consumption grew from 48 per cent in 1970 to 60 per cent by 1980. In this way the contribution of in-cash benefits to the average monthly disposable incomes of an 'average' Hungarian household had also been rapidly increasing: they represented 11 per cent of all officially registered earnings in 1967, 20 per cent in 1977 and 25 per cent in 1987 (CSO, *Statistical Yearbooks*, 1964–88; CSO, 1968, 1978, 1989).

The maintenance of the residual status of state spending on 'public consumption' accompanied by a significant internal shift toward in-cash benefits was a logical consequence of the reforms taking place within an unchanged structure. The necessary priorities that continued to be given to the everyday running of the economy had not ceased and this continued to mean that the yearly share of the funds for subsidizing the 'productive' spheres to keep them going had to remain constant. The rigidity of the structure of state spending was a consequence that could not be overcome within the existing system of over-centralization and 'centrally planned' redistribution of resources.

In this way the total of the spendings on social services plus social security remained much the same throughout the two decades after 1968, representing altogether roughly one-third of the budget. The outcome was a relatively (later even absolutely) decreasing share of the in-kind type of public consumption. Services like health care, education, personal transport, etc. suffered from the shifts of expenditures. (The consequences of this had become manifest by the 1980s in their dysfunctions and in the increasingly heated social struggles around their use. These consequences will be analysed in more detail in the example of the health care system in the next part of the chapter.) The most defenceless victims of the duality of the Kádárist social policy 'reforms' were the users of the existing services, who had to face all the consequences of increasing inequalities of access, an unstoppable deterioration of standards and of quality, a permanent overcrowding of all the relevant institutions and chronic shortages of even basic provision. Furthermore, all those negative experiences were supplemented by frequent administrative interventions of a paramilitary character, serving as fire-fighting directives to cope with the sometimes heated conflicts that arose, which were always regarded as only 'temporary' and 'transitory' by the authorities in charge.

Although the political decision to increase the available resources of private consumption through the social security system by curtailing those of the public services had serious drawbacks, it turned out to facilitate in an unintended way the gradual marketization of the economy, accompanied by quite lasting improvements of its overall performance.[5] The hidden marketization also concluded in the emergence of the quasi-owners of the services in question.

Some of these developments are outlined below.

First, the expansion of the social security scheme (both by introducing new types of benefits[6] and by extending entitlements) created significant room for manoevre for the 'socialist' enterprises whereby they could increase their independence from the rigid regulations of the central wage and employment policy. They could build lasting 'buffers' into their daily working that protected them against the direct interventions of the state. The schemes of sick pay and of the disability pension turned out to be the most usable means in their hands in this respect. Since the costs were covered by the social security fund, the enterprises could engage in creative accounting. Central wage regulations permitted them to hide the wages of those on sick leave or in the process of applying for disability pension. In this way they could create a considerable 'saving' from their yearly wages for a while, by counting such staff among their actual employees. That sum remained with the firm and could be used freely for increasing the earnings of those who really worked, without harming the strictly sanctioned rules which related only to their aggregate wage expenditures.

As time passed, the deliberate 'planning' of the annual average of those on social security (on maternity leave, on child care grant, on sick leave, etc.) had become an organic part of the employment and income policy of all the 'socialist' workplaces. 'Local' incentives (premiums, even temporary wage increases) were paid for from those planned savings, initiating both better productivity and the loyalty of the employees.

Second, social security not only helped and financed the local incentives but also offered utilizable channels for a more adaptive and more flexible use of the work force.

Since all the components of the production lay at the mercy of uncontrollable external conditions (ultimately driven by unforeseeable central political decisions), the simultaneous adaptation of the firm to fluctuating central demand and supply often had to face insurmountable difficulties. The oscillation of shortages, followed by a sudden overflow of raw materials, equipment, unmarketable products, etc., were the fundamental and continuous features of the socialist economies that the producers had to cope with, or, at least, mitigate somehow. The 'classical' means of firms' self-protection was the hoarding of all components (including the work force). That had led to tremendous wastages and could not be financed any more without facing the threat of bankruptcy amid the new circumstances of the reform.

However, manpower was an exceptional component since firms had to meet the preserved 'socialist' requirements of compulsory employment.

Social security helped here as a way out of the trap. The local costs of employment obligations could be reduced and better productivity could be attained on the level of the enterprise by sending the temporarily superfluous employees on sick leave, or negotiating their early retirement through the disability pension scheme. When they were needed once again, part-time employment (permitted only for those on social security, but strictly prohibited in the case of 'ordinary' employees) could be offered to them. They often returned to the same place, in the same position, doing just the same work (though with some relaxation in the time-schedule, conditions and duration) as before. In this way flexibility and a better adaptation to the market could be reached.

Third, all the ambiguous measures of the employers described above often matched the drives of the employees. As has been pointed out by several analyses (Kolosi, 1989; Farkas and Vajda, 1988; Szalai, 1991), there was a wide range of interests in attempting to reduce employees' contribution to the workplaces, while extending it in the second (informal) economy.

A mere 'material' or 'consumerist' explanation would be too simple here. True, the informal economy (based mainly on the co-operation of the extended family) offered the opportunity for an increase of household income, flexibly adjusted to varying needs. However, the silent struggle for autonomy, the slow elaboration of alternative paths for promotion and even for market-based, quasi-entrepreneurial routes of social mobility, people's search for self-respect to counteract the humiliating experiences of harsh exploitation and overt 'dictatorship' practised by their 'official' workplaces, etc., were equally important factors for those large groups of the society which became involved in informal production.

It should be emphasized, as probably the most significant and lasting outcome of those processes, that through the gradual expansion of informal production, people had started to build their lives on two pillars: one in the formal, and another in the informal sector. In this manner a new way of life spread in Hungarian society, and two distinct clusters of motivations came to dominate people's daily activities.

In other words, people's lives were determined by a simultaneous involvement in two contrasting sets of relationships: their formal social membership was dictated by the acceptance of subordination and 'wage-worker' behaviour, while their success and promotion depended on the strength of their entrepreneurial activities within the informal networks and non-institutionalized processes of the second economy. The combination of the two pillars and the co-existence of the two contrasting sets of relationships was helped and supported by the 'innovative' use of social security.

The case of rapidly expanding early retirement represents a clear example. In accordance with the international trends (though for markedly different reasons), people in Hungary tend to give up their employment (i.e. their participation on a full-time basis in the state-controlled spheres of the economy) some years earlier than the present regulations on retirement would suggest. (In recent years 19 per cent of all male pensioners have retired under the formal retirement age of 60.)

However, the increasing rate of early retirement does not mean that there has been an increasing rate of early withdrawal from work. On the contrary, the overwhelming majority of pensioners (both those who retired earlier, and those who did so at the 'ordinary' retirement age) work hard either in various 'branches' of the informal economy or in part-time employment in the formal economy to supplement their pensions, but usually (as was already mentioned) with much more flexibility and much better working conditions than they had before. It is important to understand that people's participation in full-time employment in the formal economy has been reduced for the sake of expanding their participation in work in both the informal economy and, on a part-time basis, the formal economy.

The data show that the economic performance of the inactive population (who are basically pensioners) has increased dramatically, and that is perhaps the most important change during the period in question. The calculations are based on the findings of the latest countrywide time-budget survey (1986), which also gives us an opportunity to follow the changes over time by comparing the information on participation rates and duration with the data of a similar survey run by the Central Statistical Office CSO in 1977 (CSO, 1987, 1990). The trends reveal very impressively how families have started to 'build' into their long-term strategies the stable existence and wide acceptance of the second economy, how they have started to plan and economize the work and participation of their members, tending to follow an optimal division between the two economies. That 'optimalization' was much supported, even subsidized, by the extensive take-up of the accessible benefits of social security.

To conclude, I have argued that the 'reinterpretations' of the functions of the social security system outlined above point in one direction. All the actors (employers and employees) gradually tended to utilize the social security funds and services as their own, thus developing behaviours, attitudes and mechanisms that prefigured a potential overt change in the existing property relations. Firms gained a degree of financial independence and individuals developed entrepreneurial skills.

That long-term hidden decomposition and erosion of the scheme has to be taken into account as an explanatory factor in understanding the contemporary heated debates around the future restructuring of social security.

The current controversy over social security

Several interest groups propose that the idea of the comprehensive and compulsory social security system should be dispensed with and replaced by a regulated network of enterprise-based insurance schemes. The proposition is especially popular among the 'new' entrepreneurs, and it is widely canvassed for by their chambers, associations and by the Entrepreneurs' Party. They argue that the present system is extremely expensive and wasteful; it works as a disincentive for capital investment and hits the new entrepreneurs, while it does not help the clients of the services. Firm-based insurance schemes would be much cheaper, and would also, in their view, express the mutual interests of employers and employees. With regard to the non-employed, the proponents of this view argue for 'targeted' welfare assistance and services for the poor, financed from taxation and run by the state.

Another proposal (pointing in the opposite direction) is the conversion of the contemporary state-dominated scheme to meaningful public ownership: social security should be run and controlled on a tripartite basis, representing the employers, the employees and the state. The idea is represented by the new free trade unions, and it is also outlined in the programmes of some of the new parties. Its most detailed elaboration can be found in the new crisis-management programme of the leading oppositional party, that is, the Federation of the Free Democrats (SZDSZ, 1991). With regard to the financing of the system, the relevant programmes demand a more just share of the contributions and argue that the social security scheme of the future should be a Western-type public investment fund. It should get a decent share from the as yet 'frozen' wealth of society, that is, by investing in the new properties emerging in the 'privatization' process (Kopátsy, 1990), and make benefits available to all.

The proposal of the present 'owner' of the social security scheme (i.e. the government) is rooted in the primary interest of reducing state expenditure and getting rid of a number of state responsibilities. The publicized ideas represent a typical compromise: the present scheme of social security should be divested of its (confused) functions: the 'classical', contribution-based tasks should be visibly separated from any social welfare function. The former should be met by the 'new' scheme, while the latter should be the obligation of separate special authorities. In concrete terms, the scheme should be converted to a national pension fund and a health insurance fund; all other services (i.e. support for families with children; aid for the handicapped or the disabled; services for the elderly, etc.) should be delivered through decentralized, community-based schemes, financed from (local and central) taxation, and complemented by a great variety of activities of charity organizations, voluntary non-profit agencies and associations, including the state-subsidized services of the church.

While the future outcome of the ongoing struggles is yet unclear, the actual latest developments in social security point toward potential lasting compromises between the strong interest groups at the expense of the most defenceless layers of society.

The recent cuts and restrictions to the state budget have been 'successfully' shifted, therefore, on to pensions, child care allowances, sick benefits, etc. which have not been inflation-proofed. The loss of their values has become an important factor in the rapid impoverishment of those living mainly from in-cash benefits: pensioners, families with dependant children, people who are chronically ill, etc. Those who retired in 1980 had to suffer a 25 to 30 per cent decrease of the purchasing power of their pensions by 1987. The loss was even more significant in case of widow or disability pensions. Another aspect of the same phenomenon was that some 60 per cent of the pensioners got a benefit below the officially declared pension minimum in 1989. In 1991 the per capita value of child benefits (calculated on constant prices) fell below the relevant values of 1988–9 (Book of Facts, 1990).

All these drastic changes were, of course, accompanied by the above-indicated new ideology of 'targeting'. The argument is well known from the history of social policy: since universal benefits do not diminish inequalities of take-up and access, there should be more concentration of the (scarce) resources on those really in need. Thus there have been significant cuts in public spendings in · the name of 'more just' social intervention. The outcome was an increase of social inequalities of take-up and of per capita incomes from benefits, while many of the poor dropped out of the benefit system altogether.

These unfavourable developments are, of course, not the 'inseparable' and 'automatic' by-products of marketization. I would argue that the worrying new trends of poverty are not the consequences of the market, as such, but are due to the lack of deliberate, protective and well-targeted social policy in the 'transition' period.

As I tried to demonstrate earlier in this chapter, marketization, even in its inconsistent form, has helped great masses in Hungarian society to gain some distance from and some self-protection against the actual crisis of the formal economy by building their lives (at least partly) on alternative pillars. That has helped them not only to compensate for the crisis, but even to build up ways of life and work that offer them future prospects.

Many of the restrictive interventions in the name of marketization, however, have led to the creation of a 'secondary part' of society. In an attempt to summarize the situation I would describe the most affected social groups as follows. They are mainly those who have based their lives and aspirations on the incentives, orientations and regulations of the past forty years of 'socialism'. Answering the challenge of industrialization, they moved to urban settlements; gave qualifications to their children that seemed to be favourably applicable in a 'socialist' economy; gave up their peasant roots and traditions by occupying the large closed housing estates built 'for them', etc. They are the very ones facing a high risk of unemployment today.

Many of them try to mobilize the 'general' protective strategies of the majority; they also have intensified their work in the second economy (though they have had access to probably the worst jobs in it) and tightened the informal network of the family by more regulated and 'targeted' internal redistribution. Daily experience shows, however, that those efforts more often fail than succeed. Their family circumstances and living conditions are too fragile to compensate for the lack of social protection. Without a parallel strengthening of the macro-social 'safety net', Hungarian society will fall apart. Serious symptoms of social disintegration indicate that the danger of a 'Third World' splitting of the social structure could be its fate in the near future. However, there is also, simultaneously a good chance for a more integrative development, depending on policies adopted. The coming years will show us whether our presently much propagated route really leads to Europe, or else leads us out of it.

Health care in the transition and after

This section of the chapter examines the impact on one of the services in kind that had been seriously eroded by the significant modifications of the structure of central state spending in favour of increased social security cash expenditure described earlier.

International comparison of long-term trends in life expectancy and mortality shows that there are not only quantitative differences between the advanced Western countries and Hungary, but that their trends have diverged from the mid-1960s onwards. At present, the life expectancy of males at birth is identical with the level of the late 1950s, and life expectancy at the age of 40 is no higher than it was in the late 1930s. From 1965 onwards the mortality rates have increased in every age group of males above the age of 15 (with the exception of the group above 80). As for women, from 1965 onwards the mortality rates of those between 40 and 60 have increased; from 1975 onwards increases also occurred in the 30–40 age group. This diverging trend is accompanied in Hungary by growing social and regional inequalities. Deterioration of the population's health status and increasing inequality in health must be understood as a part of the exploitation of human and natural resources by the state-socialist political and economic system. Moreover, the process feeds on itself: the grave social and health problems now constitute serious obstacles to building a more flexible and more efficient economy.

The near future is rather distressing – increasing poverty and unemployment are likely to lead to further deterioration in health status and further increase in health inequalities. Hungary is in urgent need of an adequate and feasible social and health policy. However, no single actor has as its primary concern the deteriorating health status of the Hungarian population. Rather, the state is primarily interested in reducing expenditures, and health care providers in serving the highest possible number of patients. Meanwhile, wide strata of the population struggle to maintain their living standards, at the expense of their health.

In 1989 Hungary spent about 5.1 per cent of its GDP on health care, of which 80.4 per cent was public expenditures. At first glance, it could be stated that Hungary is at the same level as the less developed – that is, the comparable – Western countries (e.g. Greece or Portugal). However, the comparison of the trends of health expenditures (instead of their present levels) highlights the fundamental differences.

Between the early 1960s and the mid-1970s, Western European countries experienced an expansional phase: in the period of economic prosperity, health care expenditures increased between 40 and 60 per cent faster than the GDP. It made possible the modernization of the health care system, beginning with the hospital infrastructure, extension of insurance coverage, etc. The Hungarian health care system, however, has never experienced a similar period of expansion. During the 1960s and the 1970s the share of health expenditure in the GDP stagnated (around 3–3.5 per cent of the GDP) – the modernization of the health care infrastructure failed to be realized. Moreover, the utilization of the available scant resources has been inefficient. A conclusion can be drawn that the main problem of the Hungarian health care system is not the present level of its expenditures (in terms of percentage of the GDP) but the failure to investment in the period of the 1960s and 1970s. This was the period when the expanding social security fund drained money from other areas.

Table 6.1 summarizes the main features of the state-socialist health care system and at the same time shows the main problems to be addressed by the reform. In the light of this summary, it becomes apparent that the overhaul of the health care system must embrace every component: policy-making, ownership, financing, management, service structure, patient's rights, medical education, etc.

The dual system of Hungarian health care
The phenomenon of gratitude money has a key role in enabling us to understand the Hungarian health care system. In Hungary health care is only officially and theoretically free. In fact, the majority of the patients give so-called gratitude money to the GPs as well as to the doctors in the hospitals. As a consequence, Hungarian health care has a dual system: a shadow health care, similar to the shadow, or black, economy, functioning according to different rules, has evolved beside the official health care. The phenomenon of gratitude money can be interpreted as a tacit contract between politicians, doctors and society. The doctors accepted the centralized bureaucratic management, and they also accepted a constant relative decrease of their official salary, in return for gratitude money which was several times the amount of the official salary in

Table 6.1 *Main features of the state-socialist health care system*

Distribution of power in the health care system	Exclusiveness of state control (lack of autonomy of other agents of the health care system); total lack of lay control
Nature of the relationship between the main agents of the health care system	Bargaining for individual advantages through unregulated processes
Ownership	Exclusiveness of state ownership (facilities run but not owned by intermediate and local councils)
Institutional system	A system built downwards from the top (health departments of low independence within the public administration, under strong state control)
Decision-making (e.g. distribution of resources)	Distribution of central orders according to central plans
Financing	Scarcity of resources; only from central state revenues; lack of incentives for rational use of resources; distorted by gratitude money
Habit of mind of central bureaucracy	Sole representatives of so-called general interests and expertise (paternalism)
Position of physicians	Employed by the state; low-paid (monthly salary)
Nature of medicine	Western-style, cure-centred, coupled with low level of health technology
Service structure	Unified service structure (regardless of differentiated social and spatial circumstances); hospital-centred; overshadowed primary care
Experience of patients	Imposed; lack of free choice of physicians
Lay participation	Total lack

the case of considerable layers of doctors. For a long time the patients have been under the impression that adequate treatment is available only for gratitude money.

The relationships of suppliers of services and the consumers are actually governed by this distorted market relationship. Gratitude money creates an interest similar to that of the fee-for-service remuneration. The doctors are interested in an increasing number of patients and in a growing quantity of services and not in health promotion. The 'taken for granted' practice of gratitude money is a grave barrier against any reform. While the shortages and the overcrowded facilities hinder the work of doctors as healers, as individuals many groups of doctors have a vested interest in maintaining this system. The established practice of what amounts to a fee-for-service system also shapes the nature of proposed reforms.

The reform proposals of the Ministry of Welfare
The government and its Ministry of Welfare have not yet accepted an elaborated proposal for the reorganization of the health care system. A study of the 'National Renewal Programme' issued in September 1990 (which contained only very general aims) and articles by and interviews with leaders of the Ministry and the Social Insurance Institute suggests that the following goals seem to be given the greatest emphasis:

* transformation of the state budget-based financing into a financing through insurance;
* encouraging private provision of health care;
* encouraging efficient use of resources by means of:
  * reimbursement of physicians based on productivity,
  * a new method of hospital reimbursement,
  * a new management system for hospitals;
* free choice of physicians;
* making primary care the real basis of health care delivery;
* reform of medical education.

The basic features of the state-socialist health care system justify the importance of these goals. However, the experience of 1990–1 shows that there are great differences between health policy rhetoric and the reality, concrete measures designed to achieve the declared goals seem highly questionable, and fundamental issues are ignored.

Health policy rhetoric is about a comprehensive reorganization of the health care system. In fact, the actual endeavours narrow down to changes to the reimbursement methods of doctors and hospitals. For example, there is no sign of any intention to develop adequate regulations regarding investments in new technology, nor to develop methods for the assessment of medical technology.

Despite the agreement on general goals, disagreement necessarily appears if we ask how these are to be attained. The possible alternatives and feasible means have not yet been clarified. In the case of the proposal for insurance it is not clear what should be the main features of the compulsory insurance; whether everybody or only certain groups should be the insured; whether only basic services or as wide as possible a range of services should be covered by the compulsory insurance; or what kind of institutional system of compulsory insurance should be established. Equally, if we ask how it is intended to eliminate the exclusive role of the state in financing and service provision, the answer is not yet clear. The new actors may be the compulsory and private insurance funds, the managers of hospitals, local government and the lay representatives of the communities. The share of power different actors should have in the future system is not resolved or even overtly discussed.

The reform process in practice
Uncertainty is pervasive. Proposals have been changed monthly by the Ministry and the Social Insurance Institute. Partial information filters out and becomes distorted, producing many absurd answers to particular questions. Doctors and nurses are uncertain as to the future of their jobs. Among the population disquieting rumours are spreading that patients will have to pay the total costs of everything.

A chaotic property situation evolved during 1990–1. The law on local government passed in October 1990 declared local governments to be the owners of health facilities but the concrete regulations necessary to make use of property rights have not been issued. Meanwhile the churches claim back their previous property including buildings where hospitals – owned by local governments – are functioning. The Act on the Property of the Churches might paralyse the activity of local governments. Foreign investors are appearing on the scene. The Ministry, however, does not seem to try to formulate any policy or regulation in regard to operation of foreign capital in the health care market. Uncertainty might be a 'bad decision-maker' – it might prepare the way for the acceptance of ill-considered proposals. On the other hand, it might give a free hand to the government, or, more precisely, the secret and uncontrolled bargaining between the Ministry of Welfare, the Social Insurance Institute and the Ministry of Finance might decide every important issue. In this battle short-term political interests and power relations play a more decisive role than considerations of the requirements of a workable health care system, let alone the improvements of the population's health status.

Trying to wipe out every value professed by state-socialism, the new regime is not able to distinguish between values 'abused' (merely declared and not met) by state-socialism and their intrinsic features. This is connected with the misconception of the failure of state-socialist health care system. A telling example is the current main slogan that 'health care will not be the citizen's right any more'. Health policy-makers declare it as an outstanding achievement which we should be extremely proud of. They don't add any further explanations to this slogan – it should be obvious to the public that it is the key to the best ever health care system. This slogan keeps being re-echoed in the media. By writing in these terms I commit a 'blasphemy' by asking what kind of results can we expect from the 'jettisoning' of citizen's right for health care? Is there any relationship between an efficient way of financing the service and the issue of whether health care is a citizen's right or not? It must be stressed that, in fact, this slogan (elimination of the citizen's right) is the only certain point the public know about the health care reform. The rhetoric that the citizen's right was the 'cause of every problem' is interrelated with the failure to realize that the crux of the reform is really the nexus between 'third party payer' and the providers. Furthermore, the health policy-makers have the misconception that the citizen's right and financing through compulsory insurance are irreconcilable.

According to the bill on the amendment of the 1975 Social Security Act – which is before the parliament – some of the most disadvantaged groups are likely to be left out of the compulsory health insurance. For example it is proposed that those who receive unemployment benefit are to be entitled to health insurance, but when their unemployment benefit expires they might become uninsured.

Misconception of the failure of the state-socialist health care system, a 'deaf ear' to the lessons from the Western European countries, 'over-ideologized' ways of thinking, are preparing the ground for a search for panaceas as the reform proposals unfold. 'Reimbursement proportional to productivity' is the main panacea in terms of paying the doctor. It is not clear what is meant by productivity. A majority of physicians think that the more services they provide the more money they will earn from the insurance. More services is thought to be equal with more productivity and better outcome. It is a 'blasphemy' to ask whether it is really the case that the more services that are provided, the greater is the benefit to the patient.

An intrinsic feature of the state-socialist health care system was the lack of institutions and regulated mechanisms which could permit the interests of the main actors to be adequately expressed and reconciled, that is, the lack of frameworks of consensus-making. Changes in the political system as a whole have not entailed changes in policy-making processes within the health care sector. Proposals continue to be worked out without the real involvement of the representatives of the main actors concerned. Furthermore, there is no sign that the Ministry would intend to create a new way of policy-making. Just the contrary, the Ministry seems to consider itself the sole competent body. To put it more precisely, decisions and proposals are the results of the 'power game', the behind the scenes struggle between the Ministry of Welfare, Social Insurance

Institute and the Ministry of Finance. Decision-makers have not become aware that a necessary (but not sufficient) precondition of the success of any reform is to make the actors involved – that is, to reform the process of the reform itself. In this sense, Hungarians are captives of the former political system.

The situation, however, is even more confused. The inheritance of state-socialism means also the weakness of organizations representing the main actors of the health care system. A Medical Chamber was established in late 1988, but so far it has been obsessed with inner struggles. Moreover, the physicians are deeply divided. This is shown by the establishment of the Christian Medical Chamber in early 1991. Proliferating trade unions are divided and disorganized – the old and new ones are fighting each other as are the different new ones among themselves. There is a proliferation of local government associations – hence assertion of their joint interests against the central government seems impossible. Consequently, the different interests are not formulated, or represented adequately – which is the main (although not the only) obstacle to the promulgation and implementation of an adequate health reform proposal.

Notes

1. The new government is established on the basis of a coalition of three parties: the Hungarian Democratic Forum (165 seats out of the 386 in the parliament), the Smallholders' Party (44 seats) and the Christian Democratic Party (21 seats). It characterizes itself as the trustee of 'national' and 'universal Christian' values. It has a centre–right-wing orientation.

2. The inaccurate concept is meant to embrace all the property transforming activities, regardless of whether the potential owner is (will be) a private person or a collective, and whether the form of the ownership can be related to designated individuals at all. The word 'privatization' is used more and more as a synonym for all kinds of changes in property relations.

3. The phrases 'public infrastructure', 'non-productive spheres of the economy', 'institutions and services of public consumption', 'funds of social benefits', have been used in the literature to refer to the same segment of the 'socialist' economy (since questions of control and property had no significance amid the actual conditions of all-embracing statism). I have kept that tradition, and use them mostly as synonyms in this chapter. When any particular phrase has importance in the context of the analysis, I will describe it more accurately.

4. The scope of this part of the chapter does not permit a detailed analysis of those antecedents. It has to be pointed out, however, that those reforms were the first experiments in the history of East Central European 'socialism' to combine 'planning' and the 'market', though without any accompanying social and political reforms at that time.

5. The key to a full understanding of the surprising achievements can be found in the deeply rooted socio-historical drives of Hungarian society to accomplish the once

interrupted embourgeoisement process through the re-opened pathways after the mid-sixties (Szalai, 1990).

6. The most important was the introduction of the child care grant in 1967. (The grant initially was a job-protected, flat-rate benefit helping mothers to stay at home with their babies until the age of three.) The scheme was modified in 1985 by introducing the earnings-related child-care fee, which can be taken up for the first two years after childbirth, while the original grant was preserved to extend the mother's (or the father's) temporary exit from employment for the third year.

References

Book of Facts (1990) Budapest: Ràció Publishing House.

Central Statistical Office (1964–88) *Statistical Yearbook*. Budapest: CSO.

Central Statistical Office (1968, 1978, 1989) *Income Surveys of the Years 1967, 1977 and 1987*. Budapest: CSO.

Central Statistical Office (1987) *Time-Budget: Changes in the Way of Life of Hungarian Society According to the Time-Budget Surveys of Spring 1977 and Spring 1986*. Budapest: CSO.

Central Statistical Office (1990) *Changes of the Way of Life of the Hungarian Society*. Budapest: CSO–Institute of Sociology.

Farkas, J. and Vajda, A. (1988) 'The second economy of housing', in J. Szalai, et al. (eds), *The 'Hungarian Harvest'*. Budapest: Institute of Sociology.

Kolosi, T. (1989) *Inequalities in the 1980s*, Budapest: TARKI.

Kopátsy, S. (1990) 'On the funding of social security'. Manuscript, Budapest.

Programme of the Government (1990) *The Rebirth of the Nation*, Budapest.

Szalai, J. (1990) 'Social crisis and the alternatives for reform', in L. Gabor and A. Toth (eds), *Research Review No. 3*. Budapest: Institute of Social Studies.

Szalai, J. (1991) 'Early exit from employment in Hungary', in M. Kohl and M. Rein (eds), *Time for Retirement*. New York: Cambridge University Press (forthcoming).

SZDSZ Programme of the Federation of the Free Democrats (1991) Budapest: SZDSZ.

Vajda, A. (1991) 'The prefiguration of privatization'. Manuscript, Budapest.

7

The Future of Social Policy in Eastern Europe

Bob Deacon

In this chapter we summarize the main trends in the development of social policy in Eastern Europe at the beginning of the transition to market economies. We will note the diversity of developments as well as the commonalities and reflect how the issues of social policy in transition set out in Chapter 1 are being handled in practice. Within the framework set out in Chapter 1 we shall also make initial and cautious predictions about the type of welfare regimes that are likely to emerge over the next few years. We do this not so much in the spirit of confidence that we have got it right, rather in the spirit of creating a framework within which students of the social policy of Eastern European and the several countries of the former Soviet Union might analyse developments as they actually unfold in the 1990s. The actual developments in policy over the next years will continue to provide evidence for testing and modifying existing theories of welfare state diversity and development. We also add certain evaluative comments where we judge recent social policy developments against the criteria for evaluation established in the first chapter. In drawing the threads of the book together we also include material from other countries that we have not systematically reported on in this volume; notably Yugoslavia and its successor states and Romania.

A final section of this chapter addresses the question that will be of interest to those who wonder what the implications of the collapse of communism in Eastern Europe and the Soviet Union are for any future attempt to imagine and construct a socialist social policy. We will argue that in the struggle between capitalist welfare and socialist welfare it is not that capitalist welfare won, but rather that for any foreseeable future the struggle for socialist welfare will take place within diverse types of capitalist society.

Social policy in transition: commonalities and diverse developments

From the accounts given in Chapters 2 to 6 describing recent developments in the former Soviet Union, Bulgaria, Czechoslovakia, Poland and Hungary it is evident that with varying degrees of speed and conviction all the countries of Eastern Europe and, trailing behind, the former Soviet Union are trying to replace their centralized command economies and their one-party political systems with economies governed by the rules of the market and by political systems that provide for a degree of democracy. This is having an immediate, and in some cases dramatic, impact upon social conditions across the region. Unemployment is being created and made explicit where previously it was hidden. Inflation, often initially very rapid, is eroding living standards that were already low. The removal of subsidy has led to the rocketing of rents. Previously inefficient and under-provided medical care establishments have found themselves unable to operate in the new cost-accounting frameworks imposed upon them and some have closed. Some educational institutions, particularly the Academies of Science, find themselves in a similar situation. Women's child care support systems and other rights and entitlements to, for example, free abortion services may be under threat. Ethnic minorities, while gaining the freedom to organize autonomously, find that the same freedom gives rise to increased expressions of racism and the intolerance of minorities. Foreign workers are being repatriated. There have been examples, however, of positive progress in cultural autonomy: Bulgarian Turks have regained their names, while Hungarians in Romania can learn in their mother tongue.

Table 7.1 summarizes some of the indicators that measure the immediate impact of the period of transition on the well-being of the population. It should be noted that in some countries, such as Poland and Hungary, price rises and the consequent decline in living standards began with the 'shock therapy' early in 1990. Other countries, such as Czechoslovakia, Bulgaria and Romania, only entered this phase in 1991. Russia and the other republics began to do so in January 1992 and the new Albanian government has yet to make decisions. An overall decline in living standards of around 30 per cent and an increase in unemployment to 10 per cent or more appears to be the price for transition from communism to capitalism in the short term. With the loss of the Soviet market the unemployment figures for Eastern Europe might reach 20 per cent in 1992 according to some analysts. A further reduction in Russian living standards can be predicted.

Commonalities of social policy initiatives
In response to the legacy of social problems of the past, and in recognition of the need to develop social policies that both facilitate the move to marketization yet compensate those who are paying the

Table 7.1 *The well-being of the population in the period of transition*

	Unemployment (as % of labour force)		Decline in living standards		Key price increases consequent upon free market or regulated change[a]		
	1990 (highest recorded)	1991 (highest recorded)	Date	% p.a.	Date	Commodity	% increase
Bulgaria	0.8	12.9	end 1991	30	Jan. 1991	Bread	600
						Food	700
Czechoslovakia	0.7	6.0	end 1991	20	Jan. 1991	(Details unavailable)	
Hungary	1.7	9.0	end 1990	20	Jan. 1990	Food	38
						Rents	35
						Mortgages	50–100
					Jan. 1991	Bread	38
						Milk	20
Poland	7.5	12.0	end 1990	30	Jan. 1990	Bread	38
						Meat	55
						Electricity	300
Romania	2.0	10.0	end 1991	30	Nov. 1990	Some goods	100
					Apr. 1991	Bread and meat	100
Soviet Union and successor states	n.a.	6.0	end 1991	30	Apr. 1991	Most goods	66
					Jan. 1992	Most goods	300

[a] It should be noted that in some countries, notably Bulgaria, Romania and the former Soviet Union, free market or regulated price rises were initially accompanied by percentage compensation to some workers and welfare beneficiaries. For details see text and Table 7.2.

Source: Newspaper reports and government sources

highest price for this, each of the governments of Eastern Europe are developing initial policy responses that are broadly similar. These measures and their immediate consequences include the following:

- *Ad hoc* development of services and benefits for the new unemployed. Introduction of variable measures to compensate social security recipients and employees for rapid inflation.
- Appeals to philanthropy and voluntary effort to fill gaps left by withdrawal of state services.
- Rapid removal of subsidies on many goods and services, including housing, often with limited anticipation of social consquences.
- Limited initial privatization of some health and social care services, with indications that this may speed up. Encouragement of private house building.
- Encouragement of independent social initiatives in the sphere of social care but with evident differential capacity of citizens to initiate and participate in these.
- De-secularization of education and pluralization of control over schools and colleges.
- Erosion of women's rights to some child care benefits and services and free legal abortions, although the final outcome of debate on these issues is not yet clear.
- Deconstruction of the state social security system in favour of fully funded social insurance funds often differentiated by categories of worker.
- Abolition of many health and recreational facilities provided by firms for their employees and/or their conversion into local community or private facilities.
- Ending of privileged access by virtue of nomenklatura status of old party-state apparatus to special clinics and services.
- Increase of local community control over local social provision but in an impoverished context where the state does not provide enough resources and the local authority has not yet established its own tax base.
- Shift in the nature of social inequalities in use of and access to social provision from those based on bureaucratic/political privilege to those based on market relations.

Table 7.2 summarizes some of the measures described in the preceding chapters. Policy and provision is changing often by the month in some countries in this period of transition. The table is a snapshot of a moving picture, the details of which will quickly change.

In the related fields of unemployment benefit, retraining provision and compensation for price rises consequent upon the move to marketization there are several points to note. There is diversity between countries ranging from those, like Russia, where measures to compensate the unemployed have hardly begun, to those, like Poland, where detailed schemes are now in operation. Even here, however, it must be noted that the provision, for example, for labour exchanges and retraining is often purely academic as the network of offices is only just being set up and provision is patchy and underfunded. Bulgaria, at least on paper, stands out with an exceptionally generous unemployment benefit scheme which, however, may not work in practice, or, if it does, will surely limit the drive to market efficiency. There is also a broad distinction to be drawn between those countries like the Soviet Union, Bulgaria and and Romania (the latter not shown in the table) where initial price rises were being systematically compensated for in the case of both workers and welfare beneficiaries by agreements struck or regulations about wages and prices promulgated at a national level and those countries like Poland where no such all-embracing wage compensation exists. For those dependent on state benefits (pensioners, the ill, children) the compensation situation is patchy and variable. Compensation tied to wage levels as in Poland means these categories share in the falling living standards. In Czechoslovakia compensation or valorization seems to be tied to price rises, which is preferable. By January 1992 it appeared that the systematic attempts at social compensation in the former Soviet Union and Bulgaria were being abandoned as the scale of the economic crisis made such policies unviable and the post-communist conservative corporatist governments gave way to ones more committed to shock therapy.

Housing policy, it is becoming clear, seems to be taking the same direction in all of the countries, but with the ex-Soviet republics, Bulgaria and Romania adopting initially their distinctive pace. The goal, certainly in Poland and Hungary and to a large extent in Czechoslovakia, and probably to be followed elsewhere eventually, is the removal of state subsidy on rent and mortgages over a three-year period and their replacement by specific targeted housing or equivalent benefits for those who cannot afford to pay. There are differences between countries on what is regarded as a reasonable percentage of family income to be spent on housing costs: Poland thinks 8 per cent (including heating and lighting), Hungary prefers 20 per cent. In Hungary whole categories of persons, such as pensioners, are excluded from rent rises. The other arm of the policy is to privatize building and construction and to sell off to

Table 7.2   *Recent social policy measures*

	Unemployment benefit	Retraining measures	Price rise compensation measures
Bulgaria	Benefit at 80% of previous earnings. Years of work and age generate length of entitlement. Men over 50 with 20 years' work entitled to 10-year benefit.	Being given priority.	Wages raised by inflation every 6 and monthly if in exceeds 10%. Be similarly protecte October 1991 government unlik maintain this pol
Czechoslovakia	Benefit at 60% of past earnings for one year. Small earnings allowed in addition. Means tested after one year. Benefit of 75% conditional on accepting retraining.	Benefits during retraining. Enterprise start-up allowances available.	Minimum wages. cash benefit for a Benefit levels tie price rises every quarter.
Hungary	Benefit level 70% of previous unindexed earnings for first half of entitlement, falling to 50% for second. Period of benefit related to contribution. One year earns 180 days. Four years earns maximum of 2 years.	Retraining schemes being developed. Enterprise lump sum worth 2 years' benefit available.	No systematic po wages. Benefit le inflation related. Independent soc security fund bei established.
Poland	Benefit levels are 70% past earnings for 3 months, 50% for next 6, 40% subsequently. Maximum benefit is average public sector wage. Minimum benefit is minimum wage. Registration for work obligatory. Disqualified if refuse 2 jobs or retraining or public works programme.	Six or twelve months' training at 80% previous earnings. 100% if redundant. Training allowance 125% min. wage if have not previously worked. Business start-up loans.	Measures empha prevention of m compensatory w claims. Pensions benefit levels tie falling real wage SOS voluntary f established.
Soviet Union and successor states	Not yet officially acknowledged, but minimal short-term benefit available for those 'between jobs'.	1991: 'all redundant workers being found new employment or retrained on full wages'. Policy will change in 1992.	1991 60% price compensated at level for pension students, low-wa families. Pension minimum wage 1992 300% price compensated by wage and benefi increases.

Housing policy	Medical care policy	Education policy
–	Retention of state service. Encouragement of private provision. Doctors' salaries raised.	–
Subsidy reduction in stages. Marketization of new houses. New supplementary benefit for those unable to meet higher housing costs.	Retention of state service but cost accounting. Private initiatives and church provision allowed 'under local government control'. Shift to insurance funding by 1993?	Retention of state schooling but private and religious schools now allowed.
Staged reduction of rent and mortgage subsidy. Mortgage payments raised by 100% or 50% depending on whether more than 10-year-old loan. Rents can't exceed 20% family income. Pensioners excluded from rent rises. Sale of state flats to tenants.	Retention of state service. Insurance funding planned. Private facilities encouraged.	Diversification of forms of state schooling. Religious schools allowed.
Staged reduction of rent subsidy. Tenants to meet real housing costs by 1993. Benefits available for families where rent exceeds 8% of family budget. Privatization of house building.	Initial retention of state services but cost accounting closed some services. New charges for some services and drugs. Private sector envisaged eventually.	Retention of state schooling but private schools now allowed. Introduction of religious education (optional) by priests into schools being contested.
Rents, in 1991 3% household costs, not yet raised despite cost accounting decrees. Tenants right to buy (in Moscow) not being implemented. Policy will change in 1992.	Some cost accounting in some authorities. Major anti-alcohol campaign.	Attempts to shift from too much academic education to more vocational training.

(Data compiled in December 1991)

sitting tenants the rented state sector. The development of the second of these policies would seem to depend on the capacity of the tenant to purchase.

In medical care and education policy there is, not surprisingly, a much greater intention, at least in the short term, to retain a large state stake in policy and provision. There are moves towards cost accounting, which is leading to closures, and towards allowing private health and educational facilities to be developed alongside the state sector. Religious organizations are being allowed an increased influence over both medical care institutions and policy and educational institutions and policy. Religious education is returning both as a separate provision and as a part of the curiculum in all schools. Catholic influence to change the previously freely available abortion provision is beginning to be felt. The salaries of doctors and teachers are being raised everywhere.

There are important features of policy that do not show up in the table. There is pressure to increase the pension age in Hungary and Bulgaria. In both it stood at 55 for women and 60 for men. The cost is regarded as too high. On the other hand, increasing unemployment may lead to a countervailing pressure. Indeed the new law in Bulgaria effectively lowers the age to 52 or 57, provided 25 years' work has been completed.

The existing often generous provision of child care grants and allowances for women are under discussion. It is too early to say whether these will be eroded or whether again the countervailing pressures of reducing the unemployment total by removing women from the figures of the unemployed will work in the opposite direction. Certainly in Poland when women registered for the new unemployment benefit the law was rapidly changed to disqualify from receipt of benefit those who had not worked for at least six weeks in the previous twelve months. The likely outcome is the continuation of grants and allowances for the early years of motherhood but the removal of the right to return to work without loss of status and salary. In Hungary this right was abolished in July 1991.

New services for the care of dependants and for the alleviation of new poverty and for coping with increasing homelessness and destitution are being developed within local areas in many of the countries. Often these are new voluntary initiatives. They exist, however, within or alongside presently underfunded, ill-organized local social welfare or social aid services. A large part of the social costs of transition appears to be being placed at the doors of local agencies who themselves are impoverished because of the new rigours of cost accounting. It is evident that in the short term they are often not coping.

Diversity in responses to issues of the social policy of transition

We now turn to a review of these recent developments in terms of some of the issues of transition raised in Chapter 1.

Two issues that we felt would be most pressing were the development of a new acceptable conception of social justice appropriate to market economies, and the facilitating of an active civil society capable of managing its own welfare affairs. This issue of civil society encompassed the question as to whether all or only some society members were going to be able to and/or permitted to be incorporated into active social participation. The questions of women's social, economic and political rights and the rights of ethnic or racialized minorities are encompassed in this concern. In reviewing the preceding chapters in this context, the diversity of social policy developments will come more sharply into focus.

A sharp distinction can be drawn between those countries like Poland and Hungary on the one hand and Bulgaria and the former Soviet Union on the other. Poland and Hungary from the outset were willing to let the new market determine prices and shape the new social inequalities and to trust to popular opinion coming to terms with initial impoverishment in the hope of improved standards for all emerging eventually. Bulgaria and the Soviet Union, certainly before the failed coup of August 1991, continued to operate much more in the style of the old regimes and regulate price changes by decree and compensate significantly sections of the population for the consequences of these price rises. In other words, there appeared to be, at least initially, a continued commitment to socialist egalitarian sentiments and values in certain countries which tried to juggle these in the context of the pressures to marketize. In others the old ideology was more readily abandoned in favour of the language and policies appropriate to emerging capitalist societies. At the time of writing (January 1992) it does now appear that Bulgaria and the countries of the former Soviet Union are abandoning the juggling in favour of shock therapy measures.

Czechoslovakia represents a modification of these two approaches. The debate and struggle within the Civic Forum and now between its two wings exemplified by the divergent positions of the Minister of Finance and the Minister of Labour and Social Affairs signals not so much a struggle between new liberal marketeers and old-guard communist regulators as a debate between two different views as to how best to develop a humane and just welfare capitalism. The issue here is how far there should be social regulations of markets in line with conventions of social democracy. These debates are also taking place within the Hungarian and Polish context and will probably eventually emerge within social and economic policy discourse in Bulgaria and the countries of the former Soviet Union, but they are not yet so sharply focused as in Czechoslovakia.

In terms of the viability of emergent civil societies and the policies of government to empower sections of society to participate in the new democracies, the diversity between countries is drawn differently. The contribution of Julia Szalai to the Hungarian chapter clearly articulates the case for Hungarian exceptionalism here. Under the social compromise established by János Kádár in 1956 and aided by the development of social security policy subsequently, an organic development of a bourgeois section of society took place. The issue in Hungary is only whether the other half of society that put its trust in the paternalistic 'socialist' state can be empowered to participate as citizens in the new order. There is little sign that the government is actively developing policy with this goal in mind. Local agencies of policy and provision that might facilitate this are impoverished. A passive reliance on new, albeit liberal, city and town bosses might be emerging in lieu of an active community politics, although there are signs of this too.

A rather different case is, in effect, put in the Czechoslovakia chapter for considering Czechoslovakia, or at least part of it, as being ready to extend the impetus of the Round Table days of the Civic Forum into an active community and local social politics of the future. The combination of pre-war social democratic politics and the recent mass character of the 1989 events are important here. The 'shock' of marketization appears to have had less impact. Elements of the government's social policy are also directed to the end of the empowerment of citizens.

In Bulgaria and the countries of the former Soviet Union the slow ripening of civil society under the edifices of state power has hardly begun. The democratic movements in both countries are emerging but to date the old habits of doing political business between the corporate interests of the nomenklatura, its successor enterprise managers and the workers' representatives die hard. There is a time lag and cultural lag of considerable dimension between these countries and the others. Romania, Albania and parts of Yugoslavia (Serbia) fall into this category also. After the failed coup of August 1991 and the subsequent collapse of the union the scope for the emergence of civil society in the former Soviet Union may be greater and will develop at differential speeds between republics.

Poland represents a different picture. Despite the earlier years of the mass-participation Solidarity movement, the prevailing mood described in the chapter by Frances Millard is one of collective, resigned, passive depression. Calls by the Ministry of Labour and Social Affairs for philanthropic and mutual aid civil activities seem to fall on deaf ears. Between those who cling to resigned dependence on the old state structures and the few aggressive competitors in the new market business there is a vacuum where an energetic civil society should be. The oppositional politics of Solidarity have not given way, unlike in Czechoslovakia, to an active participation in the new social and political affairs. The shock therapy of marketization has indeed been experienced as shocking and fed this sense of helplessness. The Catholic Church provides an exception to this inactivity and is a mobilizing vehicle for social solidarity of a particular kind. We discuss further the prognosis for the Polish regime in the light of these considerations in the next section of the chapter.

Within the context of this diverse picture of emergent or non-emergent civil societies the part played by ethnic diversity is important. The extent to which policies of assimilation give way first to multiculturalism and then to a self critical anti-racism on the part of the majority population can be taken as a measure of the flourishing of a non-exclusionary civil society. The desirable goal of a positive encouragement of diversity and difference with policies that empower religious and ethnic minorities is far from being reached across Eastern Europe. While the right to the autonomous articulation of social needs is being granted to, or at least taken by, minority populations of Gypsies everywhere, Hungarians in Romania, Turks in Bulgaria, Slovaks in Czechoslovakia, it is far from clear that this is positively welcomed and encouraged by national social policies. Within the countries of the former Soviet Union there is the paradoxical development whereby several republics now asserting their independence after the collapse of the union, are actively repressing the rights of minorities which had been granted the status of autonomous regions within those republics by Lenin's Bolsheviks. National self-consciousness still has the capacity within Eastern Europe to feed repressive discrimination and authoritarian policies, and, of course, has fuelled the war between Serbia and Croatia. Economic stagnation and the further growth of unemployment may yet add further impetus. The international dimensions within Europe of these developments have yet to be played out, with the prospect of a Mexican border replacing the Iron Curtain as dispossessed minorities from the East try to find economic security and acceptance in the West.

Emerging worlds of welfare

In Chapter 1 we concluded that, despite various limitations, the three-fold typology of Esping-Andersen (1990), in which he described three distinct worlds of welfare capitalism, was a useful one for analytic purposes. His liberal, conservative corporatist and social democratic regime types were distinguished on a number of grounds. These included the degree of *de-commodification* of social policy and provision. This measures the extent of citizenship entitlement to services independent of price or insurance contribution or work record. A second criteria was concerned with the *distributional* impact of policy. Regime types either generated inequalities, maintained ordered inequality or redistributed cash and services in a correction of market-generated inequality. The third criteria related to the *state/market mix of agencies* of provision as exemplified by pension schemes. How did the old, pre-1989, system of bureaucratic state collectivism and how do the newly emerging sets of policy and provision measure up against these considerations?

The old system was highly de-commodified, although benefits were dependent on work record; it had a particular and unique impact on distribution in that it combined explicit and open redistributive and egalitarian practices characteristic of social democratic regime types with implicit and hidden conservative corporatist arrangements to protect the privileged position of the party-state apparatus; and its pension system was a state system, but a state system with built-in social differentiation in terms of entitlement.

The new system, ignoring for the moment the divergencies, is being shaped precisely by its reaction to the perceived failures of the old system. Thus, in very general terms, we can say that the new system is and will become highly commodified, will generate a new system of inequalities and will place far greater reliance on the marketplace for pensions and other provisions. The commodification and marketplace features are evident from the summary of developments just given and require less discussion. On these two counts liberal welfare state regime type characteristics are emerging. The market and, perhaps to a lesser extent, private property extending into the welfare sphere have been seen by all social groups as the requirements for economic and social development. State services have been experienced as inefficient and inadequate and often as oppressive totalitarian impositions, and this is leading to their erosion. The alternative conceptualization of a public responsibility for the welfare of the poor with provision of a more enabling and less oppressive kind has been overshadowed initially by the perceived need for everyone to learn how to thrive on their own initiative. So far the emerging disquiet of the working class with some of the negative consequences of marketization and privatization has not found articulation in a new strategy for welfare that is neither the return to 'communist' statism nor the embrace of 'liberal market capitalism'. Formulations like 'workers' capitalism' and 'market socialism' have not been translated into political strategies and programmes, although, in practice, given the slow pace of actual privatization, a type of market socialism could be said to exist by default at the initial stage of transition.

The second feature concerning the distributional impact of new policies requires more extensive discussion. There is an evident political and social tension between, on the one hand, liberating and generating new social inequalities which are increasingly perceived, despite the continued legacy and attractiveness for some of egalitarianism sentiments, as necessary for efficient economic development, and, on the other hand, maintaining the privileged position of the threatened nomenklatura. The matter is further complicated by the existence of a third system of inequality based upon pre-communist property and land relations (Wnuk-Lipinski, 1992). Different ideologies of justice applied to all three systems of inequality. To the extent that the nomenklatura are able successfully to convert themselves into capitalist owners and entrepreneurs, and there is some evidence that this is happening, then their interests and perhaps some of the interests of the old capitalist class where it exists may be served by liberal capitalist welfare policy. *To the extent that this is difficult or not desired by them, then we may be witnessing in some countries the emergence of a modified form of conservative corporatism in which a 'deal' is struck between some elements of the old nomenklatura and some elements of the working class to modify the free play of market forces, at the price of less economic growth, in order to secure a greater degree of state protection for both nomenklatura and skilled worker.* Bulgaria and Romania seemed initially to be taking this path, followed by the Soviet Union and parts of Yugoslavia (particularly Serbia). Certainly in the case of the major part of the Soviet Union there is no dispossessed bourgeois class ready to re-establish its position. Events may however yet prove this post-communist conservative corporatism to be a fleeting hesitation on the path to liberal capitalism. In Russia it appeared by January 1992 to be giving way to a form of authoritarian populism.

Poland represents a variation of this scenario, in which a nomenklatura turned capitalist and a strong working class resistant to accepting the privatization of capitalism, may both see their interests represented in a particular Polish variant of post-communist authoritarian conservatism with strong populist tendencies. The strong influence of Catholicism is important here. Only in Czechoslovakia (especially in the Czech lands) might we see the converting of the statist legacy into a social democratic welfare policy strategy, but then only after an initial flirtation with liberal welfare capitalism. At this stage those arguing that social democratic welfare traditions are rooted in Czech history are dismissed as proto-communists. The future for the social policy of the former GDR is, of course, bound up with the conservative corporatism of Germany.

We hazard the following projection in Table 7.3 for the medium-term prospects for welfare policy in Eastern Europe and the countries of the former Soviet Union in terms of a modified Esping-Andersen typology. Liberal welfare regimes will emerge as well as those with social democratic characteristics. We are suggesting that, although it is still early days, a pattern of divergence in the politics of social policy is taking place within Eastern Europe. We are predicting that in time we will be able to look back and characterize the social policy of these countries in terms that reflect Esping Andersen's three-fold typology together with a new as yet uncoined term to describe the unique post-communist conservative corporatism of parts of the Soviet Union, Romania, Bulgaria, parts of Yugoslavia and possibly Poland. Time will tell how long this post-communist conservative, sometimes authoritarian, corporatism will last. It may be short-lived as the strategy is likely only to increase economic uncompetitiveness with other countries.

Our argument for the conclusions we have drawn above and summarized in Table 7.3 rests on a combination of the actual descriptions of emerging policy for each country provided in this book together with the factors that we saw in Chapter 1 were influential in shaping and explaining diversity between already existing and capitalist welfare states. These were as follows:

• Demographic need.
• Economic development.
• Economic growth.
• Working-class mobilization.
• Influence of Catholic teaching on social policy.
• Historical impact/legacy of absolutism and authoritarianism.

To these, we argued in Chapter 1, we would need to add two others that might have predictive value for the post-communist generation of welfare state regime types. These were

• The character of the (1989) revolutionary process.
• Transnational impact and societal learning.

Table 7.3 *Emerging welfare regimes in Eastern Europe*

Some relevant factors	Bulgaria	Czechoslovakia	Germany (former GDR)	Poland	Hungary	Romania	Yugoslavia		Soviet Union and successor states*
							Slovenia	Serbia	
Economic development (relative scale)	Medium	High	High	Medium	Medium	Low	High	Low	Low
Working-class Mobilization	High	High	Medium	High	Low	High	Low	Medium	High (parts only)
Catholic teaching on policy influential	None	Little	Little	High	Little	Little	Medium	None	None (parts only)
Absolutist and authoritarian legacy	High	Low	Medium	High	Medium	High	Medium	High	High
Character of revolutionary process	Mass	Mass	Mass	Mass	Quietude	Mass	Quietude	Mass	Medium
Transnational impact (larger if indebted to West)	Medium	Medium	High	High	High	Low	Medium	Low	Low (but will change)
Emerging welfare state regime-type	Post-communist conservative corporatism†	Social democratic	Conservative corporatism	Post-communist conservative corporatism†	Liberal capitalist	Post-communist conservative corporatism†	Liberal capitalist	Post-communist conservative corporatism†	Post-communist conservative corporatism⁻

* The future for welfare in the countries of the former Soviet Union will diversify with the varying degrees of independence being achieved by each republic. See text for a more detailed discussion.

† Post-communist conservative corporatism may prove to be a historically brief phase. In Russia an authoritarian populism appeared to be replacing it by January 1992. The same development is possible in Poland and elsewhere (see text).

We are describing, predicting and explaining the broad sweep of social policy developments in these countries. Hungary and Slovenia, relatively richer countries, in the absence of highly influential labour movements, under policy influences consequent upon foreign debts, and, in the case of Hungary, with less church involvement, will gradually develop into liberal welfare state regime types. Czechoslovakia, or at least the Czech lands, because of the mass character of its velvet revolution, and because of the longer training in democracy, is most likely to emerge eventually as a social democratic regime type. Our caution here would be that social democratic regime types will, as a separate and distinct type, change their character with further economic growth and become more welfare pluralist and less statist. East Germany has already joined West Germany and despite enormous initial economic difficulties will become part of this conservative corporatist regime. In the case of Bulgaria, Romania, Albania, much of the former Soviet Union and the Serbian part of Yugoslavia we are describing and projecting something new. There the old language of socialism and egalitarianism is not dead, the tradition of democracy is weak, the extent to which the state is still looked to for strong support of worker interests is high, the direct pull of Western consumer capitalism is less evident. A new, but probably historically speaking temporary, form of post-communist conservative corporatism has emerged. We are tempted to call it Socialist Conservative Corporatism to capture the ideological and practical commitment to socialist values, the maintenance in power of some of the old guard, and the social deal struck with major labour interests. It might be that this corporatism gives way to an authoritarian populism.

Within the increasingly fragmented Commonwealth of Independent States this strategy is more likely to be followed in the Slavic republics of Russia, the Ukraine, Belorussia; and in Moldavia. The Baltic troika of Lithuania, Estonia and Latvia might move more rapidly down the road of marketization and democratization with economic and social policy less dictated by accommodation to old labour and nomenklatura interests. The future for the Central Asian republics and the other trans-Caucasian republics is less clear. Here the model of a Middle Eastern or South East Asian statist capitalist development which has little regard for democracy may prove to be a necessity. The inclusion of some of these republics within the Iran-Turkey-Pakistan Economic Cooperation Organization will be influential.

For Poland we foresee a problematic future. Although a liberal welfare regime may emerge, we doubt that the high degree of working-class mobilization and the level of their representation in government can combine with the considerable level of indebtedness, the strong influence of the church and the weak tradition of democracy without a major conflict of class interests arising. History in Western Europe has offered solutions to this problem before but they fall outside the range of regime-types studied by Esping-Andersen. For the moment we simply predict an authoritarian regime with a populist character. What impact the changing character of Catholic teaching on social policy will have is not yet clear. The traditional subsidiarity principle seemed well suited to the early flush of market enthusiasm in Poland. The concern of Pope John Paul II (1991) to reform capitalism in the interests of the poor may feed this authoritarian post-communism.

The conclusion that the future system of welfare for Poland and some other countries and parts of the former Soviet Union may lie outside the three worlds of welfare capitalism described by Esping-Andersen is consistent with our initial suggestion in Chapter 1 that the price of marketization and economic growth in parts of Eastern Europe and the former Soviet Union might be the destruction of democratic pluralism. In the initial flush of enthusiasm West European political commentators assumed that societal learning would be by the East from the West. We would suggest that some of the learning will be by the East from further East. South East Asian or Middle Eastern forms of authoritarian capitalist development, with a large role assigned to the state, may offer more appropriate models than any described by students of Western welfare states. Also, as we suggested earlier, the workplace paternalism associated with the Japanese model may be particularly appropriate in those parts of the post-communist world where popular attitudes remain either apathetic or are directed to some other person or agent to solve their new life problems for them. It is not too fanciful to suggest that Western Europe will be affected by and learn from new capitalist welfare strategies devised in the East. The hegemony of the West European Social Charter may not be imposed on the rest · of Europe. Influences may be reversed. Western European pluralist democratic welfare capitalism may be put at risk by developments further east.

Evaluation of social policy developments since 1989

In the opening chapter (Table 1.5) we set out ten criteria against which the social policy of a country might be evaluated. We distinguished the value-free criteria (e.g. the level of expenditure on welfare) from our preferred evaluation using any particular criterion (in this case high). Some of the preceding country-specific chapters have attempted an initial evaluation of new social policy developments against these criteria. Here we indicate a very provisional evaluation for the region as a whole, indicating diversity where this is evident.

First was the 'degree of self-activity by civil society in shaping policy and provision'. Clearly there is wide variation ranging from countries like Czechoslovakia, where popular involvement in and interest in running the social and political affairs of the future is high, through countries like Hungary, where a dualization of society has been noted between a half that already possesses civic capacity and a half that does not, to countries like Poland, where, despite years of Solidarity opposition, a social apathy prey to authoritarian populist leadership exists.

Second was the relationship between social and economic policy. In the initial transition period economic concerns have been and continue to be dominant but these have been subjected to social considerations in two different ways. In Czechoslovakia a new ideological and political case for social concerns has been mounted. In those countries where we have predicted a post-communist conservative corporatism social considerations and actual policies (the compensation for price rises) have, at least initially, been an integral part of economic planning.

The priority given to welfare issues has everywhere been low in the initial transition phase. Previously existing services have closed down. Substitute voluntary and private effort has not yet compensated for this. Government budgets available for welfare expenditure have been reduced.

The extent to which all social group interests are being served by new developments is, certainly in the short and medium term, highly questionable. Providers of welfare such as doctors and teachers have received higher than average wage increases. Large sections of the working class across Eastern Europe have been faced only with considerable impoverishment and unemployment.

Agencies of provision have certainly multiplied, more so in some countries than others and more so in some spheres of welfare than others. These new voluntary and commercial forms of welfare seem only to serve limited social group interests at this stage.

New forms of democratic control over local services do seem to be developing in certain countries but this is taking place in a situation where those local services are increasingly impoverished. This is leading to a combination of popular apathy in local elections and a call for stronger city managers to be appointed who, it is believed, will be able to get on and resolve the huge legacy of urban problems quickly.

In terms of the relationship between provider and users of services there is little reported yet of an equalization of professional–client exchanges. Market mechanisms, where they are introduced, might facilitate this for some users.

The eighth criterion we established in Chapter 1 was concerned with the degree of social justice embodied in provision and policy. Clearly, across Eastern Europe and the countries of the former Soviet Union there is a shift away from heavily egalitarian sentiment and formal practice towards the generation of inequality in the service of efficiency and a modified conception of justice. Egalitarian sentiments and the interests they serve remain higher in some countries than others and this has influenced the degree of modification of the play of market forces that certain countries have adopted.

Insofar as the issue of the gender division of care and family form has emerged in recent policy debate it has done so in the sense of emphasizing the traditional pre-communist role for women as home-makers and carers. Catholic teaching on such issues is evident in some countries. There is little evidence yet of Western-style feminist concerns reaching a broad audience in Eastern Europe.

The issue of racism and nationalism has emerged in social policy debates in almost all countries of Eastern Europe and the countries of the former Soviet Union. On the one hand, there has emerged a strengthened articulation of the welfare needs of ethnic minorities within and between countries, and, on the other, a worrying set of exclusionary arguments have emerged resulting in the denial of social citizenship rights to certain minorities in several countries. The break up of the Soviet Union may lead to the relative social impoverishment of some of the Central Asian republics as Russia concentrates on its own development.

The ten criteria can continue to be used over the years ahead to evaluate social policy developments as they unfold.

What future for socialist welfare?

There is no a priori reason why a discussion of the past, present or future system of social welfare in Eastern Europe should address the issue of what constitutes a socialist welfare policy. As, however, writers and commentators on Eastern European and Soviet social policy have very often made a connection between the two, we feel it is important to do so. An earlier study of Poland, Hungary and the Soviet Union (Deacon, 1983) was used to argue the case that these countries did not exhibit socialist welfare policy. Many political and economic commentators have used this failure of

Eastern Europe to live up to socialist expectations to prove the unviability as well as the undesirability of the socialist project. The collapse of 'communism' in 1989 has also been used to finally lay not only Stalin, but Lenin, and even Marx to rest. In this final section we briefly address these issues.

In the immediate and foreseeable future there is little that is going to develop within Eastern Europe that socialist critics of welfare capitalism will be able to point to and say 'There, that's the socialist future for welfare.' The determined effort, against the odds, in Bulgaria to fashion a generous system of social security in the midst of economic crisis could be seen as a doomed exception to this. Equally we already knew that there was little about the social policy of the earlier bureaucratic state collectivist regimes that could be defended as socialist. What then of a future for socialist social policy as a guiding idea and a realizable practice? It is necessary to take stock, throw out the ideas and politics whose sell-by date has gone and continue to preserve those with a shelf life left in them.

The earlier (Deacon, 1983) attempt made to paint a picture of an ideal socialist social policy still has something of value but was flawed in a number of ways. Events in Eastern Europe have merely served to underline these flaws. Socialists, it argued, would applaud those countries that spent more rather than less on welfare, that provided for democratic forms of control of welfare institutions, that utilized the state as an agency of provision but not exclusively, that facilitated social relations of welfare that were reciprocally co-operative, that emphasized egalitarian principles of distribution and that facilitated non-gendered forms of care. Socialists, following Williams (1989), would also prefer policy that reflected ethnic diversity and was not based on racially exclusive citizenship rights. Lee and Raban (1988: 149) have pointed to the tension that exists between attempting to realize all of these socialist goals simul- taneously. They argued, correctly in our view, that democratic and egalitarian measures may work against each other. The extent to which trade-offs might be required between local democracy and egalitarianism, or between egalitarianism and quantity (efficiency) in any feasible socialist future, is an important point which we discussed in Chapter 1. Certainly these considerations were missing from this earlier attempt to paint a picture of socialist social policy.

To these critical points must be added the implications of the experience of Eastern Europe and the collapse of 'communism'. We do not hold to the view that Eastern Europe and the Soviet Union had nothing to do with socialism either as an idea or as a political practice. Of course, Lenin's historic 'mistake' of attempting to build socialism in conditions of underdevelopment where the working class were a decimated minority of the population cannot be taken as evidence that any socialist revolution would take that course (Feher, Markus and Heller, 1983). Of course, the Stalinist atrocity of substituting the party for the class and the general secretary for the party and then imposing that across Eastern Europe has nothing to do with the dream of communist democracy. It is not possible, however, for socialists to wipe their hands of the negative experiences that have been suffered under the name of socialism in Eastern Europe. The idea that a party can know better what the people want and, should the people not choose it, impose the idea because it knows better contains the seeds of totalitarianism. The notion that the state can plan for the needs of people without also utilizing any of the methods that are known to be able to find out what those needs are – both democratic choices and marketplaces – must surely now be abandoned. To be fair, the earlier discussion was open-minded on these questions. Thus in Deacon (1983: 29) we read:

> There is thus considerable dispute among Marxists as to whether some form of market mechanism will play a part under socialism and communism. How far a democratic pluralist political process could be constructed that permitted full expression of the continuing diversity of, and disagreement about, need under socialism that excludes any form of market as a mechanism of registering preferences is far from having been worked out in detail. Equally, it has not yet been shown how a socialist system that permitted that expression of consumer preference through a market mechanism could avoid generalized commodity production and the restoration of capitalism.

The negative lessons that must be learned from the Soviet and East European experience combine with the Western critical writings on Marxism in recent years to suggest a less certain picture of socialism and a less sure political strategy for its realization.

Where once, in the Western Marxist literature, it was presumed that the politics of a post-revolutionary society would be an unproblematic matter as all interests expressed through workers' councils would be the same, now no such certainty can be expressed (Polan, 1984). A political process for a socialistic future has still to be fashioned that acknowledges the diversity of human needs and interests. Where once, in the Western Marxist literature, it was presumed that markets would play no part in the de-commodified economy, now no such certainty can be expressed (Nove, 1983). While markets as social forces and as criteria of evaluation might still be suspect, markets as mechanisms for affording democratic choice and for facilitating efficiency are to be valued. To an extent markets *are* facilitators of the autonomous expression of need.

Where once, in the Western Marxist literature, it was presumed that the morality of the socialist future was something that could safely be left to the future to create in new material circumstances, now no such amoral position can be afforded. Marxists are enjoined to make moral choices on matters social and political (Geras, 1985; Lukes, 1985). Where once, in the Western Marxist literature, it was presumed that human needs of a certain radical kind would flourish in the new society, now no such faith can be expressed. A genuine politics of needs is all that can and must be aspired to (Soper, 1981; Doyal and Gough, 1991).

The negative lessons of actually existing socialism coalesce then with self-critical analysis of Western Marxism to suggest a socialist future that embodies a political pluralism, involves contended moral choices, envisages a role for markets and a political debate over needs.

This does not mean, in our view, the abandoning of the Marxist analysis of the dynamics of capitalist or post-communist society. Class struggle exists and will continue to exist so long as – and it will be a long time – capitalism continues to exist. The dimensions of gender and race and other social divisions and the struggles that arise out of them must, of course, be integrated with this class analysis. What, therefore, do the foregoing considerations lead us to say now about a socialist future for welfare? Four main prescriptions follow.

First, we must abandon for all practical purposes that form of politics which is guided solely by the idea that nothing can be achieved until capitalism collapses and therefore everything is measured by whether it hastens its downfall. While we may retain (if it helps) as a final vision a social transformation to a classless society, this possibility is so unlikely, and may be impossible to realize, that it is irrelevant to any socialist welfare politics of the present.

Second, we must defend and argue for the ideals of socialist social policy (e.g. the ten questions drawn up in Chapter 1 and our preferred answers) as goals and as principles to be struggled for now, both at the level of ideas and with those class and other forces in whose interests they are fashioned. These values, backed up by this democratic class struggle, can be realized by degree within capitalism. Capitalism East and West can be reformed by the struggle of socialists.

Thirdly, and perhaps a point that flows most directly from the experience of East European welfare and the struggle now to fashion a new future for welfare capitalism in its place, we must acknowledge the trade-off between efficiency and equality, and state guarantees and personal and group autonomy. What balance will exist between these and other trade-offs will vary between societies and will depend on the diverse forms of struggle of diverse interests within them. Nothing more can be said on this point.

Fourthly, and probably the point with the most exciting potential for the future, those who wish to establish within capitalism a socialist social policy need to broaden their canvas to a global level. Capitalism cannot, in the long run, be reformed with socialist values backed up by struggle in one region of the globe if it is to be undermined by an unreformed cut-throat capitalism existing elsewhere. The level playing field of the European Social Charter has eventually to encompass the globe, and when it does so it can be raised even higher. It will not matter then that egalitarianism is being traded for efficiency because there will be nowhere more efficient (because less equal) to undermine the existing welfare achievements (discounting interplanetary capitalist competition!). The collapse of the false East–West ideological political and systems posturing of the past decades liberates this potential for a global reformist politics within which socialist values will play their part and give it a real chance of success. Such a success is not guaranteed. Social policy achievements of Western Europe may be undermined by authoritarian East European developments and by the collapse of global reformist politics in the face of national and regional economic rivalry.

In the early days after the collapse of the 'communist' regimes of Eastern Europe Deacon and Szalai (1990) wrote the following about the future for socialist welfare. Nothing has happened in the intervening period to encourage us to modify this:

> We may still be allowed to paint a picture of a welfare future that is more egalitarian, whose provisions are not so closely tied to a work ethic, that facilitate forms of care that are not sexist or racist, that is less structured by nationally bound citizenship rights, that allows for variety and difference in the social needs that are articulated and in the ways in which they are met, that is more reciprocal and less paternalistic, more enabling and less dependency creating, more empowering and less stigmatizing. We may still be allowed to argue that the democratic state has a duty to guarantee some territorial justice and that international authority has a duty to guarantee some global justice. We may still be allowed to argue that markets between competing collective properties must operate within a regulating framework that tries to ensure they help achieve democratically agreed ends. What we are not able to do is to place our faith in the mysterious mechanisms whereby the universal interest in all of this is carried for us all by the working class. We require instead a re-doubling of commitment and argument at the level of social values as a necessary part of the process of realizing this welfare future. (Deacon and Szalai, 1990: 22)

It is important, and reassuring, to note that we are not alone in this! Those who have stepped outside the twin traps of either defending the past in Eastern Europe as socialist or claiming that its terrible legacy has had nothing to do with socialism seem to agree about what is now to be done. Stephen Lukes (1990), reviewing the lessons of Eastern Europe, argues that from now on the left must be guided by both the republican principle that tries to ensure equal social citizenship and the rectification principle that rectifies inequalities where they exist and makes real those existing paper equalities. He adds: 'From which I think we must conclude that the future of socialism, if it has one, can only lie within capitalism, and it can only consist of one or other version of social democracy' (Lukes, 1990: 544).

Anthony Giddens has argued that

> The left at this point has finally and absolutely to relinquish the conceptual security once offered by panoramas of historical inevitability, or by the theme that the working class is a privileged historical agent . . . there are no guarantees for the future . . . yet the reconstructive tasks which a left political programme might develop thereby actually become all the more urgent. (Giddens, 1990: 20)

Zygmunt Bauman (1990) has argued that as the era of modernism, within which capitalism and Marxism were twin sides of the same coin, both promising world redemption, gives way to postmodernist contingency and uncertainty, the part played by socialists and socialism has to change, yet also remain the same. It has to continue to act as a counter-culture to capitalism, because without it capitalism cannot deliver what it makes possible, but it now also has to act as a guardian of the changed goals of the new era. The values championed by and appropriate to post-modernism are those of liberty, diversity and tolerance. To ensure liberty becomes positive freedom for all, diversity becomes the celebration of difference, and tolerance becomes the empowerment of the other requires the challenge of socialists. Bauman concludes, reflecting on the lessons of the collapse of communism in Eastern Europe:

> The casus belli is, as before, the capitalist management of the project, which cannot but transform freedom into privilege, diversity into discrimination and tolerance into callousness . . . . The purposes of the war is, as before, to force society to keep its word: to deliver what is best in its promise and to stave off the gruesome consequences of mismanagement. (Bauman, 1990: 25)

Finally, Robin Blackburn (1991) has acknowledged the economic and democratic role that can be played by markets in social and political development, has found a common ground between Trotsky and Hayek, and calls for Eastern Europe to join the

European Community, for socialists to fight a common cause within the wider Europe, and for the establishment of a global planning authority which would socialize and regulate markets on a world scale. The goal would not be to command but to regulate the development of the world economy in the interests of the free development of all which is the precondition for the free development of each.

Our conclusion is, and it is important to clarify the point, not that in the struggle between capitalism and socialism capitalism has won, nor in the struggle between capitalist welfare and socialist welfare capitalist welfare has won. It is that socialist values and socialist welfare objectives can only be realized in any foreseeable future by struggling within capitalism to reform it in the interests of human needs. It is also that this struggle now has as an urgent priority a transnational and global dimension in the interests of socialist welfare objectives East and West, North and South.

References

Bauman, Z. (1990) 'From pillar to post', *Marxism Today*, February.
Blackburn, R. (1991) 'Fin de siècle: socialism after the crash', *New Left Review*, 185.
Deacon, B. (1983) *Social Policy and Socialism*. London: Pluto.
Deacon, B. and Szalai, J. (eds) (1990) *Social Policy in the New Eastern Europe*. Aldershot: Gower.
Doyal, C. and Gough, I. (1991) *A Theory of Human Needs*. London: Macmillan.
Esping-Andersen, G. (1990) *The Three Worlds of Welfare Capitalism*. Cambridge: Polity.
Feher, F., Markus, G. and Heller, A. (1983) *Dictatorship over Needs*. Oxford: Basil Blackwell.
Geras, N. (1985) 'On Marx and justice', *New Left Review*, 156: 47–85.
Giddens, A. (1990) 'Modernity and Utopia', *New Statesman*, 2 November: 20–2.
John Paul II, Pope (1991) *Centisimus Annus*. Rome: Vatican Press.
Lee, P. and Raban C. (1988) *Welfare Theory and Social Policy*. London: Sage.
Lukes, S. (1985) *Marxism and Morality*. Oxford: Oxford University Press.
Lukes, S. (1990) 'Comment by Lukes on Goldfarb, J.: Post totalitarian politics – ideology ends again', *Social Research*, 57 (3): 544.
Nove, A. (1983) *The Economics of Feasible Socialism*. London: Allen and Unwin.
Polan, A.J. (1984) *Lenin and the End of Politics*. London: Methuen.
Soper, K. (1981) *On Human Needs*. Brighton: Harvester.
Williams, F. (1989) *Social Policy: a Critical Introduction*. Cambridge: Polity.
Wnuk-Lipinski, E. (1992) 'Freedom and equality: an old dilemma in a new context', in B. Deacon (ed.), *Social Policy, Social Justice and Citizenship in Eastern Europe*. Aldershot: Gower.

Index

Note: Soviet Union includes the successor republics.

abortion: Poland 140, 141; Romania 4; Soviet Union 47; under state collectivism 4; in transitional period 12, 168, 170, 174
absolutism, impact on welfare regime 21–2, 180
Academies of Science, in transitional period 168
accountability, Poland 121
Adirim, I. 50
Aganbegyan, A. 37, 44
agencies, transnational, influence 2, 9, 22–3
agriculture: Bulgaria 68; Poland 120; Soviet Union 33–4
Albania, marketization 168, 176, 182
Alber, J. 20
alcoholism, Soviet Union 3, 39, 43, 44, 48, 54–6, 57, 60
alienation, political 112, 141
Andropov, Yuri 43
authoritarianism 18, 21–2, 189; conservative 180; liberal 16; populist 12, 16, 46, 58–9, 64, 183, 184
autonomy, and welfare provision 7, 9, 26, 27, 149, 188–9

Baltic Popular Fronts 45
Baltic republics: and ethnicity 58; and welfare systems 182
base-superstructure model 60
Bauman, Zygmunt 190
begging, Soviet Union 51
Belorussia, welfare systems 182
benefits: cash 4, 152, 157; child care 4, 127, 157, 166 n.6, 170; indexation 4, 113–14, 128, 134; maternity 127; one-off 103, 128; parental 113; related to party support 2–3, 98; sickness 4, 127, 153; universal 111, 158; *see also* insurance, social; pensions
benefits, work related 4–6, 10, 18, 59, 170–1, 178; Bulgaria 70–1, 73, 82–4, 86–7; Hungary 150; Soviet Union 34,

37–8, 42, 51; *see also* unemployment, benefits
Bettleheim, C. 33
Beveridge, William 114
Bielecki, Jan Krzysztof 122, 123, 129, 130, 131, 132
birth rate: Bulgaria 72, 74; Poland 123; Soviet Union 49, 55
Blackburn, Robin 190–1
Bolshevik revolution, impact 94–5
Boni, Michal 133
bourgeoisie: Hungary 12, 144, 176; Soviet Union 179
Brezhnev, Leonid 36, 38, 42, 43
Bugaj, Ryszard 132
Bujak, Zbigniew 132
Bulgaria: history 67–70; new social policies 13, 67–89, 169, 172–3, 175, 176, 179–80, 181, 182; past social policies 70–8; and Soviet Union 67, 68–9; Turks 89, 168, 177
bureaucracy: Czechoslovakia 92, 101, 104; Hungary 2; Poland 118

capitalism: and socialism 175–6, 189–91; 'workers' 179; *see also* welfare, capitalist systems
Castle-Kanerova, Mita 91–116
Castles, F. 16
Castles, F. and McKinlay, N. 19
Castles, F. and Mitchell, D. 15, 17
Catholicism 21–2, 138, 140, 174, 177, 180, 183, 185
Central Asia: life expectancy 3; as supply of labour 49; welfare provision 47, 182–3, 185
centralization: Czechoslovakia 94; Hungary 149, 152; impact on welfare regime 20; Soviet Union 32, 40, 41, 43
Centrum, Poland 129
Chavdar, Kyuranov 75
Chernenko, K. 43
Chichkanov, V. 62
child care: Bulgaria 71, 74–5; in corporatist systems 15;

Czechoslovakia 108, 113; Hungary 4,
166 n.6; Poland 127, 141; under state
collectivism 4; in transitional period
12, 168, 170, 174
Christian Democratic Party, Hungary
165 n.1
church, influence 12, 15, 20, 163, 174,
182; *see also* Catholicism; Orthodox
Church
citizenship: emergence 10–12, 114–15;
and rights to welfare 18, 24, 59, 93,
178, 185, 186, 189–90; theory 61–2
Civic Democratic Party 91
Civic Forum, Czechoslovakia 22, 91,
96, 175, 176
civil society: Albania 176; Bulgaria 176;
Czechoslovakia 92–3, 99–100, 105,
107, 176, 177, 184; emergence 1,
11–12, 25, 26, 175–6, 184; Hungary
144, 184; Poland 129, 177, 184;
Romania 176; Soviet Union 32–3,
45, 56–7, 176–7; Yugoslavia 176
class: changes in 141; and education
42, 52–3; interests 10, 14, 25, 33,
44–5, 57, 89, 96–8, 183; struggle, and
welfare regime 20, 188; *see also*
working class
collectivism, state: collapse 1, 7, 44–6;
post-bureaucratic 18; in Soviet Union
32; and welfare realities 26, 27, 178,
186
commodification of welfare services 14,
141, 178
Commonwealth of Independent States
46, 49, 60, 182
Communist Parties: Bulgaria 68–70;
Czechoslovakia 95, 96; Poland 119,
122, 131, 142; Soviet 46
Confederation of Independent
Bulgarian Trade Unions 79
conflict theory 20
Congress of People's Deputies, Soviet
Union 44–5, 50, 57
Connor, W.D. 53
contraception 4, 140; *see also* abortion
control of policy, *see* democracy, and
control over services
corporatism, conservative 14–16, 21,
26, 178–80, 182, 184; Bulgaria 67,
84–6, 88–9, 182; Socialist 182; Soviet
Union 58–9, 182
crime: Czechoslovakia 116; Poland 137;
Soviet Union 43, 60
Croatia: nationalism 177; new social
policies 182
culture, impact on welfare regime 21
curriculum, changes 138, 174
Czech and Slovak Federative Republic
(CSFR), *see* Czechoslovakia

Czechoslovakia: and democracy 22;
mass movements 11, 182; Slovaks in
177; social policy in transition 91–3,
104–16, 169, 172–3, 175–6, 177, 180,
181; state collectivism 94–104

de-commodification of welfare 15, 16,
18, 178, 187
Deacon, B. 1–28, 36, 167–91
Deacon, B. and Szalai, J. 2, 189
Deacon, B. and Vidinova, A. 67–89
decentralization: Bulgaria 81; Hungary
157; Soviet Union 43–4
democracy, and control over services
25, 57, 60–2, 91, 105, 107, 115,
184–6
Democratic Forum, Hungary 165 n.1
Democratic Platform manifesto, Soviet
Union 45
demography, impact on welfare regime
20, 21–2, 103, 180
Deyl, Z. 94–5, 96
Dimitrov, G.M. 68–9
disintegration, social 158–9
dissent, in Soviet Union 36, 39, 43
distribution: Bulgaria 80, 81; Hungary
150; impact of social policy 24, 25,
178–9, 186; Poland 133
divorce rate: Bulgaria 72, 74–5; Poland
123; Soviet Union 40, 43
Dochev, I. et al. 77
Dominelli, L. 16
Doyal, L. and Gough, I. 26

economy: Bulgaria 69, 78–81, 84–6,
88–9; Czechoslovakia 91, 92–3, 97,
98–9, 103, 104–6, 109–10, 114–15,
184; Hungary 144, 145–6, 149–56;
impact on welfare provision 19, 20,
21–2, 25, 91, 180, 184; Poland 48,
120–2, 129–33, 141–2; second 2, 74,
144, 149, 151, 154–6, 158; social
market 78–9, 80–1, 145–6; and social
rights 61; Soviet Union 31–2, 36–7,
42–3, 44–6, 48, 57, 59–60
education: adult 41, 120;
Czechoslovakia 110; higher 41–2,
52–3, 119, 124–5, 137; Hungary 149;
Poland 119–20, 121, 124–5, 137–8;
pre-school 124, 138; Soviet Union
33, 41–2, 44, 47, 52–3, 56, 58; in
transitional period 168, 173, 174; UK
42; USA 42; vocational 52–3, 110,
119, 124, 137
efficiency, economic 6, 7, 9, 26, 27, 57,
185, 188–9
egalitarianism: Bulgaria 68, 70, 175;
Czechoslovakia 92, 99, 111; Poland
10; and social democracy 15; Soviet
Union 57, 175; and under-

development 6–7, 9; and welfare regimes 18, 24, 26, 178, 179, 182, 185, 186, 188–9
elderly, care for: Czechoslovakia 103–4; Poland 141
Ellman, M. 50
employment, part-time 86, 110, 154, 155
employment policies: Bulgaria 81–3, 86–7; Czechoslovakia 92, 106, 107–11; employment bureaux, *see* labour, exchanges; enterprise allowances 12; Hungary 149, 153–4; Poland 131–2, 133; *see also* work
Engels, F. 98
entrepreneurs, emergence 8, 11, 89, 134, 155, 156, 179
Entrepreneurs' Party, Hungary 156
environment, damage to 3, 13, 101, 114
Esping-Andersen, G. 14, 16, 17, 18, 21–2, 56, 58, 178, 180, 183
Estonia: housing 52; welfare systems 182
European Social Charter 23, 189
expectation, popular 8, 9, 57, 111, 122–4, 130
expenditure, levels 19, 23, 24, 151–2, 159–60, 184

family: in Bulgaria 71–2, 74–5; in Czechoslovakia 93, 100, 108, 112–13; in Hungary 147, 158; in Poland 127; and provision of welfare 15, 25, 185; in Soviet Union 43, 49–50, 57–8
Federation of Free Democrats, Hungary 156
Ferge, Z. 46
food subsidies 2, 49, 111, 121, 127
functionalist theory 20

GDR: child care 4; mass movements 11; privileges 3; and social policies 12, 180, 181, 182
Georgia, welfare regime 182
Germany, welfare regime 15, 17
Giddens, Anthony 190
Gierek, Edward 121
Ginsburg, N. 15, 16, 17
Giorgi Dimitrov Research Institute for Trade Union Studies 70–1, 73, 77
Glapinski, Adam 135
glasnost 44, 47
Goldfarb, J.C. 43
Gomulka, Władysław 121
Gorbachev, Mikhail 34, 62; on alcoholism 43, 44, 54, 56; downfall 33, 46, 60; and Eastern Europe 69; and education 52–3; on equalizing 6–7, 48; on restructuring 43–4, 49, 59

guarantees, social 7, 9, 26, 27, 188–9; Czechoslovakia 94, 104, 105, 107, 111; Hungary 150
Gypsies 3, 4, 70, 102, 177

Harding, N. 59
health: and environment 3, 13, 54, 77, 101, 114; occupational 120; preventive measures 13, 39, 72–3, 101, 140
health care: Bulgaria 72–8; Czechoslovakia 98, 101–2, 114; Hungary 144–5, 149, 159–65; internal market 53–4, 138–9; Poland 119–20, 125–7; 138–41; primary 39, 72–3, 126, 140, 162; provision 7, 13; right to 163–4; Soviet Union 33, 39–40, 47, 53–6, 58; under state collectivism 3; in transitional period 168, 170, 173, 174; UK 39, 40; USA 39, 40; workplace 3, 39, 72–3, 127; *see also* privatization
Hicks, A. and Swank, D. 19–20
Higgins, J. 23
Holubenko, M. 99
homelessness: Poland 123, 134, 136–7; Soviet Union 51; in transitional period 174
housing: Bulgaria 171; Czechoslovakia 102, 112, 171; Hungary 171, 174; Poland 119–20, 121, 123–4, 126, 135–7, 171–4; Romania 171; Soviet Union 4, 34–5, 40–1, 49, 51–2, 57, 58–9, 171; under state collectivism 4; in transitional period 10, 170, 171–2, 173; *see also* privatization
Hungary: child care 4; and citizenship 11, 12; and class politics 22; Kádárism 2, 12, 148–56, 176; new social policies 13, 64, 144–8, 156–65, 169, 172–3, 176, 181, 182

IMF, influence on social policy 22–3; Bulgaria 85, 89; Czechoslovakia 106; Soviet Union 46, 58, 60
income distribution: Bulgaria 84–5; Soviet Union 48
income support, Bulgaria 88
individualization: Czechoslovakia 97–8, 104, 106–7, 115; Hungary 149, 151; Poland 121, 123
industrialization: Bulgaria 68; Czechoslovakia 97–8, 100–1; Hungary 149, 158; Poland 119–21, 132; Soviet Union 34, 38
inequality: and citizenship theory 61, 178; ethnic 47, 58, *see also* racism; under state collectivism 6–7, 42, 152; in transitional period 9–10, 11, 18,

53, 57–8, 92, 141, 148, 158, 170, 175,
178–9, 185, 190
inflation: Bulgaria 85, 88;
Czechoslovakia 106; Hungary 157,
171; Poland 139–40; Soviet Union
58, 59; in transitional period 168, 170
information, dissemination 92
Inkeles, A. 24
Institute of Social Insurance, Poland
127
insurance, health: Czechoslovakia
113–14; Hungary 157, 162–4; Poland
140
insurance, social: Bulgaria 79–80, 82,
87, 88–9; Czechoslovakia 94, 95,
96–8, 105; Hungary 144, 156; Poland
127; in transitional period 170
integration, social 60–1, 158–9
intelligentsia: Czechoslovakia 96;
Poland 119, 120, 125, 128, 130, 141;
Soviet Union 63–4
interest, social 57, 62–4, 151
Ivanov, V. 62

Japan, possible influence 16–18, 183
Jaruzelski, Wojciech 130
John Paul II, Pope 183
Jones, Catherine 15, 16, 17, 20
Jordan, B. 7
justice, social: in Czechoslovakia 92,
95, 105, 107, 114–15; in Soviet
Union 50, 59; in transitional period
1, 9–10, 12, 24, 175, 185

Kádárism 12, 148–56, 176
Kagarlitsky, B. 45
Kazakhstan, and South East Asian
model 18
Keane, J. 44–5
Khrushchev, N. 34–5, 36, 38, 42
Klaus, Vaclav 91–3
Kolarska-Bobińska, L. 11, 131
Konopasek, Z. 93
Kornai, J. 6, 7, 26, 37
Kostelancik, D.J. 102
Krejci, J. 97
Kuroń, Jacek 133, 134
Kyuranov, C. 70

labour: exchanges 51, 83, 86, 109, 171;
gender division 4, 16, 25, 57–8, 71–2,
74–5, 107–8, 185; migrant 13, 16, 24,
49
labour market: Bulgaria 81–3, 84;
Czechoslovakia 107, 109; Poland
118, 129, 132, 137; Soviet Union 34,
41, 42, 48, 49–51
Latvia, welfare systems 182
Lee, P. and Raban, C. 186

Lendvai, P. 70
Lenin, V.I. 33, 41, 187
liberalism 14, 21, 26, 27, 118, 129, 130,
135, 178–80, 182–3
life expectancy: Bulgaria 73, 76;
Central Asia 3; comparisons 76;
Czechoslovakia 101; Hungary 159;
Poland 125; Soviet Union 54, 55
Lissev, G. et al. 73
Lithuania, welfare systems 182
living standards: Bulgaria 69, 85;
Czechoslovakia 97, 99–100, 102–3,
105, 110–11; Hungary 151, 159, 168;
Poland 121–2, 128, 131–2, 135, 168;
Soviet Union 38, 50; in transitional
period 9–10, 168, 171, 175
local government: Hungary 163, 165;
Poland 121, 134, 135–6, 138
Lukes, Stephen 190

McAuley, A. 3, 98
Machonin, P. et al. 99–100
Mandel, E. 38
Manning, Nick 31–64
marketization: Albania 168; Bulgaria
74, 89, 168, 175; Czechoslovakia
91–2, 104–6, 108, 114–16, 168, 176;
effects on democratic pluralism 16;
effects on welfare provision 8, 9–10,
13, 178–9, 187–8; and health care
53–4, 138–9; Hungary 145–6, 147,
151, 153–4, 157–8, 168, 175; Poland
118, 129, 131–2, 168, 175, 177;
Soviet Union 43, 46, 57–9, 168, 175;
in transitional period 168–71, 175–6,
184–5
Marshall, T.H. 61
Marxism: and Soviet Union 32; and
welfare provision 20, 31–2, 60, 62,
187–8
mass movements 10–11, 69
maternity allowance, Bulgaria 71
maternity leave, Poland 127
Mazowiecki, Tadeusz 118, 122, 129–30,
131, 135
Middle East, welfare regimes 183
Mierzewski, Piotr 138
Millard, Frances 118–42, 177
Miller, Peter 92
minorities, ethnic: rights 175, 177, 185,
186; *see also* Gypsies; racism
Mishra, R. 15, 16, 17, 20, 98
Mitchell, D. 15
Mladenov, P. 69
mobility: international 110; social 20,
53, 154
modernization/convergence theory 60
Moldavia, welfare systems 182

monetarism, Czechoslovakia 91–2, 93, 96, 104
morality, social 91–2, 188
morbidity rates 13; Czechoslovakia 114; Poland 125–6; Soviet Union 40
mortality rates: Bulgaria 72–3, 76–7, 78; Czechoslovakia 101, 102, 114; elderly 77; Hungary 144, 159; infant 39, 43, 47, 54, 76, 101, 102; Poland 125; Soviet Union 40, 43, 47, 54–5; under state collectivism 3, 39; in transitional period 13, 24
Movement for Rights and Freedoms, Bulgaria 70
movements, social, in Soviet Union 11, 57, 62

nationalism: Bulgaria 68, 89; Soviet Union 45, 58, 177; in transitional period 185; Yugoslavia 177
nationalization, Czechoslovakia 97
need: articulation 10–11; and Bulgarian policy 69, 73; and Hungarian social policy 150; impact on welfare regime 19, 21; in Marxism 187–8; and Polish social policy 118, 120–1, 128; and Soviet social policy 37, 38, 41–2, 57, 59, 63
neo-liberalism: Czechoslovakia 104; Poland 141–2
Ninov, D. 89
nomenklatura: 'new' 96; under state collectivism 2, 7, 26, 129; in transitional period 10, 22, 89, 170, 176, 179–80
'Novosibirsk manifesto' 43–4, 60

Olszewski, Jan 130, 132, 133
opposition: in Bulgaria 67; in Hungary 156; in Poland 184; in Soviet Union 45, 60
OPZZ trade union 142
Orosz, Eva 144–65
Orthodox Church, influence on Balkan states 22

participation: Bulgaria 79–80, 84, 88–9; Czechoslovakia 105, 107, 115, 177; Poland 134, 141–2; under social democracy 15, 61, 175–6; under state collectivism 7
Paszyński, Aleksander 135
paternalism: under state collectivism 4, 7, 11, 176; in transitional period 16, 114–15, 183
paternity leave, Bulgaria 75
Penkov, P. 80
pensioners, in employment 38, 109–10, 128, 155

pensions: Bulgaria 73, 83, 86–7, 174; Czechoslovakia 111; Hungary 153, 157, 174; Poland 122, 127, 128, 134; Soviet Union 38, 50; and welfare regimes 4, 18, 178
perestroika: and 1991 coup 11, 32, 46; attitudes to 59, 62–3; and social policy 42–6, 47, 57, 78
Pick, Hella 69
Pinc, Karel 97, 98–9, 104
Pinkevitch, A.P. 33
pluralism, and welfare provision 16, 20, 94, 137, 183, 188
Podkrepa trade union, Bulgaria 79, 89
Poland 12, 13, 22, 176; conservatism 60; in Communist period 118–22; future prospects 141–2, 177, 179–80, 181, 182–3; mass movements 11; 'short, sharp shock' 92, 131, 168, 177; Soviet influence 119; in transitional period 122–8, 129–41, 169, 172–3; *see also* Solidarity
policy, social: compared 172–3; evaluative criteria 23–7, 56–8, 167, 183–5; future prospects 167–91; and societal policy 47; and transition 168–78
Polish Committee for Social Assistance 128, 134–5
political theory 60–2
politicization: Czechoslovakia 91; Soviet Union 35, 37, 45–6, 56, 62
politics: effects on welfare regime 19, 20, 21–2, 26; Poland 129–31; Soviet Union 31–2, 43
population, homogeneity 20
populism, authoritarian 12, 16, 46, 58–9, 64, 183, 184
poverty: Czechoslovakia 100, 103, 105, 107, 111, 112, 116; Hungary 148, 157–8, 159; Poland 128, 132, 141; Soviet Union 50–1; in transitional period 13, 174–5, 184
pressure groups, under state collectivism 5
price reform: Albania 168; Bulgaria 84–6, 88–9, 168, 175; Czechoslovakia 104–6, 168, 171; Hungary 168, 171; Poland 129, 131–2, 133, 139, 141, 168; Romania 168, 171; Soviet Union 45–6, 48–9, 56, 57, 58, 59–60, 168, 175; in transitional period 171, 172
privatization: businesses 58–9, 92–3; Czechoslovakia 92–3, 104; education 137, 174; and health care 10, 13, 138–9, 162, 170, 174; housing 10, 49, 59, 121, 123, 135, 170, 174; Hungary

146, 157; Poland 129, 137, 138–9, 180; responses to 179
privileges, under state collectivism 2–3, 6–7, 26, 120, 170, 179
problems: conditions as 35, 36; groups as 34, 35, 52–3; individuals as 35–6, 39
property: private 145, 146–7, 178, *see also* privatization; state 10
prophylactoria, Bulgaria 72–3
prostitution, Soviet Union 60
protest, social 142
provision, agencies 7, 25, 57, 178, 184, 186
psychiatry, misuse 36, 39
public opinion: Czechoslovakia 92–3, 100; in transitional period 175

racism: and unemployment 13; and welfare rights 16, 24–5, 102, 168, 177, 185
religion, *see* Catholicism; church, influence; Orthodox Church
rents: levels 4, 51, 58–9, 112, 124, 171–4; subsidies 2, 121, 127, 135, 168, 171
research: comparative studies 23–6; cross-national studies 19–23
residual principle 37
retirement: age 4, 38, 87, 111, 127, 155, 174; benefits 4, 71; early 155; flexible 7
revolutions of 1989, impact 22, 28, 182
Rimachevskaya, Natalia 47–8
ROAD (Citizens' Movement for Democratic Action) 129
Rocznik Statystyczny 123
Romania: conservatism 60; Hungarians 13, 168, 177; nationalism 89; in transitional period 169, 176, 179–80, 181, 182
Russia, *see* Soviet Union and successors
Ruzica, M. 16

Serbia: nationalism 89, 177; in transitional period 179, 181, 182
Shatalin '500–day' plan 45, 49, 59
'shock therapy' 49, 80–1, 92, 131, 168, 175–7
shortages: housing 4, 123; Hungary 2, 152, 153–4; Poland 120, 123, 140; Soviet Union 49, 50
Slovenia, new social policies 181, 182
Smallholders' Party, Hungary 165 n.1
social democracy 15, 21, 26, 27, 176, 178, 190; Bulgaria 88; Czechoslovakia 106, 176, 180, 182; Poland 132; Soviet Union 45
social market, Bulgaria 78–9, 80–1

social security: Bulgaria 70–2, 186; Czechoslovakia 102–4, 107–11; Hungary 144, 146, 150–9, 176; Poland 120–1; Soviet Union 37–8, 50–1; in transitional period 170
socialism: and capitalism 175–6, 189–91; 'developed' 35, 36–7, 42; in Hungary 145–7, 148–56, 158; 'idealistic' 94; 'market' 179; and welfare 176, 185–91
Socialist Parties: Bulgaria 69–70, 78, 89; Hungary 146
sociological theory 60–1
Solidarity 22, 125, 132, 142, 177; in power 11, 118, 122, 129
SOS Fund, Poland 134
South America, as welfare model 18
South East Asia, welfare regimes 18, 182–3
Soviet Central Asia, social policy 40, 41
Soviet Centre for Public Opinion Research 44, 48, 52
Soviet Union and successors 39; continuity and change 32, 35–6, 44–6, 64; coup 11, 32, 33, 46, 60; emerging strategies 59–64; and independent republics 177; industrial phase 34, 38; and racism 13; social movements 11, 57, 62; in transitional period 9, 31–3, 46–59, 169, 172–3, 175–7, 179–80, 181; urban phase 33–4; utopian phase 33; welfare realities 26, 182; welfare/productivity phase 35–42; *see also* Bulgaria; perestroika
Soziale Marktwirtschaft 145
Stalin, Josef 34, 38, 48, 68, 187
Stalinization 95, 97–100
Standing, G. 51
state: Czechoslovakia 115; Hungary 145–6, 153, 157; 'legal' 104–7, 115; 'organic labour' 32, 59; Poland 128–9, 130, 132, 135, 137, 141–2
stratification, social 58; Czechoslovakia 99–100
subsidiarity principle 15, 183
subsidy, removal 10, 13
Sweden, welfare regime 15, 17, 26
Szalai, Julia 2, 12, 144–65, 176, 189
Szelenyi, I. and Manchin, R. 64
Szubert, W. 121

targeting 157–8
taxation: Bulgaria 82; Czechoslovakia 112; Poland 135
theory, social 121
Titmuss, Richard 42, 114
Tomes, Igor 95, 98, 105

Toshchenko, Zh. 62
trade unions: Bulgaria 67, 69–70, 79,
82, 85–6, 88–9; Czechoslovakia 107;
Hungary 156, 165; Poland 142
training, vocational: Czechoslovakia
110; Poland 119, 133–4; Soviet
Union 48, 52–3; in transitional
period 13, 171, 172
Tropolova, Y. 74
Tsivilev, R. and Rogogin, V. 57
Tyminsky, Stan 131

UK, welfare regime 15, 17
Ukraine, welfare regime 182
Ulc, Otto 94, 97–9, 102
unemployment: benefits 12, 48, 51,
83–4, 109–10, 127, 133–4, 164, 170–
.1; Bulgaria 82–3, 86, 171;
Czechoslovakia 91–2, 96–7, 106,
107–10, 116; Hungary 158, 159, 164;
Poland 48, 131–2, 133–4, 140, 141,
171, 174; Soviet Union 38, 46,
48–51, 171; and state collectivism 2;
in transitional period 8–9, 12–13,
168, 171, 172, 177, 184
Union of Democratic Forces, Bulgaria
69–70, 79, 89
urbanization: Bulgaria 68, 69; Soviet
Union 33–4
USA, welfare regime 15, 17, 26
user, relationship with provider 4, 7,
23, 24, 25, 37, 57, 71, 134, 185, 186
uskorenie 44

Vecernik, J. 111
Vidova, M. et al. 75
voluntary sector 12, 118–19, 134–5,
157, 177, 184

wage: minimum 51, 71, 86, 93, 110;
social 113
wage levels: Bulgaria 70–1, 73–4, 84–6;
and collective bargaining 85–6;
Czechoslovakia 97, 99, 102–3, 105–6,
108, 116; Hungary 2, 150, 151, 153;
indexation 84–5; Poland 126, 131,
134, 171; Romania 171; Soviet
Union 40, 47, 48, 53, 58; under state
collectivism 2–3; in transitional
period 9, 174, 184
Wałęsa, Lech 122, 130–1
Webb, Sidney and Beatrice 7
welfare: capitalist systems 8, 14, 15–19,
167, 175–6, 178, 188–91; employer

16; future prospects 185–91;
'Labourite' 15; priority given to 25,
39, 47, 57–6; state collective system
1–7; in transitional period 7–14;
typologies 14–23, 56–7, 167, 178–83;
see also benefits; corporatism,
conservative; liberalism; social
democracy
Whittaker, R. 75
Wilensky, H. 19, 21
Williams, F. 24, 186
Wnuk-Lipinski, E. 10, 11–12
Wnuk-Lipinski, E. and Illsley, R. 13
women: caring role 103–4; in
employment 3–4, 12, 15, 37, 49,
71–2, 74–5, 93, 108–10, 115, 141,
174; and health care 40, 47;
movements 12, 37, 57–8, 74–5,
108–9, 185; in social policy 16, 24–5,
47, 108, 113, 175; welfare benefits
71, 170, 185
work: attitudes to 44, 48, 50, 59, 73–4,
99; and health 77; obligation 106,
149, 154; right to 2–3, 38, 48, 50–1,
70, 82, 106; in second economy 2,
74, 144, 149, 151, 154–6, 158; *see
also* benefits, work related;
employment; health care; workplace;
unemployment
working class: attitudes to transitional
period 9, 10; Czechoslovakia 99; and
perestroika 49, 57, 59, 62–4; Poland
119, 120, 130, 141, 180, 183; Soviet
Union 99; and welfare provision 3,
20, 21–2, 96, 99, 179, 180
working hours: Bulgaria 82, 86;
Czechoslovakia 96–7, 110
World Bank, and Poland 134, 140
world systems theory 60

Yeltsin, Boris 45–6, 49, 59, 64
Yugoslavia, in transitional period 176,
179–80, 181, 182

Zachranna Socialni Sit 110–11, 112–13
Zasady Strategie Zamestnanosti 108–9,
110
Zaslavskaya, Tatyana 43–4, 46–7, 56,
60, 62–3
Zhivkov, Todor 68–9
ZUS (Zakład Ubezpieczeń
Społecznych) 127